EXPECTED GOALS

EXPECTED GOALS

THE STORY OF HOW DATA CONQUERED FOOTBALL AND CHANGED THE GAME FOREVER

Rory Smith

MUDLARK

Mudlark
HarperCollins*Publishers*
1 London Bridge Street
London SE1 9GF

www.harpercollins.co.uk

HarperCollins*Publishers*
Macken House, 39/40 Mayor Street Upper
Dublin 1, D01 C9W8, Ireland

First published by Mudlark 2022
This edition published 2023

3 5 7 9 10 8 6 4 2

© Rory Smith 2022

Rory Smith asserts the moral right to be
identified as the author of this work

A catalogue record of this book is
available from the British Library

ISBN 978-0-00-848407-1

Printed and bound in the UK using 100%
renewable electricity at CPI Group (UK) Ltd

MIX
Paper | Supporting
responsible forestry
FSC™ C007454
FSC
www.fsc.org

This book is produced from independently certified FSC™ paper
to ensure responsible forest management.

For more information visit: www.harpercollins.co.uk/green

For Rob, who shared my algorithm

CONTENTS

VELVET REVOLUTION

Most days, Ashley Flores wakes up at about 4 a.m. As quietly as he can, he slips out of the apartment he shares with his girlfriend and makes his way down to the small gym in the building's basement. The skyscrapers that denote the financial heart of Taguig – one of the 16 distinct cities that sit cheek-by-jowl in the endless urban sprawl of Metropolitan Manila – stand sentry in the darkness.

Flores stays down there for a couple of hours. He is, first and foremost, a footballer, a forward for Mendiola FC 1991, one of the half-dozen teams that comprise the Philippines Football League. He trains with that in mind, carefully constructing workouts to improve his speed, his explosiveness, the attributes that he sees as his primary assets. Sometimes he wanders to the underground car park, to sprint up the ramps. He tries to finish every session with a half-hour swim.

It is light when he emerges. Football in the Philippines does not pay well enough for the vast majority of players to devote themselves to it full-time; a handful of superstars apart, most have to take on a second job to support themselves, too. Flores has a light breakfast, gets dressed and heads downstairs again. The apartment is expensive for Manila – £160 or so a month, manageable between two – but Flores is prepared to pay the premium for convenience: his office is nearby, so he can cycle to work, a blessing in a city where the roads are permanently choked by traffic.

He could, if he chose, work from home, but he likes the change of environment, the separation, the clear delineation between different aspects of his life. The office itself, rented from a co-working space, is unremarkable. The walls are white, the desks wooden. Decoration extends no further than the dozen or so Lenovo computers that sit on top of them, and the occasional potted plant. Two slender windows offer a dash of natural light. Outside, there is a cafeteria and a communal area and a suite of conference rooms, all decked out in the same neutral, pared-back decor that you might find in an office in London or Moscow or São Paulo, the kind that strips away any hint of time or place. Clues as to its location are seasonal, at best: in the Philippines, the Christmas decorations go up early, almost as soon as high summer has finished, and there is a tree in reception from September onwards.

Strictly speaking, Flores does not have to clock in at any particular time; one of the things he likes most about his job, he said, is the 'freedom' to set his own timetable. Still, he tries to be at his desk not too long after 9 a.m. Particularly in the aftermath of the coronavirus pandemic, many of his 127 colleagues decided that they could not bear the thought of commuting anymore; even as the Philippines slowly came out of lockdown, the majority chose to work remotely. Now, he is often one of just a handful of people who still like to come into work.

Ready for the day, he takes a seat and switches his computer on. He has been doing this job for a couple of years now. He grew up in Laguna, a city a couple of hours away from Manila, and could only attend college in the capital because he won a football scholarship. His parents could not have afforded his education otherwise: his father is retired, and his uncle has long been the one who 'meets the day-to-day needs' of the extended family, Flores said. He feels a duty to contribute, too, to send money back, and this job allows him to do

2

that. It is not lucrative, far from it, but the pay is good, way above the Filipino minimum wage. Staring at his monitor all day hurts his eyes after a while, but it is no great suffering. There are worse ways to earn a living. He enjoys the work. He does not necessarily see it as a long-term thing – he is a qualified coach, too, and wonders if he might like to do something with that – but he is in no rush. He feels a debt of gratitude to the company.

'Many people in the Philippines lost their jobs during the pandemic,' he said. 'But we stayed open. They allowed us to keep working.' His manager, Leo Lachmuth, a gregarious, fresh-faced German – Boss Leo, to his staff – remained in Manila throughout. 'It showed commitment,' Flores said. More than that, Lachmuth set about finding ways to make his employees' lives easier, setting up three regional offices outside Manila to help people continue to work.

Settled in, Flores gets to work. On his contract, he is employed as a 'data operator'. That does not, particularly, offer an insight into precisely what it is he does, and so he and his colleagues have come up with another way of describing themselves. Their job is to watch football matches. Every time something happens, anything at all, they click a shortcut on their keyboard. They do it over and over again, for several games a week. They do it for hundreds and thousands of hours of football every year. They call themselves 'taggers' and they are the very first building block in the sprawling, lucrative data industry that has, over the last two decades, come to dominate the sport.

The training at Packing Sports – the Manila-based division of Impect, a German data analysis company that counts some of Europe's biggest clubs, Bayern Munich and Paris Saint-Germain included, among its clients – lasts a couple of weeks. On Flores' first day, he was tasked with tagging the same game that all new starters get: Germany's demolition of Brazil, in front of a shell-shocked, mournful Maracanã, in the 2014 World Cup semi-final. The choice is not solely rooted in triumphalist nostalgia, according to Lukas Keppler, Impect's managing director. 'It is because it was the first game that really highlighted the difference between our data and what you normally see,' he said. 'If you looked at that game, Brazil had more shots, more passes, more corners. But Germany won 7–1. It told you that those statistics were not telling the right story from the game.'

Impect's approach is different. The company's foundational metric – the piece of information it is looking for from a game – is known by the slightly uncomfortable anglicism of 'packing'. It is, at heart, a measure of how many opposition players are bypassed by any single action on the pitch. It does not matter what form that takes: a quick, short pass that goes beyond two rival players carries the same weight as a languid, mazy dribble that does the same. It is a way of gauging, in other words, how effective a player and a team are at manoeuvring the ball up the field, at evading opponents, at creating danger. Germany's packing measures in that game against Brazil were vastly superior. Joachim Löw's team won, at least in Impect's thinking, because it took more players out of the game, more effectively, than its opponent.

Neophyte taggers do not have to gauge that immediately. When Flores sat down at a screen for the first time, he was told to go through the game painstakingly, looking out for just two things. Every time a player touched the ball, he had to count how many opponents were between the ball and the goal, and input it into the system. Next, he had to estimate how much pressure the player with the ball was under, how close the nearest opponent was when the ball arrived, and input that. Pressure, Lachmuth admits, is a little 'subjective', the sort of thing a tagger can only learn with time and experience. Impect has a 'scale' of pressure, but the company does not pretend it is absolute, objective. 'There are certain boundaries,' Lachmuth said. It is still, though, enough to give an idea of how difficult what the player did once in possession might have been.

That first experience of tagging can, Lachmuth said, take hours, even days. Once they have finished, their work is quality controlled, checked for errors, assessed. Nobody gets it right first time. They go back, again and again, until they have got it to the sort of standard Impect requires. Only then are they allowed to move on to the second phase of their training: picking any game at all in the company's archive and tagging that one. Most of the taggers are football fans; most choose a game featuring the team they support.

This time, though, the task is more complicated. They are now tagging four different metrics: as well as the number of defenders and the pressure on the ball, they must denote the height the ball arrived at the player – choosing from four options, ranging from a low pass, received on the ground, to a lofted ball, aimed at the head or the chest – and the position on the field of both the player making the pass, and the teammate receiving it. 'The whole training takes a couple of weeks,' Lachmuth said. 'We tell them to take their time. They will get quicker, but we do not want them to internalise the wrong things.' That can only corrupt the data, and the data is everything.

Two years in, Flores is good at tagging. He can do a game in a few hours; he sets himself a target of doing at least one complete fixture each day. Often, those are from the world's biggest leagues: Impect prioritises analysing games from the Premier League, Bundesliga and Champions League; it prides itself on having the weekend's Bundesliga fixtures tagged, controlled and ready for publication about 18 hours after the last game has finished. They could, though, be from anywhere: if a client has requested analysis of games in Greece or Uruguay or a regional youth competition, as long as the footage is available and comprehensible, Impect will do it. 'We did some from the Under-17 Bundesliga once,' Keppler said. 'It was filmed by just one cameraman. There was a big lamppost in the middle of the shot. So it was quite hard to judge exactly what happened at certain points in the game.'

Once Flores has finished, his work is checked – the quality control process takes up to an hour, as a colleague goes through to make sure his tags are accurate – and then, almost immediately, it is automatically uploaded onto Impect's systems, the various analysis products the company sells to its clients. They contain far more than just the packing metric that Impect's founders, two former players convinced that more traditional statistics did not quite do justice to the complexities of the game, first divined. Impect now furnishes its customers with more than 1,200 different ways to assess a player.

How that is used, of course, is not up to Flores, or to Lachmuth, or to Keppler. Data has suffused almost every aspect of how football is played, how it is coached, how it is scouted, how it is consumed. For some clubs, it has become a cornerstone of the recruitment process, pored over by scouts hoping to find a player who can transform a team's fortunes. For others, increasingly, it is a way of establishing how a team should be playing, or identifying an opponent's strengths and weaknesses, or working out whether an underperforming manager warrants a little more time, a little more patience. Coaches use it to pick their teams. Executives use it to spend their money. Broadcasters and journalists use it to understand what they have seen. Data scientists and analysts use it to spot patterns and unearth trends, and conceive metrics in the hope of nurturing a little objective knowledge among the deafening tumult of the world's most popular sport. And fans, more than ever before, lean on it as a way of assessing their side's performances, of defending the honour of their favourite players, of diminishing the legitimacy of their rivals.

But those reams of numbers and metrics, all of the figures and gauges that fall under the unwieldy umbrella known as analytics, start somewhere. They start with someone. The data that has come to affect and influence so many of the decisions in football is not created by an algorithm or by a program, but by people sitting at computers in offices all over the world. Football data is, now, a truly global business. Impect still regards itself as a start-up, but it now employs more than a hundred people in the Philippines. Its peers and rivals in the football data industry have thousands of employees, not just in the game's financial engine in western Europe, but in Russia and in India and in Laos, too, a world away from the bright lights and multi-million-pound transfer deals of the Premier League and the Champions League. It is there that the data is first drawn from the ether, first mined in its unalloyed form, before it begins a journey that might end in a Bayern Munich team-talk or a Real Madrid coaching routine or a player, beaming, being presented as Chelsea's newest recruit. All of it begins here, or somewhere like here, with the click of a finger.

There is a story, one that has passed into folklore in analytics circles, that is generally assumed to regard Michael Edwards, the sporting director who would find some measure of fame by helping to restore Liverpool to the pinnacle of English and European football. It dates to a time early in his career, when he was working as an analyst for the company ProZone.

Edwards was attached to Portsmouth. It was his job, every weekend, to collect and to interpret the information provided by the firm's software. These were the early days of data, when someone like Edwards, with his university degree and his lack of high-level playing career, might have been viewed as an outsider by the players and the coaching staff. That was not the case for him, though: Edwards, not exactly a shrinking violet, was at home in the boisterous environment of the training ground. The manager, Harry Redknapp, liked his quick wit and his mischievous streak; the players appreciated the fact that he did not mistake their friendliness for acceptance. Affectionately, they came to know him as 'Eddie'.

Part of his role was to take ProZone's data and prepare pre-match analysis for Redknapp, pointing out the strengths and weaknesses of forthcoming opponents. He was good at it, too, pairing it with video clips – also drawn from ProZone's system – so that he could illustrate the points he was making. Just occasionally, though, he would be reminded that the work he was doing was still regarded as irrelevant, suspicious, or somewhere in between. Before one Premier League game, he produced his usual report. Redknapp, not wanting to wade through it, asked him bluntly: did the computer say that Portsmouth would win? Edwards, a little flustered, replied that it did. A few hours later, Portsmouth had lost. As the squad prepared to leave, Redknapp turned to Edwards, a glint in his eye, and said: 'Tell you what. Next week, why don't we get our computer to play against their computer and we'll see who wins?'

That vignette speaks volumes for how football, for years, felt about what would, in time, come to be known as analytics. In the early 2000s, as data transformed the way baseball was both run and played in the United States – as captured in the Michael Lewis book *Moneyball*, detailing the remarkable 2002 season of the Oakland A's – football remained proudly inviolate. Baseball, the theory went, was a series of set-piece battles: pitcher against batter, batter against pitcher. It was inherently static. Football was not. Instead, it fell into the category of 'invasion sports'. It was too fluid, too relentless, too chaotic to be subject to useful analysis; it was too beautiful to be broken down into mere numbers, akin to discussing Botticelli by talking about what sort of brush he used. It was a game of intensity and industry and, above all, passion, defined not just by tactics and technique but by a series of great, revered intangibles: hunger and desire and fire in the belly. To many, the things that mattered in football were things that could not be measured. As one Premier League manager would say: 'There's no way of measuring a player's heart.'

What has happened in the last twenty years or so has, fundamentally, fatally undermined that myth. Football had flirted with data as far back as the 1950s, but it was only in the late 1990s – a few years before Bill James and his acolytes and apostles started to infiltrate and then influence baseball's thinking – that it started to gain any widespread traction. What has followed has been nothing short of a boom: a great flowering of ideas and innovations from both inside and outside the sport that has changed not only how many of the biggest clubs on the planet operate but how players play, how coaches coach and how fans watch the world's game.

A host of factors go into explaining why that has happened, and why it happened at that moment in history. Football, at the turn of the century, was changing rapidly. It had grown richer, for one, making the rewards for even the slightest edge ever more valuable, wherever that advantage might be found; advancement was incentivised. But it was also, in part thanks to increased globalisation, becoming more professional. Best practice was spreading more quickly between leagues and between clubs. In England, in particular, the drinking culture that had soaked the game for decades was starting to ebb, replaced by a fixation on nutrition and high performance. Seeking to get the best out of the expensive assets at their disposal, clubs started to hire sports scientists, many of them produced by the universities at Loughborough and Liverpool John Moores, as well as specialist fitness and conditioning coaches. They were used to dealing in physical data, looking at speeds and loads and cardiovascular output. They would go on to provide an invaluable bridge to the idea of using numbers to assess performance, linking the previously distinct worlds of elite sport and academia.

Football, though, is not quite the bubble it thinks it is. It is shaped, inexorably, by the world around it. By the late 1990s, that was changing, too. The sport's early experiments with data had always been held back by technology, or the lack of it. Collecting and collating data largely by hand was, on some level, inherently unreliable, vaguely subjective, and did not bear practical analysis. Rapid improvements in the equipment needed to gather, store and then assess the data cleared that hurdle. Cameras became cheaper, better quality. DVDs allowed information to be recorded and filed. Later, the dawn of the digital age meant that it could be dissected and disseminated at lightning speed. Football could not, on a practical level, have indulged in data any earlier. That era could only arrive when the world was ready.

By the time it did, the game's audience was receptive, too. The 1990s had changed the way fans thought about football. It is something of a cliché – and not always a positive one – to trace the sport's gentrification to the 1990 World Cup, to Paul Gascoigne's tears and 'Nessun Dorma', but it brings with it the ring of truth; it was the tournament that turned football into such a middle-class pursuit in England that, by the time Euro 1996 rolled around, the stereotype of the uncomprehending, arriviste fan was well enough established to be mocked on *The Fast Show*. That broader demographic was reflected in the media: in print, where broadsheet sports pages suddenly blossomed with football coverage, and on screen, where football was talked about more than ever before. That was matched on bookshelves, which might suddenly be stocked by the blossoming canon of football literature: not just the memoirs of Nick Hornby and Pete Davies, but the oeuvre of Jonathan Wilson and Simon Kuper and the rest. Football was, somewhat begrudgingly, being

intellectualised, moulded and shaped to fit the presumed requirements of its new breed of fans. Helped by the burgeoning popularity
of Fantasy Football, which familiarised the idea that players could be
valued, numbers poured into that void. In part, that was snobbery: a
way of covering the game in a manner that might appeal to the
professional classes that were proving such voracious consumers of
it. In part, though, it was not nearly so ideological. Newspapers had
space to fill and broadcasters had airtime. Numbers provided a point
of discussion. They helped flesh out the content.

The shift was driven not only by who was coming to the game at
that point, but how they were getting there. It is no coincidence that
analytics has grown steadily in popularity at a time when more and
more fans are introduced to football not just by watching and playing
it but by simulating it, too. Since the early 1990s, consecutive
generations of supporters have grown up playing the *FIFA* and
Pro Evolution Soccer and *Football Manager* video games. In all of
them, a player's ability is broken down into a series of attributes:
their speed and their creativity and their desire. In the early editions
of *Football Manager*, in particular, players could only follow their
games through a text commentary on the screen; to get an idea of
how your team had done, it was necessary to examine the post-match
facts, the number of shots taken and the percentage of possession
enjoyed and the amount of corners won. The impact of that cannot
be underestimated. The millions of people who play and played
them were all raised believing that the story of a game could be
broken down into statistics and that, no matter what traditionalists
might say, you very much could measure a player's heart, out of 20
or out of 100, and with a high degree of accuracy, too. To them,
the idea that football could be expressed through data was not
alien. It was, often, how they had come to understand the game in
the first place.

And yet, for all that the change that has swept through football in the last twenty years has been seismic, a great tectonic shift in the game, it has happened in almost complete silence. While baseball's metamorphosis from old-fashioned bastion of Americana to a sport that recruits not from the minor leagues but from Silicon Valley and Wall Street has been played out in public, a struggle between teams that have embraced data and those that have fervently resisted, football's has been a wordless revolution. With just a handful of exceptions, clubs remain militantly tight-lipped about how they have incorporated data into their decision-making, fearful not only of giving away secrets to their rivals and peers but also of transgressing football's in-built conservatism, its cherishing of the old ways, its reverence for tradition, the scepticism and suspicion it reserves for anything new-fangled or vaguely intellectual, or, the greatest sin of all, American.

That has allowed something of a misunderstanding to flourish. Data is not football's next frontier, not on a conceptual level. That battle has long since been won. It is now a core part of the game. Almost every club that can afford one has a data analyst on staff. The richest have whole teams of them, academics with PhDs and backgrounds in mathematics and machine learning and astrophysics, hired from Harvard and Cambridge and the Large Hadron Collider at CERN in Switzerland, where particles crash into each other in a state of pure, chaotic energy, an experience that is not entirely unlike watching a mid-table Premier League game.

Every team's recruitment department uses data to perform due diligence, at the very least, on players they might sign, checking that their underlying numbers bear some relation to what the club's scouts have decided. They will use one of the array of video and analysis platforms that have sprung up in the last two decades – Wyscout and Scout7 and InStat among them – to check in on leagues around the world. Their bosses in the executive suites might bring in a data-driven consultancy like 21st Group to understand which markets they should be targeting in the summer transfer window, or to assess whether a manager warrants more time. That manager, if they are sufficiently progressive, will use data to work out how to set up their team for a forthcoming game, or how to ensure players are not at excessive risk of burnout, or how set-pieces might be deployed most effectively over the course of a season.

That is not to say football's data revolution is complete. The game is only just beginning to explore the range of possibilities provided by the latest weapon in its arsenal. Very few clubs, if any, have been able to use data to override fully the tribal, emotional instincts laced deep into its fabric; even those held up as the poster-boys for the new wave are liable, at times, to make rash, knee-jerk decisions. Most, if not all, elite teams now use data to some degree; quite how many of them are using it well is open to interpretation.

Still, the early transformation is remarkable. The sheer speed with which football has turned a heresy into something close to an ortho-doxy has been too quick even for those at the very heart of the story; often, only when they take time to reflect, to take a step back, are they able to see quite how far they, and the game, have come. In the space of a quarter of a century, no more, football has gone from believing it could not be profitably analysed to sprouting a lucrative, globe-spanning analytics industry to service its ever-increasing demand. This book is an attempt to chart that shift, to explain how we got from there to here, to add sound to an unspoken revolution.

There were times, in the early years of football's modern data era, that Billy Beane felt like he had been cast as the Pied Piper. Beane was the central character in *Moneyball*, the book that told the story of how the Oakland A's, the overmatched and underpowered baseball team where he served as general manager, had adopted a data-driven approach and seen their fortunes transformed; despite their many and varied disadvantages, with a team of cast-offs and apparent no-hopers, the A's put together a record-breaking winning streak in the course of their 2002 season. The team did not win anything that year – they were eliminated in the first round of the play-offs – but their achievements changed the way the sport operated, and they made Beane a star.

Though it is not an especially literary culture – and though the release of the subsequent film, in 2011, arguably had a broader impact – Lewis' book did create something of a stir inside football. When it was published in Britain in 2004, Ram Mylvaganam bought 20 copies and posted one to the chairman of every Premier League team. He did not do it out of the goodness of his heart: he was the founder of ProZone, one of the sport's two pioneering data providers, and he had a vested interest in proving to his customers and clients the power of the information his company was gathering and generating. He was also not alone. Executives at Opta, the sport's other data service, had done exactly the same thing.

As word spread, it kickstarted an obsessive search for football's 'Moneyball' moment. A steady stream of supplicants and admirers beat a path to Beane's door, hoping to consume some morsels of wisdom from the master's knee. They wanted to find, just as he had, the magic formula that would change football forever, but also, and this really is just a happy coincidence, help their team win. Beane's success had come from paying close attention to undervalued statistics, the few figures in a numbers-drenched sport that nobody was interested in. The assumption was that football must have an equivalent.

That was not quite the message that those pilgrims to the Bay Area received. Beane, by his own admission, is not what baseball would come to call a 'quant'. He is not a trained statistician. Diffident and modest, he is not particularly given to analysing his 'genius', but if he has a gift, he said, it is in empowering other people to be as brilliant as they can. That was his secret. 'Smart translates to any business,' he said. He appointed people without a background in sports – people with the 'same skill-sets that Google and Goldman Sachs' demand – and let them do their thing, even if he did not understand, not entirely, the mechanisms by which they did it. What mattered, to Beane, was finding the right people. They were the ones who drove the revolution. He just opened the gates.

This is not a technical book, and it is not intended to be. There are no equations. There are no graphs or charts or tables. There are no in-depth explanations of how the algorithms that power so much of the work in the field of football analytics work. There are descriptions of what it is, exactly, that some of the most important metrics the game has developed in the last 20 years do, of course, but they are designed to be potted. This is not a book that will compare and contrast the relative merits of different xG models.

Instead, it is a book about people. Just as every single piece of data that suffuses modern elite football comes from the click of a finger from Ashley Flores, or someone like him, so all of the ideas that have done so much to change the way we play and coach and run and watch the game have been generated by someone, somewhere. They may have then taken that idea and coded it into a program that could comb through millions of data points or built it out into an algorithmic equation to find meaning in the chaos, but it all starts with a person. The artificial intelligence has a human root.

Beane takes great pride in how data has allowed baseball to diversify its marketplace of ideas. 'It is one of the smartest industries in the world now,' he said. 'We have opened up our business to the best and brightest.' He regularly competes with tech start-ups and Wall Street giants for graduate hires, despite not being able to match the salaries they can offer; people are drawn to working in sport, after all, for a passion that they probably do not feel for firms in other spheres. Nobody grows up with a JP Morgan Chase poster pinned to their wall.

The people who have been drawn to football's data revolution follow the same pattern. Though, sadly, they are not diverse in a social sense – for the most part, analytics at the professional level remains the preserve of white men, though a handful of pioneering women have played a considerable role in developing the field – they are, by football's standards, in an intellectual one. Some came straight from academia, switching their attention from modelling the migratory patterns of bison or tracking consumer habits to understanding what happens on a football pitch. Others found themselves drawn in from technology firms or large-scale betting syndicates or high finance, simply because they had a gift for finding meaning in numbers, or because they thought about the game in a novel way. That is, perhaps, the greatest change that football has experienced in the last two decades. For the first time in its long history, it has started to admit the legitimacy of a range of perspectives.

Often, that has been through gritted teeth. Many of the characters who have driven football's change have only a few things in common: they did not play football professionally; they had a moment of epiphany when reading *Moneyball*; and they have encountered fierce, ideological resistance at the ideas they advocated and proselytised. Football has not always responded well to external feedback. The idea that it could not be reduced to some binary equation was worn as a badge of honour by fans and insiders alike. That its data revolution has been quiet does not, by any means, suggest it has been easy.

But obstinacy was not the only obstacle. There is no single motivating force that unites all of the people who have helped to usher in football's data age. Some were fans of the sport, and some were not. Some became involved on purpose, and some by accident. Some wanted to find a more effective method for playing the game. Some had a deep-seated, sincerely held belief in the power of numbers; some saw it as a way to level a playing field hopelessly and increasingly lop-sided by the vast sums of money that have flooded into the sport since the dawn of the modern era in 1992, to obtain a competitive edge. Some saw, in data, a chance to understand the game they loved in the same manner as they understood the world. Some understood it simply as a way to make money, to beat the odds. They come from all walks of life: retail analysts and professional gamblers and theoretical physicists and chair salesmen and all manner of academics.

Chris Anderson and David Sally fall into the latter group. It would be hard to imagine more obvious outsiders to football. Both were distinguished scholars, emissaries of the Ivy League: Anderson a Professor of Government and Labour Relations at Cornell, Sally a Professor at the Tuck School of Business at Dartmouth. Neither would ever have imagined their lives becoming entwined with football, right up until the point that they decided to try and change it.

Their impact would not, in the end, prove quite that substantive. They co-authored a book, *The Numbers Game*, which explained how football might be improved by embracing a more data-led approach. Plenty of people inside the game read it; some of them may even have taken some inspiration from it. But they are, in the story of data in football, relatively liminal figures; there are plenty of others who had a more direct, more consequential effect.

That they are central characters in this book, though, owes more to their experiences than their influence. In the years after *The Numbers Game* was published, Anderson and Sally set out to see if their theories could work in real life; they spent the better part of a decade searching for the chance to run a club, one where data would be front and centre in everything they did. Anderson is aware of how ridiculous it sounds, but like so many of those who made the same journey, he had visions of becoming football's equivalent of Billy Beane.

It did not quite work out like that, but what he and Sally saw, heard and endured during the long, painful process of trying to gain a foothold in the sport goes a long way to explaining not only why football had held out against data for so long, but why the revolution that their book hoped to seed and capture was so vital. Football has never been an industry that functions according to logic. It is not easily understood by those outside. It has its own rhythms and rationales. As Anderson, in particular, witnessed, it often makes no sense at all. He knew, from the start, that he had no idea how to run a football club. After a while, it became clear that was not necessarily a problem, because barely anybody else did, either.

The history of data and analytics in football is not really a story about numbers; it is a story, instead, about Anderson and the people like him, the ones who set out to change a sport that did not think it could be changed. It is the story of their ideas and their inspirations, their setbacks and their struggles. It is the story of a revolution that has long since triumphed but has, in another sense, only just started, one that touches every corner of the globe, from Manila to Manchester and all points in between.

On his days off, Ashley Flores, the tagger from Taguig in the Philippines, is still consumed by football. Two glittering studs in his ears give him away: he looks like a footballer. He is a qualified coach, now, but he is some years from hanging up his boots. He remains a regular feature on the right wing for Mendiola FC 1991, the team he represents. Ever since he started work at Packing Sports, in the tight office rented off the co-working space with the white walls and the wooden desks, he feels he has changed the way he plays. 'I try to incorporate some of the things I see into my game,' he said. Watching all of that football, tagging every action in the finest detail, has given him a few ideas about how to improve: how to receive a pass, how to play one, how to take players out of the game.

He is not alone in that. Far from it. Data has changed the way everyone plays football; the numbers have helped to rewrite the code of the sport. This is the story of the people who made that happen.

THE SWITCH TO DIGITAL

Ram Mylvaganam did not mean to revolutionise football. He did not set out to launch an industry that would employ thousands of people across the globe, draw the world's biggest clubs into a frantic arms race or alter, on some fundamental level, the very nature of the game itself. That is precisely what he ended up doing, but it was not what he was trying to do, not at the start. No, at the beginning, all Ram Mylvaganam wanted to do was sell some chairs.

They were, he is clear, very good chairs indeed: acoustic massage chairs, in fact, designed in Finland, by a professor, no less, wrapped in plush leather, worth a couple of thousand pounds apiece, a cut above the dimpled, sagging efforts you might see in an airport waiting lounge. He might have gone down a different route, professionally, but he has been an engineer at heart since his university days, and those chairs were a triumph of engineering.

The spiel is compelling, even twenty years on, even with his chair-hawking days long past. Mylvaganam is avuncular, charming; he makes for easy, rewarding company. In his sixties now, he remains a natural salesman. He makes for a substantially less likely revolutionary. He does not, it is fair to say, fit the classic disruptor's mould. He is immaculately turned out, in a checked button-down shirt and pressed trousers. He keeps an office in the grounds of an old stately home, where models of Spitfires dot the grounds. He acted, for some time, as the chairman of his local cricket club, where he found himself beset on all sides by parochial squabbles that he still discusses with ill-disguised relish. He is polished, refined, old-school corporate.

An accidental revolutionary, though, is a revolutionary nonetheless. A handful of iconic managers and the occasional disgraced oligarch apart, it is hard to think of anyone who has had more of a direct impact on the nature of football in the twenty-first century than this proud alumnus of Royal College, Colombo, and erstwhile chairman of Collingham and Linton Cricket Club. He just did not do it on purpose.

Mylvaganam was never a football fan, not really. Growing up, cricket and rugby were his sports of choice; he was a keen golfer and fiercely competitive squash player, too. His only experience of football came in the form of a couple of trips to see Derby County, at their old Baseball Ground stadium, with some friends from Aston University in Birmingham. He had moved there from his native Sri Lanka in 1968, to study chemical engineering. They took him along to a game because they worried he might be bored. He quite enjoyed it, but it did little to change his mind.

He had never worked in football, either. After graduation, he took a job as an area sales manager with Mars, the confectionery giant, for no other reason than it paid him well. Looking back, he regards the role as the equivalent to 'going to business school for fifteen years'. He rose high enough, performed well enough, that he was seconded to Tokyo for several years – on the admittedly problematic grounds that, according to his personnel director, he was 'from that part of the world' – to help establish the company's expansion into Japan. He took great pains to make sure the company operated according to local custom: employees were expected to wear crisp white shirts; everyone, executives included, had to clock in and clock out; salaries were paid weekly, rather than monthly. He learned Japanese. He cherished the experience. He returned to England, handed a new patch in Yorkshire, in the early 1990s, but decided to leave in 1996, as he approached his twentieth anniversary with the company. He wanted a new challenge and accepted an offer from a group of friends to join a 'loose affiliation' of a consultancy that they had started. One of his first projects was shifting an expensive – but well-engineered – line of massage chairs.

Nor did he have some grand vision of how football might be changed, some innate sense of what this sport that he did not particularly like had been missing. He came to it, instead, by a mix of coincidence and opportunism. One day, as he worked on the chair contract, he happened to play golf with an acquaintance who mentioned, in passing, that he knew someone who worked at Derby. Mylvaganam, the natural salesman, immediately realised that a Premier League football team might just feasibly have the money and the appetite to buy some high-spec chairs, and that their seal of approval might help to shift a few more. His friend arranged a meeting with Derby's manager, Jim Smith.

Smith, too, was an improbable midwife for the future. A stalwart, first as a player and then as a manager, of the less glamorous reaches of the English game, Smith was closer to sixty than he was to fifty. He had been involved with football for close to half a century. He was, as one of his players fondly told *The Athletic*, a 'dinosaur'.

But he was also desperate. Derby were struggling against relegation, and Smith was willing to take a chance on anything that might help. 'He was looking for ways to stay up,' Mylvaganam said. The training facilities at the club were rudimentary – 'a garden shed,' as Mylvaganam put it – and the players did not linger after a session. 'Egg and beans for lunch and then they played golf in the afternoon,' he said. Smith wanted a place to debrief the players on their performances, to hold team meetings, and to run injury recovery sessions. It would function as a sort of safe space for his first team. He wanted to call it the 'Pro Zone Room'. To Mylvaganam, that all sounded like the sort of problem that might be solved by some really good chairs.

It was while he was visiting Derby that Mylvaganam ran into Smith's assistant. Steve McClaren was not a dinosaur. Far from it: in his late thirties, he was starting to earn a reputation as a progressive, innovative coach, one intrigued by sports science and video analysis, ideas then at the very cutting edge of the game. Mylvaganam found him, one day, poring over video cassettes of Derby's recent games, laboriously operating two video recorders, cutting and splicing the tape itself so he could compile the footage he needed to analyse. His guest asked why he did not get someone else to do it for him. This was a Premier League club, after all; there must be someone lower than the assistant manager who could take on such a menial task? McClaren replied that there was nobody else who knew what he was looking for.

Mylvaganam was not, remember, a football fan. He was not inculcated in the game's traditions. He did not have strident views on how things should be done. Had things been different, perhaps that conversation with McClaren would not have given him the kernel of an idea. Perhaps he could not have been a revolutionary if he had also been a supporter. Perhaps he needed to be what he was: a businessman, someone with a trained eye for an untapped market, a scent for an opportunity. Clubs, he saw, were clearly starting to use video analysis, but the coaches were not getting the things they were looking for from traditional footage. So why not provide them with it? Why not record every single thing that happened on a football pitch, note it down and package it up? That way, they would not need to sit in a darkened room, staring at a screen. They could just receive the information they wanted, neatly and conveniently presented, ready for them to dissect. That, he thought, might work. He even had a name ready to go, the same one given to the room where his chairs had been installed. He could call it ProZone.

The idea was so innovative, so cutting edge, that its inventor decided it required a foolproof, point-by-point explanation simply so that people might understand it. In the summer of 2017, Lyft, the ride-sharing app and one of Silicon Valley's start-up darlings, announced it had devised a concept called 'Lyft Shuttle'. It represented a daring new frontier for the transport company. Rather than functioning like a traditional journey with Lyft – or its rival, Uber – in which a customer orders a car to take them from one point to another, the Lyft Shuttles to be tested in San Francisco would run along specific routes. Customers would walk to a preordained stop, wait for the vehicle to appear, board, and then be dropped off at a set point further down the road. This remarkable, novel approach, Lyft said, would allow users to 'ride for a low, fixed fare along convenient routes with no surprise stops'. All they had to do was walk to the stop, and then 'hop on, hop off'. Lyft had, very proudly and seemingly without a hint of irony, invented the bus. (Two years previously, Uber had trialled a system known as 'Smart Routes', which was also just a bus.)

Football is not immune to this phenomenon. Nothing is ever really new in football, not truly. What appears, on the surface, to be innovation is often little more than the repurposing of old ideas, adapting and altering theories that have been around for decades before repackaging them for the modern game. Much of the time, when the sport thinks it has discovered some new horizon, there is a better than average chance that it has, in fact, just invented the bus.

That is true, certainly, of the idea that football might be understood through data. Mylvaganam was not the first person to have had that insight; he was, in fact, almost half a century too late. The belief that the sport might be unlocked by unearthing and understanding the data that it yielded had been around since 1950, if not before, thanks to an accountant and Wing Commander in the Royal Air Force called Charles Reep.

Starting in the 1930s, Reep devised a system of annotating each and every event that happened in a football match in the hope of discovering some objective truth about the game, something that might 'provide a counter to reliance upon memory, tradition and personal impressions'. From a perch in the twenty-first century, his dogma is familiar; so, too, are his methods. The first game Reep broke down into its constituent parts for analysis was a meeting between Swindon Town and Bristol Rovers in 1950; he had been forced to wait for 17 years to test his system in real life, thanks to his role in the RAF and the outbreak of war. Every pass, every cross, every shot was taken down in a shorthand that he had invented. That code was also applied to the nature of each of those moments: Reep made note of the 'length, direction, height and outcome' of every pass he witnessed. The work he was doing by hand – illuminated, for night games, by a miner's helmet and headlamp – was much the same as that performed by football's data-gathering companies now. He referred to his industry as 'match performance analysis'. He conceived the term 'on-the-ball event'. It became his life's work: as well as working with the RAF team, he was hired on a part-time basis by Brentford, wrote a newspaper column sharing his findings and won the admiration of Stan Cullis, manager of the great Wolves team of the 1950s. Reep would go on to annotate more than two thousand games. He was the game's first tagger.

Reep, though, did not stop there; he was also its first analyst. He interrogated his data, even publishing his findings in a paper in the *Journal of the Royal Statistical Society* in 1968. Together with Bernard

Benjamin, the Chief Statistician at the General Register Office, he found that the data generated by football could yield what would now be termed analytical insights, ones that would, half a century later, become orthodoxy for the modern game. Reep found that with every extra pass in a move, the chances of retaining the ball fell significantly. He discovered that football was a game not of possession but of turnovers, and that those turnovers were disproportionately valuable: long before Jürgen Klopp and Ralf Rangnick and even Marcelo Bielsa made it the bedrock of their playing philosophies, he could claim that the most sure-fire way of recording a shot on goal was to win the ball back in or near the opposition penalty area, and he had the data to prove it.

That data cannot, almost by definition, have been 'clean', or even especially accurate – there is only so much one man, writing on a roll of wallpaper, can do to capture every event in a game – but its existence alone should have been enough to make him a celebrated figure in football's history. Reep was decades ahead of his time, a genuine innovator and disruptor.

As early as 1997, he and Richard Pollard of California State University published a paper in *The Statistician* that sought to bring a degree of analytical sophistication to the game. 'The planning of tactics, strategies and an overall style of play still remains, for most coaches, an entirely subjective procedure,' they wrote. Nobody knew anything about football, they posited, they just thought they did; there was no systematic 'collection and analysis of numerical data', just observers watching a game and then 'drawing subjective conclusions about individual and team performances'. That paper set out to change that, by attempting to use data from 22 games at the 1986 World Cup to 'develop a method in which the effectiveness of different strategies and tactics can be quantified and compared'. If that seems abstract, faintly academic, it should not: Pollard and Reep's paper includes what is, in effect, a version of a metric, Expected Goals, that would bring analytics into the mainstream two decades later.

That the game does not lionise Reep as a pioneer is not because his data was flawed, or his thinking insufficiently sophisticated. It is because the conclusions attributed to him were.

Reep was not, it seems, an advocate of one style of play over another; his work does not suggest that he has any particular ideological commitment beyond suspecting, perhaps, that many of what we would now call the game's 'philosophies' were the product of instinct more than information. It is not even entirely clear whether he believed that there was a 'correct' way to play the game, a tactic or a strategy, as he would put it, that was more effective than all of the others. (It is fair to say, though, that he found some strategies to be wanting in effectiveness, and therefore wrote them off.)

That he became so indelibly associated with one approach – a style of play stripped of ornament and artifice, one devoted entirely to scoring goals in the most efficient way possible – was not so much to do with his conclusions, as to the way that those conclusions were consumed and contorted by those who studied his work. Reep's research was used, for decades, as justification for the idea that, since the vast majority of goals came from moves consisting of three passes or fewer, and that the longer a team had the ball the more likely it was to lose it, passing as a whole was best avoided. Those findings seemed – at least to his admirers – to advocate the most direct approach possible, and they ensured that Reep would not go down as the avant garde father of football analytics but as the brutalist theorist behind the long-ball game.

Perhaps his choice of language did not help: the emphasis on effectiveness and efficiency, the thinly veiled disregard for anything deemed elaborate and effete, do seem to betray some sort of theoretical conviction on his part. He did not particularly cherish possession of the ball; he did seem to conclude that the shortest route to goal was the most effective. But he was condemned to ignominy, to a large extent, by what others did in his name. If Reep's influence had extended no further than Brentford and that gloriously success-ful Wolves team – the one that would inspire the French journalist Gabriel Hanot to invent the European Cup – then perhaps the approach he came to symbolise might have won more acclaim, or even more sympathy.

Instead, his work unleashed a monster. The exact nature of Reep's interactions with Charles Hughes remains contested. As Jonathan Wilson notes in his book *Inverting the Pyramid*, Hughes seems to have claimed that he collaborated with Reep at some point but disa-vowed any suggestion that he built on his research; they simply, in Hughes' telling, reached the same 'major conclusion' from 'different routes'. Whatever the truth of it, there is little question that Hughes and Reep came to preach almost exactly the same gospel. Hughes just had a larger congregation.

Hughes was a Football Association lifer. His playing career had been short-lived – a handful of games for Blackburn Rovers' reserve team – and he had left football, eventually, to study physical educa-tion at Loughborough University, before going on to teach at Brad-ford Grammar School. Having obtained his coaching badge from the FA, he was plucked by Allen Wade, the organisation's head of coach-ing and another Loughborough graduate, to act as his assistant in 1964. His responsibilities included taking charge of Britain's Olympic team and overseeing England's amateur international side until, a decade later, both were discontinued. He remained at Lancaster Gate, taking up a post as director of youth coaching and, later, the role of director of coaching itself. At one point, he was even inter-viewed for the chief executive's job.

He was, clearly, fascinated by the minutiae of football and the mechanisms of coaching itself. He published two books while at the FA, *Football: Tactics and Teamwork* in 1973 and the equally imaginatively titled *Soccer Tactics and Skills* seven years later. He did not, though, appear to be especially dogmatic in terms of how the game should be played. Wilson described both as little more than 'practical manuals'. 'They are a touch over-pragmatic, but they are largely unobjectionable,' he wrote.

At some point, though, Hughes experienced some sort of Damascene conversion. Quite what brought it about is unclear: Reep seems to have harboured suspicions that it was as a result of discovering his work; Hughes himself claimed it was rooted in his own analysis of the 'library of 16 mm films of FA Cup finals and international matches' that was held at Lancaster Gate. However it happened, by 1990, Hughes was utterly convinced of the primacy of the direct approach. The key to winning, he felt, was getting the ball into dangerous areas as swiftly and efficiently as possible. 'The first objective is to get into the attacking third of the field more often than the opponents do,' he wrote in his conclusion to *The Winning Formula*, the treatise he published while in situ as director of coaching. It would serve as the ur-text for the long-ball game, and Hughes, with his academic bearing and his pseudo-scientific talk of Positions of Maximum Opportunity, would come to be known as the 'Professor of Kick and Rush'.

Hughes was right, at least, on one thing: he and Reep did seem to come to the same conclusion. What he did not notice was that he was wrong; he had not examined the data at his disposal (however he had gathered it) as he might have done. The difference was that, while Reep was never in a position of direct influence, Hughes was; he occupied one of the most powerful posts in English football. He always rejected the characterisation of his beliefs as unsophisticated – in an interview with the *Independent* in 1994, he quoted his own works to prove that he did not favour 'playing long balls forward to the exclusion of all else' – but it made little difference. Hughes' doctrine suffused the English game and, in time, would be accused of wreaking untold damage. An entire generation was raised on the misguided principles he seemed to espouse. He helped to justify and popularise an agricultural style of play that set back both the England national team and the country's club sides by a decade, perhaps more. It was only with the advent of the Premier League, and its attendant wealth, that his impact could begin to be unpicked, as England set out to import, at a high tariff, all of the technical and tactical knowledge that it had wilfully cast aside.

Hughes did not just manage to turn long-ball into an insult, though; he did more than just make a single style of play toxic. The nature, as well as the outcome, of his work was declared guilty by association. His influence meant that the use of data to understand football became inextricably linked with the long-ball, as though the former could only inevitably lead to the latter. By the late 1980s and early 1990s, it was not just Hughes' conclusion that was considered heresy, but his method, too. Football had seen what happened when it was broken down into its constituent parts, and did not like it. The numbers stripped the beauty from the game.

Elsewhere, the experience had been different. Valeriy Lobanovskyi, the great Ukrainian coach, had used a fearsome, futuristic arsenal of tools to turn Dynamo Kyiv into the dominant team in the last two decades of the Soviet Union; the dynasty he created would last, in effect, from the early 1970s to the emergence of Andriy Shevchenko in 1999. Like Reep, Lobanovskyi was a creature of his time, making his name in the Soviet Union at a time when it was obsessed with the capacity of technology to help it match and overhaul the advances being made in the capitalist West. He started coaching at the height of the space race; his work reached its zenith when the KGB was spending millions to acquire illicitly blacklisted technology from the United States and Europe. Together with Anatoly Zelentsov, a Professor of Physical Sciences, Lobanovskyi experimented with sports science, computer analysis and what we would now call 'brain training' to improve his team. More than anything, though, he leaned on data. He divined that a team that makes errors in 'no more than 15 to 18 per cent of its actions is unbeatable'. He provided his players with not just statistical analyses of their performances, but targets for how many sprints they should complete, how many shots they should take and how much pressing they should do. Zelentsov devised a program that broke the pitch into a set number of zones, analysing how many touches players should take in each one, and how fast they needed to be running while they were there. His side was not renowned for its great artfulness – Lobanovskyi was accused, at times, of using science to sap the soul from football – but nobody, in the Eastern Bloc, questioned its usefulness.

He was disadvantaged, of course, not so much by what he was doing but by where he was doing it. His teams might have made an impact in the West – he was in charge of the Soviet Union side that made the final of the European Championship in 1988 – but there was little opportunity and quite possibly scant appetite to understand what made them tick. Certainly, it was only after the fall of the Iron Curtain that quite how advanced his work had been started to come into focus. Nobody, in the 1970s or 1980s, was wondering whether the teams of the Football League or Serie A had something to learn from a side in the Communist Bloc. There is precious little reason to believe that, even had there been interest, Lobanovskyi would have been in a position to share his methods anyway.

Instead, Western Europe's early experiences of data in football were unhappy ones. The utilitarian approach of Reep and the reductive commandments of Hughes seemed to be the root cause of the rise of the likes of Graham Taylor's Watford, Wimbledon's Crazy Gang, Howard Wilkinson's Leeds United and John Beck's Cambridge, the kings of kick and rush. In one light, they were feel-good fairy tales: breaking football down into its component parts, emphasising product over process, was an undeniably effective way for David to compete with Goliath. But in another, they provided a warning that football's beauty would be stripped away if art became industry. Slowly but surely, the game became predisposed to believe not only that its true essence could not be captured by mere numbers, but that doing so was a sure-fire way of diminishing its form. Those first exposures forged a cognitive link between the use of data and not just an ugly, banal, basic sort of football, but an ugly, banal, basic sort of football that was dragging English football backwards.

The job advert caught Duncan Alexander's eye straightaway. After graduating from university with a degree in history in the summer of 2000, he had moved to London with no real plan, no real aim, beyond a broad intention of finding work in that slightly nebulous sphere where football and the media brush up against each other. He spent his first few weeks idly flicking through the *Guardian* Media, hoping to see something that might allow him to earn a bit of money, but drawing a blank. And then, one day, he saw it: a listing that might have been written for him. A company was looking for fans of lower league football teams to fill out its staff. A lifetime as a Wycombe Wanderers fan was all the qualification he apparently needed.

The interview process was surprisingly gentle. Rather than a formal grilling from a panel of executives, Alexander and his fellow prospective recruits were handed what was, essentially, a pub quiz. It was designed to test their knowledge of the less glamorous reaches of England's professional game. Alexander was no statistician, but he had a memory for and a mastery of the slightly arcane trivia that most fans – particularly those who devote their lives to some of the game's lesser lights – acquire over the years. He got the job. He would start work at a company called Opta Index.

The company he had joined was still relatively young. It had been founded in 1996, an offshoot of a management consulting company that shared its name. They had hired Suzie Russell, a sales and marketing executive, to help brand the group. Russell was a Southampton fan, but she was no ardent believer in the power of statistics to change football. Instead, she saw an opportunity to promote her firm's work. A few years previously, another consulting company, Coopers and Lybrand – an accountancy firm that is now the Coopers element in PriceWaterhouseCoopers – had been approached by Ted Dexter, the former chairman of selectors for England's cricket team, with a view to compiling some sort of system for rating Test cricketers. The company agreed: not out of any particular love for cricket, but because it believed the sport might be a way of turning the game's 'more educated and business-minded' fans into potential employees. 'It would be sensible for the human resources departments of accountancy firms and big businesses to use cricket as a way of attracting the best workforce,' as Robert Eastaway, who helped develop the ratings, told *Accountancy Daily* in 2003.

That Russell saw football as a similar opportunity is clear from how she approached the task. According to the autobiography the company itself published in 1999, it was only after she had contacted the Premier League and Sky Sports, to assess whether they might support a ratings system, that she turned her attention to how it would actually work.

That was, of course, the difficult part. Football only collected the most rudimentary data: the number of goals scored, the identity of the players who scored them, the number of yellow and red cards, the amount of corners won by each team. As Graham Kelly, the former chief executive of the FA, would later note, it was only after the 1994 World Cup in the United States that the word 'assist' entered the sport's already 'tortured lexicon'.

Russell's solution – understandable, as a management consultant – was to hire outside help. She recruited Don Howe, a former Arsenal and Coventry City manager and one of the most respected coaches of his generation, to define a series of metrics by which players might be judged. By modern standards, his criteria seem basic: passes completed, crosses attempted, shots taken, tackles made. At the time, though, they were groundbreaking. He drew up a list of 92 separate categories by which a player might be assessed. For every pass made or shot taken, a player would be assigned a certain number of points. The player with the most points, the thinking went, could be said to have contributed the most to the game. What would become known as the Carling Opta Index – Russell also thought to get corporate sponsorship – was ready to go within two months of its founding. It was a quick turnaround. But then this was not supposed to be a strictly academic exercise.

Opta's methods bore testament to that. The company occupied a rabbit warren of offices near London's Victoria Station, a hot, sticky, cramped sort of a place, where employees squeezed past each other in subterranean corridors and crashed out on sofas as they worked through the night. Every weekend, it would be sent the same tape of a game used by referees to assess their own performance; how quickly they arrived depended, largely, on how far they had to travel. Games in London would invariably be watched first; those coming from Newcastle, Sunderland or Leeds might not arrive until the next day. Once they had the footage, an analyst would spend four hours poring over the footage, annotating each and every action on a vast sheet of paper filled with boxes to be ticked. That would then be fed into the single computer the company had at its disposal for analysis; the machine would be left running overnight, with the completed report delivered by the morning.

More problematic, though, was the end result. Opta tallied each and every action a player completed on the pitch to compile their 'Game Score', the number of points they had accrued for an individual fixture. They would then add that to the scores they had been given for their previous five games to establish how many Index Points they had; it was that number which was pushed out to Sky Sports or to the *Observer*, the newspaper that had agreed to run the Index in its first year of existence. The issue, of course, was that number was almost entirely meaningless. The example Opta used on its website to explain its approach was that of Dennis Bergkamp. The Dutchman had an average score of 1455. 'These Index Scores can be used to compare players' performances over those six games, with the player who has the highest average being the most in-form,' the company said. No allowances were made for comparing strikers to defenders, or attacking midfielders from more cautious ones. It was just a number.

That did not stop it catching on. By the time Alexander joined, in 2000, Opta Index had been bought out by the Sports Internet Group, a company that ran a series of football-related websites. It had immediately celebrated by moving to an expensive office complex on Threadneedle Street, opposite the Bank of England. It was glass-fronted, modern, lavishly equipped, the perfect home for a start-up enjoying the fruits of the first dotcom boom. It was still not modern, not in any recognisable sense: only one of the many computers arrayed on the desks was connected to the Internet; Alexander remembers having 'to queue up like a villager at a well' any time he had a query that required some sort of research.

But more and more newspapers were demanding Opta's services; though the Index had fallen from favour, there was an ever-increasing appetite for the underlying data that had powered it. To some extent, Alexander believes that was a result of the popularity of fantasy football; readers wanted to know who was playing well in order to change their teams, and newspapers wanted to meet their needs; the burgeoning number of football-themed computer games, too, might have played a role. Mainly, though, newspapers wanted it because it was cheap, easy copy. Opta shared all of its information with the media for free, provided it was accredited; though it had quickly outgrown the management consultancy that had conceived it, it retained the attitude and approach of an exercise in publicity. 'It became pretty clear, pretty quickly that it was a way to fill up a page,' Alexander said. 'You'd get calls from the *Mirror* or the *Sun* before games had even ended asking you to send the numbers over. You'd explain that the final whistle hadn't even gone yet, and that it took time. They'd tell you they had ten minutes to deadline, that they didn't fucking care and just to send whatever we had, and put the phone down.'

That Alexander was not a statistician, he thinks, probably helped. Fleet Street's newsrooms were populated then, as they are to some extent now, by grizzled curmudgeons, largely men of hair-trigger tempers and little tolerance for academic rigour. They were rarely polite to the students and graduates they spoke to at Opta; Alexander suspects, probably rightly, that they regarded them as effete nerds. But, as time went on, they were at least reassured that they had football as a common language. 'I could tell them that I knew the point they were trying to make, and here is a number that kind of supports it,' he said. That would not have been possible, not really, if Opta had taken a more puritanical approach.

The company paid much less attention to making inroads into the game itself. Every club had access to its data, of course, and some even claimed to find it useful: Graeme Souness, at Southampton,

Manchester City's Frank Clark and David Pleat, Sheffield Wednesday's manager, were all described as 'enthusiastic clients'. 'We certainly take notice of it,' Jim Smith, the Derby manager and unlikely data evangelist, told the *Observer* in 1997. 'We can look at the statistics on the opposition to see how they measure up. The surprising thing we found was the number of our shots on goal were well down and Wimbledon were bottom. Yet in terms of strikes-to-goal percentages they were top.' Harry Redknapp, then at West Ham, used it to 'show up the good passers, who don't give the ball away'.

For the most part, though, the reaction was lukewarm. 'We published a yearbook at one point, and got a couple of managers to give quotes for the cover,' Alexander remembered. 'One was from Jim Smith, and it said: "We like it, and we use it." But my favourite was from Alex Ferguson. It just said: "It is of benefit." So, you know: thanks Alex.'

The reticence, perhaps, can be attributed to the fact that managers felt what Opta could not tell them was far more significant than what it could. They were, certainly, keenly aware of the system's limitations. Rather forlornly, the *Observer* noted that 'not every part of a player's performance can be analysed. For instance, there is no way of measuring the off-the-ball running of a player.' By the time that piece was published, in February of 1997, that was no longer true. Measuring the distance a player covered was most definitely possible, and another company was starting to do it. Opta's priority had always been establishing a presence in the media. That left a gap in football itself, and ProZone was quick to fill it.

Simon Wilson was swimming against the tide. As soon as the final whistle went, as Southampton's fans started to file out of The Dell, he was scurrying up into the stands. The moment that the game was over, his long weekend's work began.

First, he had to pull the discs from the eight cameras he had set up around the stadium, positioned so that between them they might capture and record every single thing that happened on the field. Next, he had to dismantle all of his equipment, neatly storing it away, ready for use in a couple of weeks' time. And then he had to get in his car, the discs safely packed in his boot, and drive the 230 miles or so to Leeds. Often, he would arrive at two or three in the morning. It did not matter: the building on Roseville Road in Harehills was always open. He would drop the discs off and find somewhere to sleep. Some of his colleagues shared a cramped, noisy house nearby, but Wilson generally found that there was better rest to be had at a hotel. By the time he woke up – as late as he could get away with – the discs would be ready. He would stop off at Roseville Road, pick up the package that was waiting for him and hit the road again. He would be back in Southampton by nightfall, ready to pore over the information the discs had yielded. Wilson was young and enthusiastic and working in football, but he was also exhausted. The life of a ProZone analyst was not, it turned out, an especially glamorous one.

Wilson, and a dozen or so analysts like him, were the backbone of the business Mylvaganam had set up. ProZone had grown steadily since he had first been struck by the idea at Derby. He had poured everything he had into the venture: he was so heavily indebted, he would later tell *The Athletic*, that even 'the dog and the cat owed the bank'. It had cost him, he thinks, somewhere in the region of £2 million. There was all of the camera equipment that had to be set up in the stadium, of course, but there was also the building on Roseville Road, a disused warehouse that he had managed to get cheap through a friend in the rag trade. It was, Mylvaganam said, something of a Tardis. He had not wasted time or money beautifying his headquarters; everything had gone on the vast banks of computers that sat inside and the wages of the staff that sat at each terminal.

Some of them were students, picked up from the three universities in Leeds, looking for part-time work. Others had been recruited from the local unemployment office, convinced to take the jobs either because of an interest in football or because, at the time, computer proficiency was seen as a valuable skill to be acquired.

Derby had acted as his first client, though the club did not have to pay for Mylvaganam's work. Instead, he did a deal. Mylvaganam would set up his camera system and provide the information from the video footage, compiled by his small staff at Roseville Road, to Smith and McClaren for free. In exchange, he would be allowed to use the analysis suite he had persuaded Portakabin to construct at the club's training ground to pitch the idea to executives and managers from Derby's opponents. Every other Friday night, before a home game, he would invite a delegation from the visiting team to dinner and a chance to watch Derby's previous fixture. (It is not clear what, if anything, happened to the chairs.)

The response was, generally, one of muted interest. Clubs seemed intrigued by the concept, but 'nobody was prepared to cross the Rubicon,' as Mylvaganam put it. There was, after all, no proof that what he was suggesting made the slightest bit of difference to a team's performance; there were no high-profile advocates for it; even Derby did not exactly provide a compelling reference. The club, after all, was not paying for ProZone's insights. The only revenue the agreement generated came in the form of fines: if a player was late to the 10.30 a.m. analysis sessions Mylvaganam laid on for Derby, they would forfeit £50. That money would go straight to ProZone.

It required a *deus ex machina* to get the company off the ground. One morning in 1998, as ProZone's year-long trial agreement with Derby was coming to an end, McClaren called Mylvaganam. He was on his way for a job interview: he was under consideration for a role as assistant to Alex Ferguson at Manchester United. Mylvaganam knew McClaren well enough by that point to know that he was nervous; he was, after all, still a young coach, and Manchester United would represent a major leap for his career. Mylvaganam was long enough in the tooth, even then, to know that his friend was worrying about nothing. 'Steve, it's not an interview,' he told him. 'I hope you've packed. If they're seeing you, then you've got the job.' The prediction proved true. One of the first things McClaren did, after being told the post was his – it did not even occur to Ferguson that he might say no – was to suggest to his new employers that they might like to start to use ProZone. Mylvaganam was summoned to see Ferguson and United's chief executive, David Gill. Neither was prepared to pay for the service, not yet. 'We're Manchester United,' Gill told him. 'We don't pay people. People pay us.' Still, Mylvaganam knew this was his chance. Ferguson's seal of approval could be a game-changer. He agreed to another trial. United would have to pay £50,000 for ProZone's work if the season ended with a trophy. It did not. It ended with three.

Mylvaganam was there, at Camp Nou, as Ferguson's team completed their treble. He had never been a football fan, but he was fully invested that evening. He felt he had played some small role in taking the club there: he had prepared a report on United's semi-final opponents, Juventus, that Ferguson would later say had helped him know exactly how to overcome the star-studded Italian champions. He called his wife, Millie, when Teddy Sheringham equalised; he was still talking to her, not looking at the pitch, when Ole-Gunnar Solskjaer scored the winner. After two years, ProZone was finally going to get paid for its work; his dog and cat could start to pay back their loans to the bank. But that was not why Mylvaganam was celebrating. When he had pitched to clubs in the Portakabin at Derby, he had been told often that data was just a 'fad', that it would soon pass. That, he knew, was how football worked: at heart, it is an industry built on trends, on keeping up with the Joneses. Within a few weeks of United's win in the Champions League, he had four more clubs lined up as paying customers, as well as United and Derby. ProZone was, all of a sudden, in fashion.

Over the next couple of years, spread as much by word of mouth as anything else, the clients kept rolling in. Sam Allardyce brought ProZone into Bolton Wanderers; the day after his team beat Preston North End in the First Division play-off final in 2001, Preston's manager, David Moyes, called Mylvaganam and signed his club up.

ProZone's services did not come cheap. Clubs paid between £100,000 and £300,000 a season, depending on how many games they wanted to be analysed by the 40 or so staff at Roseville Road. That money bought not just ProZone's camera equipment, but a permanent attaché, seconded by the company and ensconced at the client club. ProZone, effectively, had for the first time introduced the concept of an analyst to elite football.

Wilson, a sports science graduate of Liverpool John Moores University, was one of ProZone's first wave of analysts. He still, then, considered himself a player: he had been playing part-time for teams like Southport and Marine, and was due to be flying out to Finland to join another club on trial the day after his first interview at ProZone. In agreeing to take the job, he was effectively calling time on his career.

His early months were spent at Roseville Road, learning how ProZone's software worked, and pitching the idea to clubs who were yet to adopt it. It was all just a touch Heath Robinson. The presentations would take place in hotels to unnamed executives and anonymous members of a team's coaching staff. Wilson often did not know how he had been granted access, or who he was speaking to, or whether they had any actual authority.

When Preston, on Moyes' directive, brought in ProZone in the summer of 2001, though, his role changed. Wilson was sent out by

ProZone to act as the club's analyst. Nobody – not Wilson, not Moyes, not anyone at the club – seemed quite sure what his duties were, or what his week should look like. Like all of ProZone's analysts, he was told to deliver a 'blue sky' document to the coaching staff on a Monday morning, containing a run-down of the statistics churned out by the firm's software. But beyond that, it was his to shape as he saw fit. It was, after all, more than just a new job; it was an entirely new field, at the sort of club that could not really afford to carry passengers. Sometimes, thanks to his education in sports science, he found himself helping out Mick Rathbone, the club's physio. Occasionally, he would be asked to join in with training; he was still good enough not to embarrass himself alongside the professionals.

And then, sometimes, without warning, Moyes would summon him to deliver an analysis session. Again, the whole set-up felt somewhat jerry-rigged: he would find a room, remove all of the pictures from the walls, tape over the windows, and set up his projector. Often, it was not clear to Wilson quite when he would be expected, or when Moyes would decide he was needed. There was more than one occasion when he got a call while he was in the office in Leeds, only to be told that Moyes was expecting him on the other side of the Pennines in an hour, maybe less.

It may have been ad hoc, piecemeal, slightly chaotic, but Moyes was a firm believer in what ProZone – and its human face, Wilson – could tell him. 'He was curious,' said Wilson. 'He was into it.' He would often interrupt his presentation, peppering him with questions that Wilson could not always answer. The main benefit of the system in Moyes' mind, though, was that it represented a way of making his players accountable. 'He wanted his team to run,' he said. 'He wanted them to outrun the opposition.' ProZone was a way of highlighting who had, and who had not, fulfilled that basic criterion.

That experience was one that many of the early ProZone analysts found: though the software the company used meant that on the ball events were tracked and recorded, most managers and coaches honed in immediately on the physical data. To some extent, that was because the analysts and the fitness staff at clubs shared a language. A lot of the early analysts had studied sports science; all of the fitness coaches were familiar with the idea that there were some things that could be measured. Even those managers who did not have that technical background, though, who were vaguely, instinctively sceptical towards the idea of 'sports' and 'science' sharing a sentence, saw what Moyes did: this was a tool that allowed you to spot who was shirking. 'The fitness data was the battering ram,' Wilson said. The managers may not have been using ProZone's full potential, but they were using it, and that was what mattered.

Indeed, by 2003, ProZone was so ingrained in football that ITV – having won the rights to show highlights of England's top flight on its channels, striking BBC's *Match of the Day* from Britain's television schedules for the first time in more than a decade in the process – decided to incorporate ProZone analysis into its flagship programme, *The Premiership*. That contract, in turn, helped Mylvaganam to expand, hiring more staff to code games, hiring more graduates to go out in the field and work as analysts at clubs.

That was not the only great leap forward. The process was becoming more streamlined, too. Michael Edwards, the analyst installed at Portsmouth, eventually decided that the prospect of driving from the south coast to Leeds every other week was not an especially appealing one, and persuaded Mylvaganam to shell out for a courier to carry his footage back to Roseville Road for analysis; that way, after all, he would have more time to go through the information to see what he could learn, rather than being forced to spend most of his time on the motorway.

But the real transformation was not within the company, or even the sport. Mylvaganam's initial insight had come from seeing McClaren painstakingly cutting video cassettes together. ProZone might have saved a coach from having to do that work, but someone still had to do it: each game was recorded by eight cameras, which meant eight video cassettes, which meant analysing the footage by pressing pause and play and pause and play on eight separate VCRs. All of that bulky equipment did not just eat up space: it cost Mylvaganam a huge amount of money, and required vast tracts of time to operate, too.

The story of data and football is, to some extent, a technological one. The game could only embrace new horizons once it was feasible for it to do so. Reep's work had been hamstrung by his technological limitations – a single person, noting down a whole game in shorthand by the light of a miner's lamp – as much as his ideological proclivities; ProZone was, to an extent, no different. It could not transform the game, fulfil its founder's ambitions, while it was reliant on a technology as cumbersome as video. It was only with the dawn of the digital age that it could truly flourish.

That arrived, first, with the widespread ascendance of the DVD in the early years of the twenty-first century, allowing ProZone first to digitise all of its footage and then, later, to record directly onto discs; by the time Wilson had left Preston for Southampton, he was no longer carting video cassettes back to Leeds. Suddenly, analysts could use the system not only to present coaches with raw data, but to provide them with quick and easy visual proof. At Portsmouth, Edwards spent much of time producing clip reels both for the coaches and the players themselves, allowing them to pinpoint mistakes that were being made and what they might do instead. He could shift his attention, too, to opposition analysis, going through footage from forthcoming opponents to produce detailed montages on what to expect, allowing managers to show players, rather than tell them, about the challenges they were likely to face, and the opportunities they were likely to find. In that single moment, ProZone had gone from analogue to digital. In time, it would sweep football along with it.

Jaap Stam's three glorious years at Manchester United came to an end in a hurried conversation on a petrol station forecourt. That morning, he and Alex Ferguson, the manager under whom he had won three straight Premier League titles and lifted the Champions League, had been involved in what might best be described as a full and frank exchange of views during training. Stam, a taciturn, phlegmatic Dutchman, stormed out. He was almost back at his home in Wilmslow when his phone rang: Ferguson's secretary. She put his boss on. They had to talk, the Scot said. Where was he? Stam directed him to the petrol station.

Ferguson arrived half an hour later. He jumped into Stam's car. He did not mince his words: Stam had to leave, and he had to leave now. An unhappy player risked his team's chemistry; insubordination compromised his authority. Lazio had made an offer. United intended to accept. They just needed Stam, who had settled in Manchester and had, until that morning, harboured absolutely no intention of leaving, to acquiesce.

His departure took everyone, including his teammates, by surprise. 'We were as mystified as anyone,' Gary Neville wrote in his autobiography. 'All kinds of conspiracies swirled around.' Among them was the notion that Ferguson had taken exception to Stam's own memoir, *Head to Head*, published earlier that year and serialised, for four straight days, by the *Daily Mirror*.

It was not, in truth, particularly scurrilous fare, though it was perhaps a little more indiscreet than a player in the middle of their career might ordinarily publish. Stam, characteristically blunt, gave an unvarnished account not just of many of his opponents – Filippo Inzaghi was a cheat, he suggested, his brother Simone Inzaghi was less threatening 'than a Teletubby,' Patrick Vieira moaned – but his teammates, too. Writing in the *Observer*, Simon Kuper described it as a 'compendium of tabloid headlines'. David Beckham was not especially bright, Stam 'revealed', while both Gary Neville and his younger brother Phil were known in the United dressing room as 'busy little c***s'. (The older Neville would later say Stam had used exactly that description of him to his face, 'with affection', countless times.) Perhaps most damaging of all, he had also laid bare the details of the meeting with Ferguson at which he had agreed, in 1998, to move to Old Trafford from PSV Eindhoven, an encounter that he had been told to keep quiet and that was, strictly speaking, unauthorised.

Stam was surprised by the furore the book – and in particular its serialisation – created and was 'a bit embarrassed by it all', as Ferguson said at the time, playing it down as much as he could. 'He's had some making up to do in the dressing room.' A few weeks later, Stam was gone. The explanation seemed obvious: Ferguson had not been able to tolerate such a flagrant transgression of the dressing room *omertà* he worked so hard to maintain. His departure was his delayed, but ultimate, punishment.

Correlation, though, is not causation. Gary Neville, at the time, had felt that the book was likely a 'minor' factor in his teammate's sale; his intuition would later be proved right. Stam had been struggling with an injury to his Achilles tendon for a year or so; his performances, previously so imperious, had started to wane just a little. 'When he came back, Steve McClaren and I thought he had lost a yard of pace,' Ferguson would say, years later. United's first game of the season, in the summer of 2001, was against Fulham. Stam played, and the champions won, but he seemed a shadow of his former self. It was after that match that the offer from Lazio came in, and Ferguson and Stam met on the forecourt, and everything came to an end.

Ferguson, though, had not made his decision on the back of a single game. Concerned about Stam's form, he and McClaren had checked his data from the previous few months. They found evidence that seemed to support their conclusion: Stam was making fewer tackles than he had a couple of years earlier. It appeared, to them, proof that he was diminishing. The £16.5 million on offer from Italy represented more than fair value for a player starting, very slowly, to decline. It may, as Kuper would later write, have been the first transfer deal in football history driven at least in part by data.

With the benefit of hindsight, of course, it is easy to see where Ferguson and McClaren went wrong. Even Ferguson would admit, a few years later, that it was a 'bad decision'. Stam did not drift into oblivion in Italy. He performed well enough to earn a move from Lazio to AC Milan in 2004; a year later, he was playing in the Champions League final. United had read the numbers wrong. Or, more accurately, they had read the wrong numbers.

The amount of tackles a player has made is an exceptionally crude measure by which to judge defensive performance; it is an intrinsic truth in football, after all, that the best defenders do not need to make many tackles. The tackle itself is an act of last resort; great defenders intervene long before anything so tawdry is required. That Stam was making fewer tackles was not a sign that he was getting worse; if anything, it may have been a sign that his anticipation and his positioning and his reading of the game were all improving.

That a coach as wily and as wise as Ferguson could still be wrong-footed by data is illustrative of the problem that football faced in that first great rush of analysis around the turn of the century. It was, in many ways, simply an updated version of the issue that had turned Reep from a pioneer into a pariah, a digital version of an analogue problem: the power of the data relied largely on the ability of people to read it. Clubs, managers and players understood that there was a value in having all of this information at their disposal. But just having the numbers was only the first step; the sport as a whole was still grasping at air trying to work out what to do with them, how to parse and interpret them, how to separate the ones heavy with meaning from the ephemera. The data pouring out of ProZone and Opta had a Pythian quality. As with all oracles, the content and the meaning often diverged.

There were exceptions. Sam Allardyce was written off as a dinosaur even while he was, by managers' standards, relatively young. He was bluff and bullish and a touch boastful, and he played the sort of football that was, by the time his Bolton team made it to the Premier League in the late 1990s, considered deeply old-fashioned by the football's newly gentrified audience. The self-imposed caricature of 'Big Sam', though, concealed not only a fiercely inquisitive mind but a surprisingly innovative approach. Allardyce had spent time late in his playing career with the Tampa Bay Rowdies, the Florida outpost of the now-defunct North American Soccer League. There, he had been captivated by the unapologetic modernism of American sport; when he moved into management, he was determined to bring some of the ideas he had encountered back across the Atlantic. At Bolton, he was one of the first elite coaches to explore the idea of sports psychology, appointing Mike Forde, a psychologist, to oversee the club's performance culture. He became an ardent devotee of the relatively new field of sports science. He experimented with Chinese medicine techniques and hired nutritionists long before they were *de rigueur*. And, in the late 1990s, he was the first manager in England's second tier, the First Division, to persuade his club to sign up to ProZone.

Like all of the company's clients, Bolton were provided with an analyst, a sharp-witted sports science graduate called Dave Fallows. Allardyce, though, did not stop there. His time in the United States had taught him that having access to the numbers was not enough; he needed to mine the information for insight. He recruited two more analysts, Gavin Fleig and Ed Sulley, to help Fallows do precisely that.

What emerged from Allardyce's laboratory was – at least outside of Lobanovskyi's Dinamo Kyiv – the first data-driven team, certainly in football and possibly in sport more broadly. Two years before Billy Beane's epiphany in Oakland started to transform baseball and a decade before football clubs started investing heavily in their data departments, Allardyce was writing almost exactly the same story in strikingly similar circumstances, distilling what he had found in the data into a set of unorthodox principles that defined how his team played.

He called them his 'fantastic four'. He knew that, if his team kept 16 clean sheets over the course of a 38-game season, it would not be relegated. He knew that if his team scored first, it would have a 70 per cent chance of winning a game. He knew that if his players covered more distance at a speed above 5.5 metres per second than their opponents, their chances of winning would go through the roof. And he knew that a third of all goals came from set-pieces. He knew all that, rather than believed it, because that is what the numbers told him. And so he built a team in accordance with the knowledge that he had gleaned.

Data suffused almost everything Bolton did. It went beyond the fact that Allardyce and his assistant, Phil Brown, drilled their players relentlessly on set-pieces, defending them and attacking them. He learned that, in the average game, the ball switched between teams – what we now call turnovers – more than 400 times. That highlighted, to him, the importance of switching immediately into a defensive mindset once possession had been lost, or sparking into life as soon as it was won back. Ten years later, a succession of German coaches would have the same insight and develop the counter-pressing game in response. Allardyce, in some lights, got there first. What Bolton did, in the early 2000s, seems sophisticated even 20 years on; at the time, it is not too much of a stretch to suggest it was revolutionary.

Unlike Reep – and even, heresy though it may be to say it, Ferguson – Allardyce's great gift was that he did not stop at the first, most obvious, conclusion. He took the oracle and examined it to divine its true meaning. He understood that set-pieces were important, but he wanted to know what kind of set-pieces. His analysts found that most goals from corners came from crosses that swung towards the goalkeeper, rather than away from them, and so that is what Bolton did. Next, they asked what happened to all the unsuccessful attempts: if the ball was cleared, where was it most likely to land? Did that spot change depending on the nature of the corner? If the initial cross went to the near post, rather than the far, it was cleared to a different spot. All of that information bled into Allardyce's approach. He stationed players in specific areas around the box for different types of corners so as to give his team the best chance of regaining the ball should it break loose.

He was among the first, too, to use data to influence his transfer policy. Though Allardyce's teams were always regarded as functional, he had a strange and in some ways counter-intuitive habit of finding a way to incorporate the likes of Jay-Jay Okocha and Youri Djorkaeff, ageing, creative stars who did not fit the broader template. Data was at the heart of that decision, too. In 2004, Bolton were given the chance to sign Gary Speed. By traditional football logic, Speed was a risk: a lauded, much admired Premier League midfielder coming to the end of his career. He was 34. He had been playing at the top level for more than a decade; he had hundreds of games in his legs. Most managers, particularly those who preached an industrious, high-intensity style, would have seen that as a red flag. Not Allard-yce. He tasked his analysts with going through Speed's physical data from the last couple of years. They found that he was running as much, as fast, as the likes of Steven Gerrard and Frank Lampard, players more than a decade younger than him. Age had not wearied him. Speed played for Bolton for four productive years, until he was 38.

And yet nobody ever thought to turn the story of how Bolton overturned football's natural order, how they managed to survive among the elite against all odds, into a glitzy Hollywood block-buster. And if they had, they certainly would not have cast Brad Pitt in the Allardyce role. Partly, of course, that is down to how the rest of his career, away from Bolton, played out. Allardyce was reviled at Newcastle and Everton. He earned a lucrative but limited repu-tation as a relegation specialist, football's equivalent to the Hail Mary, the coach you appoint when all else is lost. And then, just as he seemed to have been granted a reward, he was removed as England manager almost before he had got started, brought low by secret recordings made by the *Daily Telegraph* that seemed to show him advising reporters posing as businessmen on how to get round rules banning third-party ownership of players. Most damaging for his reputation, though, was not what he said but what he was drink-ing: Allardyce appeared to have been sitting at a dinner table, order-ing wine by the pint.

That particular charge was not accurate, but that it stuck regard-less was telling. The image Allardyce had in English football was of exactly the sort of man who might drink a pint of wine: unsophisti-cated, boorish, a relic from a bygone age. It had proved such a compelling characterisation that it had effectively overwhelmed the more complex reality, that Allardyce was – in his own way – a trail-blazer and an innovator, albeit not an especially telegenic one.

That it had taken hold, and taken hold so firmly, can be attributed not to Allardyce's working but to his conclusions. His methods were, without question, far ahead of their time; his influence, too, is often vastly underestimated. Fallows, his ProZone-appointed analyst, is now head of scouting at Liverpool. Fleig runs Manchester City's analytics operations; Sulley was a long-term colleague there, too. Forde, his psychologist and performance guru, would go on to work at Chelsea before leaping across the Atlantic to conquer the NFL.

But the ultimate outcome of their work, valuable and pioneering though it was, remained essentially counter-cultural. Allardyce's football bore all the hallmarks of the game as espoused and envisioned by Reep and, especially, Charles Hughes. Bolton were derided – not entirely fairly but not without reason – as a long-ball team at a time when English football was in thrall to a more exotic aesthetic, imported from continental Europe and inflected by South America. Allardyce was written off as just another exponent of Positions of Maximum Opportunity. He might have been a coach for the digital age, but his team was distinctly, irredeemably, analogue. He would never get his film. Not the sort of film he wanted, anyway, one shot on something other than a concealed camera carried by an undercover reporter.

Instead, Allardyce is perhaps best understood as a harbinger of the change that now hovered on the game's horizon. He was the first coach in Western Europe to begin to harness the industrial-scale information that was, thanks to the data factories at Opta and ProZone, starting to pour into the game. He was not the first to realise its potential and power, but he was the first to explore in a meaningful, scientific way what it could do. That journey, though, would be completed by others. Allardyce had not been deemed a suitable fit for the role of football's Billy Beane. He had a stigma that he could not, or perhaps would not, shake. That left a vacancy to be filled. There was no shortage of willing candidates.

TROJAN HORSE

Kathleen O'Connor did not take it seriously, not at the start. If anything, she and her sons, Nick and Eli, found it funny. The sudden transformation of her husband, their father, from Ivy League academic into football obsessive became something of a running joke. They would find Chris Anderson sitting on the couch of their home in Ithaca, a picturesque, leafy college town in upstate New York, watching yet another Premier League game, and ask him how his 'work' was going, emphasis on the air quotes. They would mock him, affectionately, about the contents of his latest blog post. They treated his new hobby with the blend of tolerance and teasing merited by what appeared, on the surface, to be a largely benign, and slightly premature, mid-life crisis.

There did not seem to be any reason for O'Connor to read anything deeper into it. Her husband had always been a football fan in some nominal, cursory sense – he described himself, more than anything, as lapsed – but his true interest, his real passion, was his work. Anderson had spent near enough thirty years immersed in the political and behavioural sciences, the study of why people make the decisions they do, and how the two intersect. He had held posts at some of the most illustrious universities in the United States: Rice, Northwestern and Syracuse. He had been a visiting fellow at Oxford. He had published half a dozen books and written a welter of weighty, peer-reviewed papers with catchy titles like 'Losers' Consent: Elections and Democratic Legitimacy' and 'Political Institutions and Satisfaction with Democracy: A Cross-National Analysis of Consensus and Majoritarian Systems'. He had been invited to speak at highbrow conferences and deliver lectures at Harvard and Princeton and the London School of Economics. Anderson was also credited with creating the term 'barometer election' to describe things like by-elections in Britain: votes that can be used to gauge how an electorate feels about its incumbent government but do not have the power to change it. He was, at the time his interest in sport was suddenly reawakened, a tenured professor at Cornell, one of the most prestigious universities in the world.

It was a post that Anderson had worked all of his life to achieve, and a life he could scarcely have dreamed of as a child. He had spent his formative years in what he described as a small, conservative town in Germany, not far from Cologne. It was Catholic, almost exclusively, entirely devoutly, a little oppressively. Like all small German towns, it shut down entirely on Sundays. He had always felt a little like he did not quite fit. His mother was German, but his father was an American GI. He was, as far as he knew, the only child in town with an American surname and an American passport. He was also the only child in town whose parents were divorced. His father had moved back to the United States when Anderson was four. Growing up, he had no relationship with him. Instead, he lived with his mother and his grandparents. His mother, unable to work because of a disability, looked after her parents, and the German welfare state looked after the family, as best it could. Anderson remembered months when ends did not quite meet.

Academia, and America, had been his way out. He had studied first at the University of Cologne – political science, history, English – and then applied for a master's degree at Virginia Tech. The United

States, the thing that had always loomed in his mind as a source of difference, provided him with a career, and with a home. He took a PhD at Washington University in St Louis, a post as a junior fellow at Stanford, and then his first assistant professorship at Rice University in Houston. There, he met Kathleen, an assistant professor in the university's psychology department. They married, had kids, moved on and moved up.

It was hardly surprising, then, that Anderson's job blurred the lines between career and identity. He relished the intellectual demands of his work, enjoyed his study and his teaching, found the subject matter and the methodology of his field fascinating, but academia is not a place full of pure souls interested only in the betterment of themselves and mankind. Status matters. Esteem matters. It always had to Anderson, anyway. To be a Professor of Government – and at Cornell, no less, a bastion of the Ivy League – was to be someone, something. Most important of all, perhaps, it was proof that he belonged.

Anderson did not quite fit the stereotype of a serious academic. He was not particularly stuffy or pompous. He had a ready laugh and a quick, occasionally profane wit and an easy, self-deprecating manner. He was, though, most certainly an authority in his field. It was that, really, which made his almost overnight conversion into an ardent follower of football seem so inherently comic to his wife. Anderson spent his time wrestling with complex, nuanced thoughts, and yet here he was, blogging about how many corners teams won, talking earnestly to like-minded strangers on the internet about passing statistics from the French top division. It was harmless, of course. But it was also funny.

Both Anderson and O'Connor would have been familiar with the work of Robert K. Merton, the renowned, pioneering sociologist; Merton was, after all, a giant in a field at least contiguous to that which Anderson occupied. The scale of Merton's influence is impossible to exaggerate. He invented the focus group. He transformed the public perception of scientists from unruly, erratic geniuses into quiet, surgical detectives. He helped bring about an end to the policy of racially segregated schools in the American South. He not only coined the term 'self-fulfilling prophecy' but 'role model' too, the sort of achievement that feels like it belongs in Dr Evil's soliloquy from the *Austin Powers* franchise, the one in which he details how his father claimed to have invented the question mark. In Merton's case, of course, it was true. He was also the first person to capture the idea of what we now know as the Law of Unintended Consequences, the concept that an action's impact ripples out in all sorts of strange, unexpected ways. Anderson did not know it, but as he sat on the couch watching the Premier League and writing his blogs, he was on the verge of becoming something close to the perfect case study.

It all started with a book. O'Connor had heard about *Moneyball*, the Michael Lewis book that detailed how Billy Beane, the general manager of the Oakland A's, had used data to turn one of baseball's poor relations into record-breakers, overturning the sport's established financial order and transforming the way the game was both played and operated in the process, and she had thought Anderson might like it. Not so much for the context – he was not much of a baseball connoisseur – but for the message. He studied the biases and prejudices that drive our decision-making; it was, at least in part, by recognising them that Beane had succeeded. *Moneyball* was the perfect light read for a behavioural economist.

Anderson read it, enjoyed it, thanked his wife for the recommendation. And that might, really, have been as far as it went, had it not been for Merton's law. *Moneyball* made Anderson realise that not only did he not know anything about baseball, he did not know anything about football, a sport with which he was at least theoretically much more familiar, either. He did not know what the most frequent final score was. Maybe one-all? Maybe a two-one home win? How many corners were there in an average game? How many shots? He could estimate it, just by instinct. He might even be able to make an educated guess. But he did not know, not in the sense that an academic wants to know. His curiosity stimulated, he set out to find out. It would be a search that would, in short order, result in him giving up his job, moving his family across an ocean, and trying to persuade some of the richest men on the planet to spend tens of millions of pounds on a volatile asset and put him, an academic with absolutely no experience of running a business, in charge of it. One simple gift from his wife was all it took to change the course of Chris Anderson's life. He had spent three decades rising as high in academia as he could. He felt at home in his ivory tower. He was about to give it all up to try and become football's answer to Billy Beane.

The halls of the Boston Convention and Exhibition Center were packed. The corridors were filled not just with insiders from every major sport – from baseball and basketball, golf and ice hockey, both stripes of football – but with those who, until recently, would have been considered the ultimate outsiders. The MIT Sloan Sports Analytics Conference was only a few years old, but it was already well-established as the place where coaches and executives and scouts mingled with thinkers and theorists, academics and analysts, mathematicians and physicists and economists. It was where the best and brightest gathered to push boundaries and accelerate progress and sharpen the very cutting edge of sport. It was so advanced that Google and Goldman Sachs had both sent representatives to scour the corridors for talent and ideas. It had become known, in those circles, simply as 'Sloan', but the spirit and scale of what was effectively the sports analytics Super Bowl was perhaps better captured by the nickname it had been given by the writer and regular attendee Bill Simmons. He called it, affectionately, 'Dorkapalooza'.

How much it had grown in the few years of its existence mirrored the surge of interest in the field it covered. By 2011, analytics were big business across all of the United States' major leagues. Baseball had led the way, transformed by the success of Beane and the A's and the subsequent widespread interest in and adoption of what was known as sabermetrics. 'Baseball analytics is now a mature field, with debates revolving around details, not general principles,' as the official MIT review of that year's conference noted.

Other sports were lagging behind, just a little. Basketball, the conference's co-founder Daryl Morey admitted, was a few years behind; ice hockey and the National Football League were a little further back still. They knew enough about their own limitations, though, to have accepted that they needed to catch up. Sloan's guest list proved that. The previous year, the conference had attracted a thousand delegates, but this time around there were half as many again, among them emissaries from more than 50 professional teams. At the entrance to the convention center, 1,500 gift bags – each one containing a t-shirt, a pen, a flash drive containing that year's presentations, a copy of *ESPN: The Magazine* and the book *The House Advantage* by the MIT graduate Jeffery Ma – were piled high on a trestle table. The opening keynote, delivered by Morey and the author Malcolm Gladwell, was standing room only. Every single seat in the cavernous main hall was taken. Latecomers, those who had dawdled too long over the complimentary breakfast of orange juice and muffins that had been laid on outside, were forced to lean against the walls to listen to a discussion over the validity or otherwise of the 10,000 hours theory of practice, popularised and promoted by Gladwell's most recent work.

It was the same for all of the big-ticket talks that year. A talk on the extent to which home advantage essentially boiled down to referees favouring the hosts drew a huge crowd. So, too, did a presentation by Ma, the inspiration for one of the characters in the Ben Mezrich book *Bringing Down the House*, the story of how six MIT students used card-counting techniques to win millions on the Las Vegas Strip.

Football's reception was a little different. That year, for the first time, the game was the focus of a dedicated panel, one featuring representatives from Manchester City, Chelsea and Decision Technology, a company that was, strictly speaking, involved in research for the retail industry. A handful of other Premier League teams had sent delegates to listen to the talk, to make connections, to pan for ideas.

That the sport was represented at all showcased that it was starting, gingerly, to accept and internalise the importance of data. That it was represented on such a small scale showed how far it had to go.

The single football-themed event had a much more intimate, acoustic sort of an affair than the main events taking place in the main hall. The talk was held instead in a small room, at the other end of the corridor. Nobody had to stand. There were a few dozen attendees, mostly those already employed in football, together with a few curious outsiders. One of them was a Cornell professor who had used his academic credentials to wrangle an invite.

Chris Anderson had approached his dawning interest in football data as he would any other intellectual challenge. Over the previous couple of years, he had read as widely as he could on the subject, before realising that he could not read very widely at all. 'As an academic, you read first, always,' he said. The problem was that there was 'very, very little' to read. A colleague handed him a copy of *Soccernomics*, the book by Simon Kuper and Stefan Szymanski that represented the first beachhead for analytical thinking in football, but anything more rigorous, anything more academic, was thin on the ground.

What literature he could find tended to be written by a small enclave of British academics focused on the statistics of betting odds, using 'notational analysis' – counting up the number of times certain things happen – to work out what was happening on the field of play. There was some work by sports scientists, too, who had used early ProZone data to examine players' physical output; that, after all, is what most of the coaches using the software were obsessed by. There was no canon of work detailing even the relatively simple questions he wanted to answer first of all: how many corners teams won, how many shots they took, let alone anything more complex, more analytical.

He had more luck finding information from public sources. Though much of football's data remained confidential, proprietorial, fiercely guarded either by the clubs using it or the private companies providing it, Anderson found that some of it had filtered out online. And so he took the next familiar step: he started writing. 'That's how academics communicate,' he said. 'Thinking happens when you write. That's when you realise what you do and don't know.' To his family's ill-concealed amusement, and in keeping with the fashion of 2009, he started a blog. 'It was a totally selfish enterprise from me,' he said. His expectations, his desires, were not especially high. 'But I thought it was cool,' he said. 'Now I knew how many shots there were.'

He was not, it turned out, alone. Anderson soon found himself part of a niche but thriving ecosystem of fans using data to try to carve out insights into the game. They were mostly engineers, by background, though they specialised in all sorts of different areas: data engineers and chemical engineers and an aeronautics and astronautics engineer, a real-life rocket scientist. They were all trying to engage with the sport they loved through a prism that came intuitively to them in other spheres of their lives: numbers.

In his fellow bloggers, Anderson found a tight-knit, supportive community of like-minded souls. They read and commented and critiqued each other's work. They were quick to praise anything novel or innovative that any of their number had produced. They magnified each other's efforts on an up-and-coming 'micro-blogging' site called Twitter. They shared tips on what sources of data were publicly available, and banded together to try to persuade data providers to let them have access to that which was not. That was the big, common problem that they all faced: a shortage of material. Unlike in American sports, there was not a vast trove of freely available data to play with; most of it rested in the hands of private data gatherers and providers, companies like Opta and ProZone, or the teams themselves. Neither group was especially enthused by the idea of giving it away to amateur enthusiasts for nothing.

But while supply was an issue, demand was not. From what Anderson could tell, his blog and those like it appeared to be finding a small audience. It should be no surprise that an academic on a quest for data should have carried out a little analysis of who was reading his blog and who was interacting with him on Twitter. He identified certain common threads. His readers skewed younger. They tended to be college or university-educated. Close to half were in North America. That did not surprise him, particularly. Over the previous decade, football had boomed in popularity on that side of the Atlantic, driven not just through the slow, deliberate growth of Major League Soccer, North America's professional league, but by increased exposure to the Premier League and Champions League, in particular. For the first time, thanks to broadcast deals with Fox Sports and ESPN, fans in the United States had been able to watch European football regularly since just before the turn of the century. Gradually, more and more had been won over to the game; audiences were booming sufficiently for a rival channel, NBC Sports, to have taken notice: a couple of years later, it would pay $250 million for the rights to show live Premier League football in the USA.

That new audience was far more familiar with a statistical approach to sport than the game's traditional fanbase in Europe. American sports were suffused with numbers: batting averages and on-base percentages and runs above replacement and all the rest, and had been long before Bill James and Billy Beane appeared on the scene; the reason, indeed, that the sabermetric approach James pioneered could take hold was because all of those numbers existed anyway. Beane's revolutionary insight had not been to use numbers, it had been to see the values in the numbers everyone else ignored. As America took to football, it was only natural that the new arrival got the old treatment. American fans – particularly younger ones, those who might have come to the game through or at least with the FIFA video game series – wanted to talk about this sport in the same language in which they discussed all the others. They were hungry for the sort of statistical approach and context they would expect elsewhere.

Anderson was more intrigued by the fact that there seemed to be demand from Europe, too: principally Britain, but occasionally the Netherlands or Germany or Ukraine. He would field a steady stream of correspondence inspired by his blog. Most of it came from fans, eager to find out if he could tell them something about their team, or give them a little insight into a particular player. He turned the best ideas, the most interesting or illustrative challenges, into posts. But just occasionally, someone from inside a club would get in touch. 'Some of it was very much "give me your secret",' he said: people who were looking for some magic number that would solve football. Others, though, were less acquisitive. 'There were two or three people from lower league clubs in England that got in touch,' he said. 'They wanted to know where they could get data about their team, or what

I knew about them. They weren't executives or coaches. They were video analysts, sports scientists. They were casting around for like-minded people. They had been hired as technicians, really, to look after the ProZone stuff, but the clubs didn't know what to do with them. They couldn't get an audience within their clubs. They were lonely, looking for a network.'

It was the first sign he had that there might be an appetite for what he was doing within the game itself. That impression was only confirmed when, along with 1,500 others, he filed into the Boston Convention and Exhibition Center in March 2011. Going to Sloan seemed the natural next step: attending a conference to learn more about a field was what an academic, after all, would do. His bona fides had been more than enough to get him a ticket. He did not need a reason, was not asked to show his hand. There was nothing especially unusual about a Cornell professor wanting to attend a conference at MIT.

The night before the conference started, he and his fellow bloggers had gathered in a bar to meet, in person, ahead of the event; half a dozen of them had made it to Boston. Once inside the convention center, though, it was impossible not to notice how under-represented football was compared to the major US sports, but that there was even a handful of people there encouraged him. 'The people from football were the ones who were curious to find out how they could use analytics in football,' he said. He found them all more than willing to talk. They tended to huddle together. They did not know any of the other delegates. Ideas from different disciplines, at that stage, had not yet cross-pollenated, networks had not been established.

Anderson felt more than comfortable asking the few dozen people he found in attendance for the one football panel at the conference who they were, what they did and who they did it for. Generally, they were happy to talk. With only a couple of exceptions, he found, they were grateful for an opportunity to vent their frustrations. 'It was a chance to moan,' he said. Analytics in football was not quite as backward at that stage as public perception had it – many of the advances were kept under lock and key by the clubs making them – but the impression he formed was that most analysts were frustrated by the resistance they faced internally.

'A lot of them found that nobody listened to them, that nobody in their clubs really got it,' he said. 'They felt like they didn't have any colleagues. They'd all been so enthusiastic when they came into it and then they had seen their spirit, well, crushed.' They pointed out that there was nothing even similar to Sloan in Europe. They felt at home among all of their fellow delegates – 'knee deep in nerds,' as *Business Insider* would slightly unkindly put it – but that they had travelled so far to be there only highlighted how alien they were in their own field. 'Sloan was important to them to confirm to themselves, really, that they were doing something worthwhile,' Anderson said.

He had much the same reaction. He knew that the readerships of his blog, and those of his fellow travellers, were growing. He could see, now, that there were people receptive to this form of thinking within football. There was interest in football and data and how the two might combine. It was lagging behind baseball, in particular, but that was as much an opportunity as an obstacle. 'It felt like there was a wave growing,' Anderson said. He started to wonder, as he looked at the hundreds of delegates milling around the convention center, at how much sports analytics had grown in the United States in just a few years, how far and how fast it would go, and whether he might be able to ride it.

Scott McLachlan has always been the sort of scout who goes to games. Even now, when he is in a job when he does not strictly speaking have to, when there are other people who might be able to do that for him, he still finds his way to four or five a week. 'I don't want to lose touch with the essence of the game,' he told the journalist Michael Calvin in his book *The Nowhere Men*.

That was the way he had been taught to do his job. His background was an orthodox one, the traditional rise from youth football to the lower leagues and, teeth cut and instincts honed, on to the big time. He had started work at Wimbledon in its post-Crazy Gang era, the team that represented the last stand of English football's love affair with the kick and rush era. He had moved on to Northampton, taking a job in youth development, and then Southampton, before moving into recruitment at Fulham.

McLachlan's time-honoured résumé, though, was something of a red herring. He was not, by any stretch of the imagination, a traditional scout. Instead, he was something of a new breed in English football, and not just because he was university-educated. He had worked at Southampton at the time that the club's chairman, Rupert Lowe, was in thrall to what is probably best described as performance culture, appointing as Performance Director Sir Clive Woodward, the man who had steered England to victory in the Rugby World Cup in 2003, despite the rather troubling fact that he did not have any experience within, or even knowledge of, football. McLachlan had been brought into the club in the same vein, hired as a performance analyst in an era when clubs across the country were seeking people like him – those with some sort of qualification in sports science – to fulfil that role. At Fulham, though, McLachlan became something much rarer indeed: he was the club's technical scout, a member of the recruitment team dedicated to gathering and collating and parsing information on potential signings. He was tasked with judging players not just by what he saw on the field, but by what he saw on the computer screen, too. He was among the first, if not the first, person with that job description in English football.

It was with that in mind that, in 2011, he had travelled to Sloan, hoping to keep himself apprised of the advances in the field of data analytics in American sport, and keep in touch with what some of Fulham's rivals in the Premier League were getting up to. He had been in the small auditorium in which the conference's sole football-related panel had been held; he had been one of the people Anderson, comfortable in the sort of setting he knew well, had happily approached and asked, with a smile: 'What do you do?'

The pair had quickly struck up a rapport. Anderson was enthused to find a forward-thinking, progressive character who not only worked in football but was very much of football, too. McLachlan is the sort of person who chooses his words carefully, who can seem a little guarded, who is far more comfortable away from the spotlight than drifting into its glare: all the characteristics of someone who has worked, for years, in an industry which cherishes its discretion, at least as far as outsiders are concerned.

But McLachlan was intrigued to encounter an academic interested in his nascent field, the sort of external influence who might be able to find a signal in all of the noise that would otherwise have been missed. That had value to him: job security does not come easily in football, particularly to those who seem to threaten the established order. He knew he had to justify his existence in a way in which a more traditional scout would not. He was, as Anderson recalled, 'fighting a really hard fight' inside the club to make his voice heard among those who felt the new dawn he represented was a false one. He hoped Anderson might be able to add a little weight to his argument. They made plans to keep in touch; a few weeks later, Anderson flew to London to visit McLachlan at Motspur Park.

Fulham's training facility, set in a sedate part of south-west London, was not, then, among the most advanced in English football – it did not have the same space-age air as Cobham, say, where Chelsea train, or the bespoke design of Arsenal's Colney base – but it was among the most refined. Its central building had a distinctly academic air, testimony to its heritage as the changing rooms for the University of London athletics track. The world mile record was set there in 1938. The track, long since grassed over, was a filming location for *Chariots of Fire*. It sits on a quiet street in a leafy suburb, the dull roar of the A3 dampened by trees.

McLachlan had invited Anderson with no motive other than to 'hang around'. He gave him a tour, introduced him to a few people, treated him to lunch in the canteen. It was low-key, but to Anderson it felt like a bold new horizon. Sitting at home in Ithaca, 'playing around with a blog and a spreadsheet,' as he put it, the idea that he might be able to gain access to football's sanctum sanctorum seemed impossible. And yet, in the space of a couple of years, he had gone from being an academic whose football fandom had lapsed to being a central player in a blogging community to being invited into a Premier League club, so he could be granted an insight, up close and personal, into what life was like inside the game. He had made it through the gates. The problem, he quickly surmised, would be whether he could do anything once he was there.

Anderson's early encounters with football functioned, essentially, as a series of realisations. He noticed, as the readership of and the wider interest in his blog soared, that there was an appetite for an analytical approach to the sport that firmly believed it could not and it should not be coded. He spotted, at Sloan, that there was a burgeoning market within the game for that kind of information. Thanks to McLachlan, he wondered if Fulham was his chance to tap it.

After that meeting at Motspur Park, Anderson returned to the United States and set to work, seeing what he might be able to tell Fulham about their squad that they did not already know.

Fulham were performing well in the Premier League – they were destined, that season, for a third top-half finish in four years – but Anderson wanted to find out which players were most central to the club's success. He looked at what little data he could access, and produced an analysis of who was contributing most to Fulham's attacking output: which players were having the best chances, which ones were underperforming, who was suffering simply from a little bad luck. He did not use the term, but what he had effectively created was an Expected Goals model. 'Some of it was actually quite advanced,' said Anderson, as though surprised by himself.

Fulham's reaction, though, was muted. Clint Dempsey, a busy, bustling American forward, was the team's standout player that season – he would finish with 17 goals in the Premier League, and a move to Tottenham – and, unsurprisingly, he came out well in Anderson's analysis, too. In hindsight, perhaps that was less than ideal. It made it easy to assume that this complex, new-fangled data-based approach was simply confirming the blindingly obvious. All of that study and analysis and energy had proved was that the leading goalscorer had also had the most chances. 'They didn't really know what to do with it,' said Anderson. 'It was sort of like: "That's interesting. What is the point of it?"'

That response prompted Anderson's third realisation. 'For the industry to take you seriously, you have to become someone in that industry,' he said. 'You can't do it by showing up with your little briefcase at Motspur Park and saying, "Hey, I've got a product for you, I have some insight and knowledge."' Not least because, at that stage, Anderson was not especially clear on what he was selling, and Fulham had no concept of what they might want to buy. 'I could help them make sense of football data, but they didn't know what the data did, exactly,' Anderson said. Nor did he have a product, something he could point to and say: this is what I do. 'That was kind of a problem,' he admitted, ruefully.

That was a major obstacle, but it was not the only one. Anderson had never expected to be able to make connections within football; that he had managed, in short order, to traverse the vast chasm that separated his couch in Ithaca, New York, and the alien world of the Premier League was not enough. The contacts he had made were mostly further down the pecking order than McLachlan. They were video and performance analysts, sidelined members of coaching teams, sports scientists, progressives in a conservative world. 'The people who were interested were scouts and analysts, those types of people,' Anderson said. That was an achievement in itself, of course, but it was not achievement enough. 'But they had no money to spend. They had no power to do anything. The people who made any kind of decisions over money were not the people who were interested in what we could do.' To have any influence, Anderson needed to find a way to appeal to the people who held the purse-strings. To find out if his ideas worked, if the wave he had detected at Sloan might lead anywhere, he needed access to the money, and the power.

At first glance, Chris Anderson and David Sally have a cookie-cutter similarity. They are tall and slim and possess a distinctly Ivy League air: sports jackets and easy conversation and a professorial polish. But though they were close, Anderson had always been dimly aware of the differences between them. Sally had not always been an academic – he had spent three years at the start of his career working for the consulting firm Bain & Company – but he was a natural fit. He had, after all, been born to it: his parents were professors of mathematics. His siblings were high achievers. One of his brothers had taught at Stanford. The other ran an entire school district in Illinois. He met his wife at Harvard, where he had gained his undergraduate degree. He had gone on to take a PhD from the University of Chicago, work as an assistant professor at Cornell for almost a decade, and then take up a post as a Professor of Management at the college that counts as its fiercest rival, Dartmouth. In Anderson's eyes, Sally moved seamlessly through the world he inhabited in a way that he simply could not, and he envied him for it, in that affectionate, secret manner of friends.

Anderson had, deep down, always felt like an interloper. He had never quite been able to shake his background: an absent father, a single mother, the months that ended without quite enough food on the table. It was a source of pride that he had made it as far as he had, of course, but it also felt a little like a stigma. He had worked his way into the world of conferences and lectures and symposiums, but it was not his, not really. He had spent most of his professional life trying to ensconce himself as deeply as possible into it, to swaddle himself in it, surround himself by it, because on some level he worried that he would never be of it. He had risen further than he could ever have believed possible. He was a professor with a chair at an Ivy League university; he had the financial stability he had lacked as a child – the tenure he enjoyed effectively means employment for life, a guaranteed income – and, more importantly, he had the status that he had always craved. His position was not just reward for a quarter of a century of dedication, the result of his entire working life; it was, to some extent, who he was. He was Chris Anderson, professor; Chris Anderson, academic.

Giving any of that up – giving all of it up – was anathema to him. He had not started his blog in the hopes of one day abandoning the life he had built and the career he had so painstakingly constructed. He had not disappeared further down the football data rabbit-hole expecting it to lead anywhere, not really. But the deeper he went, the harder he found it to turn around. The reward that seemed to lie just around the next corner, just out of reach, was too precious to ignore. Not financially, not particularly, but intellectually: to Anderson, the chance to run an experiment in real world conditions was too good to turn down. He was enthralled by the prospect of finding out if he could do what Billy Beane had done, and use data to overturn the inefficiencies of conventional wisdom.

He began by recruiting Sally. His friend's primary sporting interest was baseball; he was something of a footballing ingenue. But he had been sufficiently intrigued by Anderson's reignited zeal for the game not to dismiss his mounting enthusiasm as a pastime or a pipe-dream. He, too, saw the appeal in the intellectual exercise; he, too, found that it piqued his curiosity, not just academically but profes-sionally. Sally's time at Bain had left a lasting impression; at heart, he still heeded to the doctrine he had been taught by the firm's founder, Bill Bain, about the way companies should be run, about the way they should think, about what good performance looked like. 'His focus was always about asking what can we actually do,' Sally said.

Their first step had, again, followed the established academic path: they started work on a book, one that detailed their vision of what data might do to change football. It seemed the obvious move: they had seen that this was a field that was of interest to people, a land-scape full of unconquered peaks. But they did not want it to be an academic exercise.

'We could easily have got a contract from an academic press in the USA,' Anderson said. 'But nobody would have ever seen it. Nobody in football would have ever read that book, heard of that book, taken it seriously, taken us seriously. It would have been pissing in the wind. We needed to write a football book that was recognised as a football book by football people in the country with the biggest league in the world. It needed to be in England before the USA. It needed to have an English tone.'

Their motivations were more than just reaching the widest audi-ence possible. Indeed, in a sense, Anderson and Sally were not writing for a mass market. At the same time as they started putting the manuscript together, they had founded a consulting firm, Anderson Sally. It was designed to combine their theoretical skills to create something of practical value: Anderson's knowledge of gleaning insights from data, and Sally's expertise in putting those insights into place. The book was to serve as a 'calling card', as Anderson put it, to show people in football – and more particularly, the people in power in football – the sorts of things data might be able to do. They did not know football. They did not know anyone in the world of football. 'We didn't have the right connections, the right qualifications,' Anderson said. 'You're nobody. Like literally: you do not exist.' The book was designed as an advert, a way to create a demand for their services, a chance to overcome that first hurdle.

Quickly, though, they realised that was not enough. The book, *The Numbers Game: Why Everything You Think You Know About Football Is Wrong*, was a success when it was published in 2013. There was considerable press interest. It was reviewed in the *Guardian* and the authors were interviewed by *The Times*, among others. There were invitations to conferences and lectures, slots on television and radio. It seemed, in a sense, like the book football had been waiting for. There had been mounting awareness, in the media, about the data revolution across the Atlantic. The lessons of *Moneyball* had not gone unnoticed within the game: copies had been dispatched by the founders of both ProZone and Opta to almost anyone they thought might be interested, largely as a sales technique. Still, the natural question for almost a decade had been how this grand idea might be applied to football. The previous year, in late 2011, the film adaptation of *Moneyball* had been released, adding further fuel to the debate: football is a far more visual culture than it is a literary one. If these methods were good enough for Brad Pitt, then surely they were good enough for the Premier League?

The roadblock was within the game itself. By 2012, football had long since accepted the idea that data was of use. There was no shortage of the stuff. Any club worth its salt had a subscription to ProZone. They all had access to the information pouring out of Opta, too. In their databases, they could build a complete picture – although not necessarily a perfect one; the quality of the data was still questionable in some cases – of everything that was happening on the pitch. They knew where the players were running and how fast they were going and which of them were completing the most tackles or taking the most shots or finding teammates with the most passes.

Collating the data, though, was only the first phase of the revolution. Data and analytics are, often, used interchangeably within sport, as though the two are synonyms to be deployed in pursuit of elegant variation. In most contexts, that is no great crime; the use of one, after all, generally indicates the existence of the other; the meaning, as a rule, is clear.

But it would be helpful, in football's case, to separate the two. The sport's data age had begun with the advent of Opta and ProZone in the late 1990s. Even if the information they provided was of limited accuracy, particularly in those early years when it was still collated by hand, and even if only a handful had used it to have any impact on the way their teams functioned, most managers had, eventually, found some sort of use for it.

Mostly, as one former ProZone analyst said, it was a way of gauging 'accountability', particularly physically. Those players who were not running as far and as fast as they might could be picked up on it. Players who gave the ball away too much could be spotted and either improved or, more likely, dropped. Data gave managers evidence. At times, it was merely circumstantial. At many clubs, that week's ProZone statistics were printed out and pinned to the wall of the changing room or the gym at the training ground; players knew that, even if they would not face censure for what was perceived as a poor physical effort, their teammates would notice. Given a stick, most footballers have an in-built instinct to beat someone with it. And so players, in an effort to stave off the displeasure of their manager or their teammates or both, engineered ways to game the system. Manchester City's squad noticed that Pablo Zabaleta, their dogged and industrious right-back, had a habit of sprinting across the field during lulls in play. He had worked out that doing so helped him improve two key physical metrics: total distance covered and the number of high-intensity sprints he had produced. Others shuttled across the field while their own team was taking a corner. Tal Ben Haim, an Israeli central defender who played for both Bolton and Chelsea, won a reputation for playing endless short passes to his defensive partner to ensure his pass completion percentage was as high as it could be.

What football had not witnessed, Anderson and Sally felt, was an analytics revolution. Plenty of people were reading the numbers and taking note of what they said: these are the players who have sprinted the most, these are the number of shots we have taken and the rest. But nobody – as far as they could tell, at least – was trying to find out what they meant. Nobody was attempting to do what Beane had done and searched for something that told you some deeper truth about the game. Everyone was listening to the noise. Nobody seemed concerned about finding the signal. In Anderson's eyes, 'there was no Moneyball'.

That is not to say they went unnoticed. People within the sport were paying attention. The call that meant the most to him came from Graham Taylor, the former Watford, Aston Villa and England manager; he got hold of Anderson's number, somehow, and got in touch to say how much he had enjoyed the book. That, perhaps, should not have been a surprise: Taylor had, of course, sought the counsel of Charles Reep in his early days in management. But it was acknowledgement that they had created something of interest, something of value, from someone who wielded considerable clout within the sport, and that in itself was not common. 'The people inside clubs who read *The Numbers Game* were really excited,' Anderson said. 'There was a lot of fan mail we got from those people, thinking alright, something's happening now.' The problem, though, was the same; the book, like the broader analytics movement, had not cut through with the executives who made the decisions. They showed, Anderson said, 'mild interest and mild amusement. From the people who mattered, it was a bit of a pat on the head.'

It was enough to convince them that they needed to change tack. What had started out as idle curiosity had crystallised into something more concrete, more vocational. Anderson, in particular, had become so invested in the idea of analytics that he felt a desperate urge to put his ideas, his theories, his academic certainty that this approach should work – would work – to the test. 'The dream was to see it come to life,' he said. 'I wanted to prove a point. It was always about proving a point.'

Pitching the idea of analysis to clubs in the vague, vain hope their football departments might take an interest, both he and Sally knew, would not be enough to do that. 'We were academics sitting in Ithaca, playing around with our little blog and our little spreadsheets,' Anderson said. 'Nobody is going to give a flying fuck about that.' Even if someone had read their book and was interested in their work, there was little scope of anyone actually paying them for it. 'Departments didn't have budgets for that kind of thing,' he said. 'There was no money in doing analysis.'

It was Sally who first suggested a far bolder strategy. 'We were sitting in Caffè Nero in Manchester, the one not far from the train station,' he said. 'We'd been there for a conference, and we had our laptops out and we were looking through data, working on spread-sheets, doing analysis of our own, pretty rudimentary stuff. We started talking about how we could ever actually make any money off this. And the only answer we could think of was that we would have to buy a club.'

If they could not build a revolution from the ground up, they would have to impose one from the top down. As absurd as it sounded, even to them, they needed to own a club; or, since that would not be possible on the salary of two academics, they would at least need to run one, on behalf of an owner who shared their evangelism for data, one who 'believed in the mission,' as Sally put it.

As they sat at their table, not far from Piccadilly, they tried to map out how they might find their Magwitch. Sally had one connection: through a friend of a friend, he could at least pitch the idea to Mark Cuban, the bombastic entrepreneur who owned the Mavericks, the Dallas NBA franchise. Over the next few weeks, they exchanged emails. Cuban seemed keen. 'But there is interest and there is interest,' Sally said. 'He got the idea. He was sold on it. He said he wanted to be part of it, but he would not lead.' He would only be involved if the risk was spread. Anderson and Sally were going to have to put together a consortium.

And so, just a couple of years on from the days when he would sit on the couch, his wife and his children gently mocking him, Anderson found himself preparing to overturn his life, their lives, for the sake of an idle dream. He and Sally had decided that they could not make their plan work, bring their vision to life, from a distance, and so Anderson decided he would have to ask Kathleen, with her own career to consider, to leave Ithaca behind and move their young sons to Europe, plucking them from their schools, their friends, their home, and start all over again in London. Not only that, he would have to give up the job that he had worked so long to secure, the one that provided the bedrock of his sense of self.

It was, by his own admission, an uncharacteristic gamble. He told himself that he would not suffer, not at first, anyway: he took a year's sabbatical from his post at Cornell – a perk of academia due to him every seven years – and told himself that if he could not make considerable headway in 12 months, he would return to the life, and the career path, that he had spent a quarter of a century painstakingly building. Even with that apparent safety net, though, it was a risk. 'It was completely counter-normative,' he would reflect, later. 'It was really strange. People thought we were nuts. You just don't do it. It is saying to your profession: "I'm done." It goes against everything you have been trained to value in your professional life. It is not how it works. You are channeled into that path and there is no turning back. You work for 25 years to get that kind of a job, and then to walk away from it is really strange.' Anderson knew, though, that he had no choice, not if he was to pursue this project to the end.

His instinct was right, though he had no way of knowing it then. Football had not been quite so slow to realise that the reams of data it had been generating for years might have a power beyond establishing how hard players were working, or what the best way to take a corner was. One club, at least, had enjoyed access to sophisticated data analysis for five years or so before Anderson and his family arrived in London. It had passed unnoticed, in part, because it was of no benefit to anyone involved to talk about it publicly; all clubs guard anything they even suspect might be an edge from jealous rivals and prying journalists fiercely and furiously. But that it had not sparked a widespread revolution was down, too, to the fact that its impact had been limited. Not because it was of no value, nor because it was not sufficiently advanced, but because its prominence was in the gift of whoever happened to be manager at the time. If they did not care for it, then it faded from view. Anderson had hit upon a truth that Decision Technology, and Tottenham Hotspur, had known for a while. 'For me personally, the conclusion was simply that unless you own the club, there is no point,' he said. 'There is no other way.'

3

TOMORROW'S WORLD

By his own admission, Henry Stott was not a football fan. He did not support a team. In the spring of 2002, as the rest of England fretted about how the state of David Beckham's second metatarsal would affect the chances of the country's golden generation in that summer's World Cup, he was completely unmoved. Not only did Stott not know anything about football, he did not care about it, either.

He was, though, 'a passionate statistician'. That year, he had helped to found a start-up, Decision Technology, which would help businesses use insights gleaned from the burgeoning field of behavioural psychology to improve their customer service. The company would, for example, use sales data and psychological principles to study how many different ranges of toothpaste or cheese or bacon should be stocked on the shelves at Tesco, the giant chain that became its earliest retail client. It would assess what sort of offers would help the supermarket shift more melons, or what the best formula for displaying the price of milk might be. They were all, to Stott's mind, 'good statistical problems'.

The mention of an office pool on the World Cup had much the same appeal. He did not have any real interest in the outcome. He did not know whether Ronaldo, the iconic Brazilian striker, had fully recovered from two injury-scarred seasons or whether France had a genuine chance of becoming the first nation for 40 years to retain the trophy. But he was intrigued by the academic exercise, the chance to show that statistical analysis could be just as much use in sport as it was in retail. The fact that it would bring him just a hint of contrarian glee to do so was just an added bonus. 'I wanted to enter,' he said, 'to demonstrate that someone who knew nothing about football could beat the experts.'

A few weeks before the tournament began, he began to build a model. He had precious little to work with: he had no access to the data that ProZone had been painstakingly and expensively gathering for the past five years, and he could not justify paying thousands of pounds for the figures Opta provided to the media for what was, ultimately, just a friendly sweepstake. Instead, he scraped together what little information he could: a few years of results for all 32 teams to have made it to the tournament in Japan and South Korea, entered by hand into nothing more sophisticated than a spreadsheet. Then, he set about analysing it, using an approach he had borrowed, and then fine-tuned, from two academics. A few years earlier, Mark Dixon and Stuart Coles had published a paper that sought to use mathematical principles to predict the results of games with more accuracy, with the central aim of 'exploiting inefficiencies' in the betting market. It was published in the *Journal of Applied Statistics* in 1997; their work was considered sufficiently groundbreaking to be featured on *Tomorrow's World*, the long-running BBC science show that had first introduced the British public to such cutting-edge ideas as the mobile phone and chip-and-pin.

But while his work was rooted in science, his approach was – by his own admission – a little artisanal. Stott did not have access to enough meaningful data to make the system watertight. It did not matter too much, of course: it was not a serious professional project, just a little bit of fun. To his delight, though, and presumably to his colleagues' chagrin, it worked. Or, rather, it worked well enough.

In the tournament's opening game, France, the defending champions, would be facing Senegal, a team competing in the World Cup finals for the very first time. To most, it looked like a cakewalk for a French side that could call on a cadre of the world's finest players and the core of the team that had won the tournament four years previously: Thierry Henry, Patrick Vieira, Lilian Thuram, Marcel Desailly. The fact that Zinedine Zidane, the finest player on the planet, was only selected as a substitute did not seem to matter.

Stott, though, had seen something in his analysis that suggested Senegal should not be seen as nothing more than easy marks. Bruno Metsu's side had no little pedigree. The French, meanwhile, had been a little more volatile than their status as defending champions might have indicated. Stott estimated that Senegal had a one-in-four chance of shocking the world.

He would, a few days later, be proved correct: after half an hour of the opening game of the tournament in Seoul, Papa Bouba Diop, an unheralded midfielder playing for the French club Lens, put Senegal ahead. No matter how many superstars the French coach, Roger Lemerre, threw on, there was no way through. Senegal held on to win. The volatile team Stott had seen in his crude data would go on to make the quarter-finals on its World Cup debut. The French, meanwhile, were eliminated at the group stage, the defence of their world title ending in humiliation and regret.

Stott's little victory might have remained private – nothing more than a point proven in pursuit of mischief – and his life, and that of his company, taken a very different course had it not been for the sort of pure, random chance that a statistician would always take into consideration. A couple of days before the World Cup started, the colleague who had organised the office pool was telling a friend about Stott's attempt to prove he could know something about football without knowing anything about football.

EXPECTED GOALS

The friend, a producer at Radio 5 Live, was intrigued. World Cups absorb as much content as anyone can throw at them. The bar for what counts as legitimate filler is, in the early days of the tournament, remarkably low, and imbuing an unlikely creature with the power of foresight is a long and apparently proud tradition in coverage. The 2010 World Cup had a psychic octopus. By 2014, there were all manner of clairvoyant livestock. The 2018 tournament nominated a cat as its official animal oracle. A statistician who could predict results despite having no interest in the game whatsoever fitted the bill nicely; after all, it is entirely possible that Paul the Octopus quite liked football. Stott was booked to appear as a guest on Fi Glover's late-night show on the network, as nothing much more than a little bit of light relief. He duly revealed that he thought Senegal, rank outsiders for the bookmakers and written off as a gimme for the mighty French, were being underestimated. Or, more accurately, that France's superiority was not quite as clear cut as assumed.

In the car on the way back from a meeting in Westminster, a Conservative Party grandee was listening in, intrigued. The idea that you could use mathematics to discern patterns in football matches was blindingly obvious, now that he thought about it. He wondered why it had never occurred to him before.

There is just a touch of serendipity to the story, the way that Billy Beane tells it. In the summer of 2003, he decided to surprise his wife, Tara, with a trip to Europe as a birthday present. He chose London as the perfect destination, and booked a room at the Four Seasons hotel in Mayfair, not far from the buzzing cafés and thronged pubs of Shepherd Market. Every morning, he would flick through the newspapers over breakfast as they planned out their activities for the day. And every morning, he noticed that they were packed to the brim with breathless, screeching coverage of the Premier League.

Beane had not grown up watching football. He had what he regards as the 'classic American' sporting upbringing: baseball, American Football and basketball, with time set aside for tennis and golf in the summer. As a child, he knew of precisely two football players: Pelé, then serving as the headline act of the glamorous, tumultuous North American Soccer League, and the rather less famous Kyle Rote, Jr. The son of an iconic NFL player, Rote was arguably the first true star of America's nascent football scene. He had been the first homegrown player to finish as the NASL's top scorer, earning him the title of Rookie of the Year; he would, later, be sold by the Dallas Tornado to the Houston Hurricane for $250,000.

Beane had not been watching any of that. He had, instead, come to know Rote because of his appearances on the television show *Superstars* in the mid-1970s. The show pitted athletes from any number of sports against each other in various, unfamiliar disciplines, in an attempt to find out who was the most complete sportsperson. Bob Seagren, a pole vault gold medallist, won the first edition. Rote won the second, and the fourth, and the fifth (his streak was broken by OJ Simpson). Beane never watched him play football. He just knew he was a 'tremendous all-around athlete'.

By 2003, of course, football had made considerable headway in the United States. The NASL had collapsed, but it had been replaced in the mid-1990s by the less exotic, more sustainable Major League Soccer. The country's national team was the undisputed force at the top of the women's game. Their male counterparts had become a regular feature of World Cups. And audiences for television broadcasts of Europe's major leagues, particularly the Premier League, were growing steadily.

Still, as he looked through the morning newspapers, Beane was struck by two things: first of all, quite how much of England's sporting consciousness was dominated by football. The sport was bigger than he had, perhaps, been able to appreciate from California. And second, more intriguing still, was how frenzied it all seemed to be. 'I thought that if there was that much emotion going into it, there must be a lot of inefficiency,' he said. 'And that meant that there was a lot of opportunity.'

When he returned to the United States, Beane set out to explore the subject further. He may not have had much prior exposure to football, but he is a sports lover in the truest sense of the word; he is instinctively drawn to sport, regardless of whether he knows the rules or the background or the storylines. Baseball is his first love, of course, and it is his work, but sport as a whole is his pleasure: the television screen in his office at his home in the Bay Area is, for example, now quite often tuned to the Indian Premier League, proof that he has become that rarest of things, an American evangelist for cricket.

It did not take long for Beane to see the parallels between baseball and football, to determine that while the sports are starkly different – one based on the discreet battle between pitcher and hitter and the other in the more chaotic genus of 'invasion sport' – they operated along similar lines. He discerned, in football, what he termed an 'embedded culture', a particular way of doing things that cherished tradition, spurned new thinking or outside opinion, and prioritised the views of longstanding members of the tribe. Players retired and became managers or coaches or scouts, perpetuating the ideals they had been taught, locking the game in a sort of self-satisfied stasis.

It was by overturning that model that Beane had made his name, of course: that summer, *Moneyball* had yet to hit the shelves in the United States, but the revolution his success with the Oakland A's had inspired was already under way in baseball. The previous year, the team had won 20 games in a row on its way to winning its division, the American League West, despite lacking the financial firepower of most of its rivals. It had done so by using a data-driven approach to break free of baseball's longstanding dogmas.

His initial research convinced him that, to all intents and purposes, there was nobody within football doing anything of the sort. Clubs had access to some forms of data – provided largely by ProZone – and the media could cover basic statistics thanks to Opta, but there was no concerted attempt to use any of that to uncover any basic truths about the game, to see if received wisdom was flawed, to seek even the slightest advantage. The only thing he could find, in fact, that seemed to dovetail with his approach with the A's was a newspaper column, running every Saturday in *The Times* of London.

Beane was painfully aware that he knew nothing about football, but he knew, too, that knowing nothing about a sport was not a bar to being able to change it. He saw no reason why the lessons he had learned at the A's could not be adapted and applied to football. Within a couple of years of those lazy mornings in Shepherd Market, Beane was convinced that football was his next frontier.

The guest list's intended message was clear and unambiguous. As the programme for a business conference, it made little sense: Bill Clinton was on it, and so were John McCain and Shimon Peres, the former Israeli Prime Minister. But then Nicole Kidman and Bono shared similar billing to Bill Bratton, the chief of police in Los Angeles. At one point, Arnold Schwarzenegger was due on stage apparently with the sole purpose of introducing Tony Blair. But then it was not designed to be read as a programme for a business conference. It was designed to be read as a statement of power, as incontrovertible proof that nobody, nobody, turned down Rupert Murdoch.

In the summer of 2006, the Australian mogul and all-purpose potentate laid on a five-day management retreat for a select group of News Corporation staff at Pebble Beach, the luxury golf course not far from his sprawling cattle ranch in California's Carmel Valley. It was News Corp's first company-wide executive get-together for eight years – the 2001 edition had been cancelled after the 9/11 terror attacks – and Murdoch wanted to put on a show. It was modelled along the lines of a similar event organised by the investment firm Allen & Co. in Sun Valley, Idaho: inspirational talks from the great and the good in the morning, golf and chit-chat in the afternoon.

Murdoch had invited just a select few actual members of staff to attend: only a couple of leading figures from each of his newspapers, broadcasters and studios had made the cut. The contingent from *The Times* of London comprised Robert Thomson, the paper's editor, and Danny Finkelstein, its most influential political commentator and, on the weekend, its football savant.

Finkelstein had come into football journalism almost by accident. He had only started with the paper in 2001, joining its editorial board after a long and distinguished career in politics. He had acted as an advisor to John Major, served as director of the Conservative Research Department and oversaw several prominent think-tanks.

A devout Chelsea fan, Finkelstein had happened to catch Henry Stott discussing his analytical approach for predicting the results of football matches on the radio on the eve of the 2002 World Cup. The way Stott explained his methodology, the way he framed his premise, immediately struck a chord: Finkelstein had long believed that to understand what was happening in politics, the media needed access to the information politicians gleaned from focus groups. To understand the data, in his mind, was to understand the pattern. The same principle applied to football.

The next morning, Finkelstein happened to be invited to a meeting with the sports department, in which the paper's editors hoped to map out their coverage of the 2002 World Cup. He mentioned, in passing, the statistic that Stott had mentioned the previous night:

that Senegal had a 25 per cent chance of beating the French. Keith Blackmore, one of the newspaper's senior executives, loved the idea. They would, he decreed, run the number on the front of the special pullout section on the day of the game.

Finkelstein knew, of course, that the probabilities were in France's favour. There was a 75 per cent chance that the defending champions would not lose the game. But that was not how it had been presented: *The Times* had seemed to be the only newspaper to suspect that Senegal might cause an upset. Diop's goal ensured that Blackmore's bold call paid off. He wanted Finkelstein to provide more numbers with which to illustrate the paper's coverage. Finkelstein immediately called Stott and asked what else he had.

By that stage, statistics were hardly a rarity in the British media. Opta had been providing data to newspapers and broadcasters for five years: the company's Index had made its debut in the *Observer*, and on Sky Sports, in 1996. Since then, the change had been substantial, and it had been rapid. In the early 1990s, it was not even guaranteed that viewers tuning into the live broadcast of a game would be provided with a box score – the unobtrusive line in the corner of the screen keeping track of who was winning. There were no on-screen graphics detailing how far each team had run or the number of passes they had completed or the amount of shots they had taken. By the time Finkelstein and Stott started work on the column that would, in time, become the Fink Tank – a title coined by Blackmore – those raw statistics were a regular feature of every broadcast. Football had started to accept the idea of numbers.

In 1994, when the comedians David Baddiel and Frank Skinner had launched *Fantasy Football League*, a wry, late-night talk show tangentially related to the booming popularity of Fantasy Football, they had included a character called 'Statto', played by the commentator Angus Loughran. Statto, clad in dressing gown and slippers, spent the entire show in the kitchen, occasionally barking out facts and figures at the hosts, a sort of poindexter-in-residence. He was there, largely, to be the butt of the joke, to represent a strand of football fan that Baddiel and Skinner, all Britpop-era cool, mocked: not so much a nerd as a pub bore, obsessed with the detail but ignorant of the feeling of the game.

It is tempting to suggest that, by the time *Fantasy Football League* aired its final special in 2004, Statto had had the last laugh: it was, by then, no longer strange to see a game represented by its basic numbers. There is some truth in that, but it does not quite tell the whole story: the reason that Statto worked as a concept was precisely because that type of fan already existed, even in an era when football was adopted as a central part of Britain's burgeoning lad culture, and quite probably had always existed. Baddiel and Skinner, like everyone else, knew a Statto. That was what had made the joke land.

It would be nice to think that, perhaps, seeing themselves represented on-screen – being given an idol in a silk dressing gown – allowed Britain's Stattos to reclaim their identity, but the likelihood is there was a more profound shift in the nature of fandom. Fantasy Football, the game at the heart of the show, had boomed in the early years of the Premier League era. So, too, had management simulations: first in the form of games played by mail, and later in the shape of *Championship Manager* and then *Football Manager*. Both the *FIFA* and *Pro Evolution Soccer* video games were on their way to becoming a key point of entry to the sport itself.

What joined all of those things together was numbers. *FIFA* and *Pro Evolution Soccer* gave players ability ratings in a variety of skills. *Football Manager* offered users details of how each of their teams' games had gone: the number of shots taken or corners won or possession enjoyed. Fantasy Football worked on rewards for clean sheets and goals scored. The 1990s marked the first time that an entire generation of fans were raised with the instinctive understanding that football could, at heart, be boiled down to numbers. The prominence of statistics in the media reflected that: this was now a language that many fans spoke.

Still, the column that Finkelstein and Stott launched as a regular feature of *The Times'* football coverage in November 2002 was a trailblazer in its sophistication. Armed both with whatever academic literature he could unearth and Decision Technology's own research, Finkelstein began to examine whether there was any truth in much of the sport's accepted wisdom. Were teams really harder to beat when they had been reduced to 10 players? ('No. Of course not. You idiot,' as Finkelstein's conclusion put it.) Was a two-goal lead really the most dangerous scoreline? (Again, no.) Was just before half-time actually the worst time to concede a goal? The Fink Tank was, most likely, the first public attempt not just to use numbers to illustrate football, but to attempt to explain it.

For all the work that ProZone and Opta had done in suffusing the sport with data, it was also the first time anyone with an academic background in the various fields of mathematics had turned their attention to football. At first, Decision Technology drew its information from the work of a statistician called Alex Morton; when he left, to take up a post at a gambling company, the firm advertised for a replacement. The job advert landed in the email inbox of Ian Graham, a bespectacled Welsh physicist then in the middle of post-doctoral research post at Cambridge. He was also, in his spare time, a Liverpool fan. He thought the job looked fun; the interview process convinced him that Stott was carrying out sophisticated, rigorous analysis, not trawling for trivial tidbits and passing them off as insight. He was also paying roughly twice what Graham earned from his academic contract. In November 2005, he accepted the post. He set about refining and developing Decision Technology's work, the information it was feeding to the Fink Tank, constructing complex models to analyse first teams, then players. It was high-level work.

That did not always make it popular. In 2005, after the column had been running for nearly three years, Stott had the chance to pitch a similar idea to Vic Wakeling, the managing director of Sky Sports. Wakeling was not averse to new ideas: he had agreed, after all, to use Opta's data in his broadcasts as far back as 1996. But his meeting with Stott, along with Sky's frontline pundit, Andy Gray, did not go well: Stott's opening gambit, of dismissing much of football commentary as hot air and cheerleading, infuriated Gray. When he asserted that many of the numbers the broadcaster relied on meant little or nothing, and had no bearing at all on the outcome, any impression of cordiality evaporated. Gray demanded to know how many medals Stott's computer had won, and left the meeting in a rage, Stott's suggestion that he might like to have some information that was actually insightful firmly turned down. Wakeling seemed to enjoy the whole thing. As Stott got up to leave, he said: 'Well, that was fun, wasn't it?' Sky's relationship with Decision Technology never really got started.

The Fink Tank's impact on football would, instead, be much more subtle. One of the talks scheduled for Murdoch's glitzy weekend at Pebble Beach was a conversation between Michael Lewis, the author of *Moneyball*, and Billy Beane, the book's hero. Beane remembers being nervous as he took to the stage: he had walked past Al Gore on his way up, and when he sat down he saw, right in his eye-line, Murdoch sitting there, waiting to be impressed.

They were scheduled to discuss radical approaches in traditional businesses, but Finkelstein's interest was a little more direct. He had read the book previously and drawn the obvious connection between Beane's story and his own work in football. He managed to snare Lewis after his talk, and Lewis agreed to put him in touch with Beane.

A few days later, the two spoke by phone. Finkelstein told Beane about the insight of Stott, the brilliance of Graham, and Decision Technology's work. And Beane told him of his burgeoning interest in football. He had, as it happened, spent much of that summer at the World Cup in Germany in the company of an executive looking for someone just like Finkelstein. Or, more to the point, someone just like Stott, and Graham.

The task that Tottenham Hotspur had set Damien Comolli was a straightforward one. The club's chairman, Daniel Levy, wanted his team to be competing with the four teams who had established themselves as the Premier League's unquestioned elite in the early years of the twenty-first century: Manchester United, Chelsea, Liverpool and Spurs' hated rivals, Arsenal. The club had commissioned Comolli, an urbane, intelligent Frenchman, to close the gap, making him the first technical director in its history.

There was just one slight hitch. Chelsea, Arsenal and the others generated at least three times as much revenue as Tottenham did, which meant they could afford to pay three times as much in wages. Comolli would have to make his new team competitive on the cheap, without the financial clout to attract the finest players in the world. Not that the club wanted to fish in those particular waters anyway: Levy had told him that he should concentrate his efforts on finding players under the age of 24, the sort of recruits that might be sold on at a vast profit in a few years' time.

Comolli's immediate instinct was to try to find out exactly what he was up against. He had been, by football's standards, an early convert to data. He had first arrived in England as an adjutant to Arsène Wenger, the Arsenal manager, operating as his European scout, quickly establishing a reputation as a gifted talent-spotter. In the winter of 1997, he had happened to be making a visit to Colney,

Arsenal's training facility on the outskirts of London, the day that ProZone arrived to pitch its products to his boss. Comolli was young – only 25 – but Wenger liked and trusted him. He invited him to sit in on the presentation. Both men were 'gobsmacked' by what ProZone could do, even at that early stage. On the way back to London that evening, Wenger told Comolli that he was certain the technology would 'revolutionise football'. Arsenal agreed to take ProZone on board.

In his seven years at Arsenal, Comolli got used to reading ProZone's reports of the team's games; after the club agreed a deal to take data from Opta, too, he added their findings to his reading list. When he left London, in 2004, to take on a role as technical director of the French side Saint-Étienne, he made it a priority to make sure he had access to the same resources. A year later, when he was appointed at Tottenham, one of his first moves was to make sure the club had access to as much data as it could find. Spurs took on ProZone and subscribed to Opta for access to its event data, too. Comolli's idea was simple: he wanted to know, first and foremost, how the Big Four – as they were then known – won games. The roots of their dominance self-evidently lay in their financial power, but he wanted to know how that translated onto the pitch.

He sifted through the data provided to him by Opta and found a handful of metrics where England's biggest teams stood out. United, Chelsea, Liverpool and Arsenal had more possession in the opposition half than anyone else. They made more passes in the final third than other teams. More importantly, a higher percentage of those passes were completed. And that, in turn, led to more shots on goal.

His findings were hardly revelatory – it is intuitive to any fan that the more time a team spends near the opposition's goal, the more likely it will be to score goals – but they at least gave him an idea of what Spurs needed to do, and to be able to do, in order to keep pace with the clubs at the top of the table. He could see that Spurs were better than the teams below them in the table; he could see, too, where they needed to get to if he was to be considered a success.

At that point, he did not necessarily know what his next step was. Comolli is not a trained statistician or data scientist. He was not qualified to interrogate the data much further. He had concentrated all of his energies on analysing the way the Big Four played, contrasting that with what Spurs were doing; he had not so much as thought about using data to help with recruitment. As luck would have it, though, it was around the same time that a package arrived at his London home from his younger brother, Loïc, in California. It contained a book that Loïc was certain his brother would want to read.

Both Comolli brothers had developed an interest in baseball as teenagers. Their mother had been relocated to California to work, and they had spent two years studying at a French *lycée* in San Francisco. They had been to watch both the Bay Area's Major League teams, the San Francisco Giants and the Oakland Athletics, play.

What struck Comolli about 'Moneyball', though, was not so much the nostalgia as the lesson. The A's had managed to overcome a stark financial disparity by finding an edge elsewhere. It had been leaner, smoother and smarter than its rivals, and its approach had been rooted in numbers. That, Comolli realised, was precisely what Spurs needed to do. To find out how to do it, he thought he might as well ask the book's central character. More in hope than expectation, through a mutual friend, he got in touch with Beane.

Comolli had no idea what Beane's response would be, of course. He did not know that emissaries from other sports had already started to beat a path to his door. His first call after the publication of *Moneyball*, in fact, had been from Bruce Blair, on behalf of New Zealand's cricket team, who wanted to know if Beane might be able to help the country achieve its lifelong dream of beating Australia. And he did not know that Beane had long been interested in seeing what sort of impact his ideas – or at least the ideas that he advocated – might have in football.

The two spoke by phone, exchanged emails, and decided to meet up when Beane travelled over with one of the A's ownership group for that summer's World Cup. They arranged to touch base at the United States' opening game of the tournament, against the eventual champions, Italy, in Kaiserslautern. Neither seemed to have grasped the impracticality of such a meeting: Beane walked around the stadium for some time, trying to catch sight of a man he had never met among the milling crowds. They found each other eventually, and Comolli volunteered to drive Beane and his colleagues – including the A's data analyst Farhan Zaidi, who would go on to take the Los Angeles Dodgers to the World Series – to the next game they were scheduled to attend, in Munich. They spent five hours in the car comparing notes, exchanging ideas, Comolli picking Beane's brain for every last scrap of wisdom as he tried to work out how he could do for Spurs what his passenger had done for the A's. Later that year, Comolli would travel back to the Bay Area, scene of so many happy memories from his adolescence, to spend time in Oakland, learning at Beane's knee.

Moneyball's release, a few years previously, had cemented Beane's reputation as the smartest executive in baseball, and perhaps all of sport. He was the visionary who had seen that there was another way, that there were inefficiencies to be exploited and that doing so could level the playing field. He had been the first – at least the first in a position of power – to see that there was a truth in the numbers.

But that had never really been how Beane saw himself. 'I was just the vehicle,' he said. 'If I have any genius at all, it is in my recruitment, in choosing smart people to surround myself with, and letting them do their work. I am just the sausage-seller. They are the people who actually make the sausage.' In Comolli, he wondered whether, at last, he had found his equivalent in football.

Just after midday on 30 August 2010, Harry Redknapp wandered outside to speak with Rob Palmer, the Sky Sports News reporter stationed outside Tottenham's training ground in Chigwell. Redknapp did not particularly enjoy the reputation he had earned, over the years, as football's premier wheeler and dealer – at some point over that weekend, he would tell Palmer to 'fuck off' for using the term – but he could never quite help himself. Whether through a selfless desire to help desperate reporters or an inability to resist the magnetic allure of a television camera, he had a tendency to stop and talk when other managers might remain silent; the image of Redknapp leaning out of a car window to proffer some insight was already, by then, one of the great traditions of transfer deadline day.

Sadly for Palmer and for Sky, Redknapp informed them that there was not much going on. Spurs, he said, were 'not close to signing anyone'. A bid for Luis Fabiano, a Brazilian striker at Sevilla, had failed a few days previously; the club was still trying to work out where Sandro, a midfielder signed earlier in the window, actually was. (Redknapp had, at one point, wondered aloud whether the player was, in fact, mythical.) He seemed relatively unfazed by the news. 'Lionel doesn't want to leave Barcelona,' he joked with Palmer.

A few hours later, it seemed as though Redknapp had been just a little economical with the truth. That evening, Tottenham had tabled an offer for Rafael van der Vaart, an impish, inventive playmaker deemed surplus to requirements at Real Madrid. As the clock ticked down to the deadline, the deal had gone through, though it had run so late that Spurs had to be afforded an extension. That happens all the time, of course: managers regularly answer the media's enquiries with something less than absolute honesty. Deals can be fragile; going public too early can change their terms or grind them to a halt completely. It is a ploy Redknapp has certainly used before. That day, though, he might have been telling the truth. Or, at least, he might have been telling the truth as far as he knew it.

Introduced by Beane and Finkelstein, Stott had met with Comolli in his office at Spurs' training facility in the autumn of 2006. The meeting had gone well: Finkelstein had explained that he was happy to arrange the logistics, but that his involvement would go no further. Stott, after all, was the one who might be able to help Spurs. They had pored over the data that Comolli had available, speculated on what they might be able to do with it, and agreed to work together. For the next two years, Decision Technology served as a consultant to Tottenham. Comolli, conscious of the example set by the A's, wanted the link to be closer than that: he advocated buying Decision Technology whole. It never went quite that far, but in 2008 the club signed an exclusive agreement with the firm, effectively bringing Stott, Graham and their team in-house.

Stott had never been a football fan, of course, but from that point on, he 'became passionately in favour of Tottenham winning'. The company he had started was consulted on almost every decision the club made. Tottenham not only provided Graham and his team with the information they gleaned from Amisco, a French competitor and early rival to ProZone, but arranged a separate deal with Opta to allow Decision Technology to start analysing its data as a third party. The company built systems to piece together whatever other data it could access from any source it could think of: if it was publicly available, then Decision Technology tried to 'scrape' it.

All of it was fed into the models that Graham had designed. Initially, he had concentrated on assessing team performance: that was all that the data at his disposal allowed him to do. By 2006, though, football data had quietly taken another great leap forward. At that year's World Cup, as Beane and Comolli had been speeding down the autobahn, Opta had unveiled a real-time data collection system. The company had changed a great deal in three years. It had been effectively shuttered in 2003, after its most recent owner, Sky, had 'effectively decided there was no future in football data,' as Duncan Alexander, now Opta's Chief Data Editor, put it. The rump of the firm was sold to Aidan Cooney, a sports media entrepreneur. He had seen an opportunity that Sky had missed. Opta's value was not in finding a corporate sponsor for its media outreach. It was in selling the data it had gathered. And the way to sell it, he realised, was to make it as clean and as fast as possible.

The World Cup provided the dry run for the system he had designed. Opta, for the first time, would be able to provide its clients – still, largely, broadcasters, but increasingly clubs, too, as well as Decision Technology – with live data: not just the number of shots and passes completed and all the rest, but where each shot had come from, where each pass had landed; all of the data would come complete with X and Y co-ordinates for where each action took place on the pitch. The company believed it could provide it all with 98 per cent accuracy, immediately, and 99.9 per cent once it had been checked.

It was not easy work: it took the company four or five months to train each and every analyst, and only a small percentage ever made it all the way to collecting data from live matches. In the course of 90 minutes, they would be expected to code somewhere in the region of 2,000 pieces of information. They were expected to be good enough, Alexander said, to be able to tell every single player apart from just a glance. 'The test was always the Bender twins, Lars and Sven, who played in Germany,' he said. 'They were identical. The only difference was that one of them wore tags on their socks. That was the level.'

For Ian Graham, though, it was crucial. Now that he had access to true event data – not just how many passes each player had completed, but where they had passed to and from – he could start building a detailed model to assess each player's individual performance. It opened up a whole new world of possibilities for Decision Technology's work with Tottenham.

Now, thanks to Opta's data and Graham's model, they could start to delve in depth both into which players Spurs should recruit, and which they should retain. The club sought Decision Technology's view on whatever business it was trying to conduct in the transfer market, even if, occasionally, it did so at just a few hours' notice. When Spurs were looking for a new goalkeeper, Decision Technology spotted a young prospect at the French club Nice. His numbers jumped off the page. They were beaten to the punch, though, by Lyon: it would be a couple more years before Spurs finally got their hands on Hugo Lloris, the player who would go on to become the club's captain.

In August 2010, when Redknapp informed the club's board that he wanted them to move for Ryan Babel – a Dutch winger who had fallen out of favour at Liverpool – Decision Technology hesitated. Babel's skillset, according to their systems, did not meet the team's needs. They suggested moving instead for another Dutchman, one who was available for sale from Real Madrid. Daniel Levy, the club's chairman, went with the data. That evening, Redknapp was effectively presented with Rafael van der Vaart, a player signed, essentially, by the models Graham had built.

Redknapp, doubtless, resented being handed a player he had not requested – though van der Vaart, of course, would prove to be a resounding success – but he could not complain too loudly, or too bitterly. He, too, had benefited from Decision Technology's work: the company had also built a model to ascertain how well certain managers would fit with Tottenham's requirements. When Redknapp arrived at White Hart Lane in 2009, it is almost certain that it was with Decision Technology's acquiescence, at the very least, or its outright approval.

By the standards of the time, the work Decision Technology was doing for Tottenham was at football's absolute cutting edge. Most elite teams had enjoyed access to some form of data for years, largely drawn from ProZone. A handful, like Bolton under Sam Allardyce, had used the insights they could glean to establish how they should approach set-pieces, or which shots had the best chance of leading to a goal. They had used the information they had at their fingertips to make their style of play more efficient, a modern – and by no means illegitimate – version of the work Charles Hughes and Charles Reep had done decades previously. A couple more, such as Chelsea – under the aegis of Mike Forde, Allardyce's erstwhile performance consultant at Bolton, and Steven Houston, his data guru – had started to investigate what advantage could be gained by assembling and interrogating huge tracts of data. But Tottenham was, almost certainly, the first team to use data in what now seems a recognisably modern way; it was the first club to try something that bore some resemblance to what Beane had done at the Oakland A's.

Graham built a model utilising what Opta called its F24 feed: one that included every single piece of event data, each on-the-ball action, recorded by the company. The idea behind it was to try to work out what impact every decision a player made had on the likelihood of their team scoring a goal. From that, Graham could start to reverse engineer which sort of shots had the highest probability of leading to a goal, and which sort of passes had the highest probability of leading to a chance. Four years before it was given a name, and almost a decade before it was sufficiently well known to feature on television, Graham was already working with the concept of Expected Goals.

And yet Spurs were not, as they might have been – as they should have been – the seat of football's data revolution. Comolli, the man who had brought Decision Technology to the club, would depart White Hart Lane after three years, dismissed along with Juande Ramos, the club's manager, after a disappointing start to the 2008/09 season. Redknapp was appointed to represent a changing of the guard, and a breaking of the model. Decision Technology remained in place for far longer – its contract with Spurs only came to an end in 2018 – but the fruits of their labour never seeped into public consciousness. Stott was, under the terms of his contract, forbidden from discussing his work at Tottenham. The exclusivity deal they had signed did not just prevent anyone else from using their approach, dulling Spurs' edge. It meant that the broader football world, to a large extent, did not even realise their work was happening.

The messages poured in through the day, as hundreds of thousands of Liverpool and Tottenham fans gathered in the streets and plazas of Madrid, as they boarded the metro to take them up to the Wanda Metropolitano, as Mohamed Salah gave Liverpool an early lead, as Divock Origi sealed a sixth European Cup, as Jürgen Klopp and Mauricio Pochettino embraced on the touchline, as Liverpool's players communed with their travelling fans. That day, dozens of people got in touch with Damien Comolli to congratulate him on the small part he had played in both teams making the Champions League final.

Comolli does not seek to monopolise credit for the transformations of Tottenham and Liverpool. He does not pretend that it was all down to him that, in the summer of 2019, both found themselves in the biggest game in club football. He is more than happy to cast himself as a footnote in the long and illustrious histories at White Hart Lane and Anfield.

But it is worth pausing to consider the impact Comolli had on that game. He had spent just a couple of years at Liverpool, acting as the club's Director of Football Strategy between 2010 and 2012, but while his influence had faded a little seven years later, it was still tangible. It was Comolli who had championed the signing of Jordan Henderson, the captain who lifted the biggest trophy in the game that night, a player sufficiently grateful to the man who brought him to Merseyside that he makes a point of thanking him whenever the opportunity arises. The two front-office staff credited with shaping the club's success and transforming its fortunes, the sporting director Michael Edwards and the Head of Research Ian Graham, both had links to Comolli. It was the analysis Graham, in particular, had done on Jürgen Klopp that had gone a long way to convincing the club to hire the German in 2015.

Comolli's time at Tottenham, in contrast, seemed to belong to the distant past. The Frenchman had left the club more than a decade previously, and by the time Spurs arrived in Madrid, it felt like a relic, an emblem of all the wrong steps Tottenham had taken before the arrival of Mauricio Pochettino galvanised everything.

It is not quite that simple. Comolli's fingerprints might have faded a little by that stage, his effects now only felt at the second or third remove, but they had not been erased completely. It was not just that he had first urged the club to sign Hugo Lloris, the team's captain on the night. It was not just that the vast profits from his signings – players like Luka Modric and Gareth Bale – had been used to acquire some of the team that had taken the club to its first-ever Champions League final. More than anything, it was that he had brought Decision Technology to Tottenham, and that had changed everything.

Few at Spurs had mourned Comolli's departure in 2008, particularly when the manager who came in after his dismissal – Redknapp – and the more traditional model that he represented seemed to revive the club, helping a team that had been struggling against mid-table mediocrity for years become a contender for a place in the Champions League. Football rarely has time to consider long-term factors. The success of what came after was used merely to highlight the failure of Comolli, his ideas, his regime.

Stott, though, proposes an alternative timeline. 'If you were to make a graph of our ten years with them, the success would overlap precisely with our time working at the club,' he said. When Decision Technology first arrived at Spurs, the club was trying to work out how to compete with the Big Four. By the time the company's contract ended, in 2018, England's top flight was dominated by the Big Six. Alongside oil-fuelled Manchester City, Tottenham had joined the club. Spurs were now a regular contender for a Champions League place. A year later, the team would make it all the way to the final. Twice, under Pochettino, the club had challenged for a Premier League title, falling short first to Leicester City and then Chelsea.

Stott, like Comolli, sees the transformation of Spurs as vindication not just of the appointment of Decision Technology, but of the work they did. That it is not seen like that by the wider world – that barely anyone noticed when Spurs and Decision Technology parted ways; that this is not a book about how Tottenham kick-started football's data revolution – is the source of a modicum of regret to both.

Comolli bridles, just a touch, at the suggestion that Spurs missed their opportunity, spurned their chance to find a competitive edge. That, in his mind, is the wrong reading of history. The Oakland A's did not win a championship in the season detailed by *Moneyball*. They did not even make the World Series. They were beaten by the Minnesota Twins in the first round of the play-offs. What caught the attention of baseball, though, was the streak, that run of 20 consecutive wins. Football does not quite work like that. It does not have much of a gauge for comparative success. It does not know how to read subtle, consistent glory: the only type that counts, according to its zero-sum logic, is the kind that can be measured in silver and gold. For a team of Tottenham's scope, if it does not end in a trophy, it is not true success.

'The revolution did happen,' Comolli said. 'It gave Spurs a competitive advantage. They broke into the top four with the smallest revenues and the smallest wage bill of the top six. They kept that advantage, kept over-performing their wage bill.' He is in no doubt that was down to Decision Technology's involvement, to the head-start Spurs had on everyone else. He had been set a challenge when he arrived: to find a way to help the club overcome the financial deficit to its rivals. He found it. That football did not realise is an indictment of football, not the revolution in its midst.

The lesson Stott learned is slightly different. Every week for ten years, Decision Technology sent a report to the club, monitoring both the team's underlying performance and that of individual players, as well as casting an eye over whatever opposition they were scheduled to face in the next few days. The company kept a log on how Spurs were faring compared to their expectations, whether they were above or below where the data suggested the team should have been. A couple of times, Stott or Graham or a member of their team would spot a mistake in one of the reports – a typo, or a figure out of place, or some minor error – and dutifully, assiduously send in a correction.

As far as they knew, the club was on board with their methods. Daniel Levy, the chairman, had been convinced enough by their work to sign a contract with them, to demand that they did not work with any of their rivals in the Premier League, although he stopped short of Comolli's suggestion of buying Decision Technology outright. Decision Technology were consulted on transfer targets – though they were by no means responsible for all of the signings made by Tottenham over the course of that decade, and their advice was not always heeded – and they had an input on the appointment of managers, too.

Even after Comolli had left, Decision Technology had found allies. Redknapp had hired his former analyst at Portsmouth, Michael Edwards, to help reshape the club's analysis department; he might, once, have joked about letting Edwards' computer play the opposition's to find out who wins, but he clearly felt there was something of value on that particular laptop. He had found Edwards' way of working – listening intently to pre-match and post-match team talks, as well as whatever was said at half-time, making notes, and then preparing a video presentation for the players that tallied up with what Redknapp and his assistant, Joe Jordan, seemed to be accentuating – useful, and wanted him to do much the same at Tottenham.

Levy, though, handed Edwards an extra responsibility. He would also serve as the club's point of contact with Decision Technology. His first meeting with Graham, at Spurs Lodge in Chigwell, was a fractious one. Edwards had looked at Graham's modelling and found that many of its recommendations did not quite fit with his own assessment of either Tottenham's squad or the sorts of players they should be pursuing in the market. Edwards is not the sort to hold his tongue or allow courtesy to get in the way of accuracy; he asked Graham what, exactly, his model took into account, queried its weighting, suggested where it was going wrong.

If it felt like an omen, it proved misleading. Edwards met with Graham and Stott regularly at Tottenham; they would speak for hours as he tried to learn how, exactly, the modelling worked, and how it might be used. He needed to know, after all, if he was going to have to account to Levy, in particular, why it was worth heeding or ignoring. Quickly, he realised that he was dealing with a different type of organisation to either Opta or ProZone. To Edwards, their work was far beyond the data gathering that his former employer had long been doing. It was more sophisticated, and more worthwhile, by an order of magnitude.

Stott knew that, in Levy and first Comolli and then Edwards, he had advocates inside the club, figures who wielded considerable power and influence. What he could never quite work out was how much difference it all made. Decision Technology sent in its reports every week, but there was rarely, if ever, a reply. Nobody confirmed its receipt or said they had read it. And, crucially, not once did anyone at Spurs spot a mistake before Decision Technology did.

'A lot of the managers and technical directors did not really know what to make of us,' Stott said. He felt, as a rule, that their input was not necessarily welcomed by the managers and coaches who – in some cases, at least – had jobs in no small part because Decision Technology had recommended them. He would not have been entirely surprised if many of the reports were printed out and immediately stored for safe keeping in the bin.

Like Comolli, Stott is proud of the work he did at Tottenham. He is convinced that his team played its part in the most successful chapter in the club's history since the 1960s. His time at Spurs may not have made a football fan of him, but he found in it conclusive proof that you can know a lot about the sport while having no knowledge of, and no interest in, the part that involves 22 people kicking a ball around on a field.

But he is sure, too, that he might have been able to do so much more had circumstances been different. Marc Andreessen, the Silicon Valley investor and founder of Netscape – one of the dominant browsers of the early internet – has a dictum that, in his business, 'being early is the same as being wrong'. The timing of technology is as vital to its success as the substance of it: the world has to be ready to accept and embrace your idea. The examples he is thinking of all come from his sphere of experience: Friendster and Six Degrees and all of the social networks that pre-dated Facebook and yet never caught on like Facebook; Loudcloud, Andreessen's own cloud-computing service that crashed in the dotcom boom and so never had a chance to become Amazon Cloud Services, a profit-churning titan of 'distributed computing'.

There is some solace, for Stott, in the idea that he and Tottenham were just too early, too far ahead of their time: when he and the club first joined forces, in 2006, football was not yet ready. The data needed to feed it was hard to access, and incomplete. The technology required to support it was expensive, or did not exist. And, as Beane might put it, the culture was just too embedded to be challenged. Football was not yet a place ready to break out of its century-long orthodoxies. Coaches had not yet grasped the idea that outsiders might be able to help.

What prevented Tottenham being the seedbed of football's data revolution was not a lack of support from the top – Levy and Comolli were on board – but a lack of support from within. The idea that ultimate responsibility lay with the manager remained sacrosanct, certainly in England; they were still the final repository of power. For the revolution to take flight, for football to experience its true 'Moneyball' moment, there needed to be complete buy-in at every level. Managers and coaches needed to be told that data and analytics were not optional, an added extra that could be disregarded at will, but central to everything they did. It was the same epiphany that Chris Anderson would have, several years later. The data, or at least the experts who corralled it, had to have control.

4

PROOF POINT

As the clock ticked towards 5 p.m., the Masters of the Universe started to file into the wood-panelled boardroom. They greeted each other amiably, helping themselves to coffee, taking in the view from the floor-to-ceiling windows looking out over Mayfair, the rest of London fading into dusk beyond.

The mood was relaxed, convivial. Most of the men – and they were mostly men – in the room were technically rivals, representatives of the blue-blood and the cut-throat world of private equity, emissaries from all of the funds and the firms that use money to make money, the pillars of global capitalism. They competed for clients and accounts and for commissions, but they shared an esprit de corps, too. They were all former colleagues or passing acquaintances or useful connections. They knew each other socially. Some might even have classed each other as friends. They were here for business, but this was, at least, the sort of business that might offer a little fun into the bargain.

Each one, as they entered, paid subtle obeisance to the executive who had invited them here. The room was full of money and power, thronged with men whose personal fortunes ran into the tens of millions, and who had billions of other people's money at their command. In the curious, inverse hierarchy of high finance, though, the one who had access to the most money, the one who wielded the most power, had made the least sartorial effort. Everyone was dressed in immaculately tailored suits and ties except David Blitzer. He had dressed down: shirt, jeans and backpack, a peacock display of informality.

As they took their seats around the boardroom table – staff had needed to bring extra chairs into the room to accommodate everyone – the two people they had come to hear waited fretfully to get started. Chris Anderson and David Sally had arrived early, their impatience betraying their nerves. Blitzer had not been available to greet them, so instead they had noodled in the boardroom, watching the catering staff set up, waiting for him to arrive.

Unlike their audience, they were not comfortable in these sorts of surroundings. This was not their world. Neither had any real experience in pitching business ideas, or in high finance, or any particular interest in acquiring and investing vast sums of money. They were every inch the uncertain entrepreneurs walking into the Dragons' Den. They were far more at home in lecture halls and ivory towers than they were in teak-lined boardrooms. Their suits made them feel like cosplay businessmen. They felt more at home in open-neck shirts and sports jackets.

Neither had slept especially well the previous night. They had been poring over their presentation for days, finessing and fine-tuning it, trying to pick holes in their own argument so that they might have some sort of response when the inevitable fusillade of questions came their way. They had done what they could to find answers that at least sounded convincing. They knew they could not afford to waste this opportunity. They had put years of thought, and months of networking and pitching, persuading and cajoling, into this project. Anderson, in particular, had upended his whole life, moving his young family across an ocean, placing his career on hold, to see if he could make it work. This was, he thought, the best chance he would get.

Once everyone was seated, and the chatter had died down, Blitzer took the floor. He did not waste any time. He thanked everyone for coming. He said he was sure they would be interested in what they heard. He had met the two gentlemen standing next to him, both Ivy League professors, and he thought they had some good ideas. And then, without further ado, he handed over to Anderson and Sally. This was the moment of truth. They stood up at the head of the boardroom table and looked out on a room full of money. Here, at last, was their chance to persuade one – or more – of the richest people on the planet to take a few million pounds from their own, vast pockets and use it to buy a football team, and then hand control of it to them. The feeling, Sally remembered, was the same as you might experience at the crest of a rollercoaster, anticipating the imminent plunge. 'That intense fear,' he said, followed by an irresistible sense of: 'Here we go.'

If Wembley is pretty much universally accepted as the home of football – a rare case of boastful English exceptionalism that is allowed to go generally unchallenged by the rest of the world – then the sport's office lies a few miles further south, in a lopsided triangle that spans much of central London.

A series of hotels serves as its border posts. To the north, there is the Landmark on Marylebone Road, all whispered pleasantries and cream tea luxury. On Park Lane, to the west and south, there are the Dorchester and the Connaught; all the way across town, to the east, something of an outpost on the Strand, the Savoy. These are the places where football goes to do business: the locations for clandestine meetings and power summits and coded, speculative cups of coffee, the places where agents meet to thrash out transfers, executives gather to gossip, where owners hold court when they are in town.

All have their particular appeals. The Landmark is a remnant of old football, long regarded as a convenient and suitably grand spot for officials travelling to the capital from the game's heartlands in the north, sitting just up the road from the train stations at Euston, St Pancras and King's Cross, all neatly lined up in a row. The Connaught is a bastion of quiet refinement; the Dorchester and the Savoy act as a flex, their names an indicator of money and power and status.

In the middle of it all is the place that acts as football's financial engine: Mayfair, with its grand Georgian facades, its private members' clubs, its dazzling veneer of money. The Square Mile – together with the soaring glass towers of Canary Wharf – might be where London makes and trades its money, but it is in Mayfair that it is stored and nurtured and cherished. The area's roads are lined with discreet gold plaques, each one marking out the office of one of a welter of private equity funds. Those plaques denote the presence of billions upon billions of pounds. This is the place where the money starts the day, and the place where the money goes to bed.

Anderson had, over the previous few months, come to know those streets extremely well. In the summer of 2012, he had taken a sabbatical from his post at Cornell and moved with his family to London. They had taken a flat on Wheatley Street, a stone's throw from the artisanal épiceries and boutique fromageries of Marylebone High Street. Every morning, he could step out of his front door and, within a few minutes, walk into Mayfair, the heart of London's world of money.

It had come at a cost. What, for him, was a harmless sacrifice – he had vowed that if he could not make headway within the 12 months of his allotted sabbatical, he would return to Cornell, go back to his normal life and write the whole thing off as a pipe dream – involved uprooting his family. His wife, Kathleen, could take a sabbatical, too, but their sons, 12-year-old Nick and 9-year-old Eli, would have to be pulled out of school, removed from their home, to start again in a new city, across an ocean.

But he knew, too, that it had to be this way, if he was to see it through to the end. His early experiences in football had taught him two things. Firstly, that there was an audience out there, a community within football that was keen to examine and adopt the sorts of insights that data could offer. And, secondly, that almost nobody within that community had any power whatsoever to institute that sort of change. Analysts and scouts within clubs wanted more information, more knowledge. They were data converts or data zealots or, at the very least, data curious. But they were also, in all but a handful of cases, overlooked by their managers, and regarded as non-entities by their owners.

He had realised quickly that the revolution he was proposing, then, could not come from the bottom up: it had to be from the top down. He had to find someone who would buy a club, and then run it according to his principles. He had to land himself a whale.

Quite how to do that, though, was a mystery. Anderson's first gambit was to work his Cornell contacts book: embed himself with those of his university's alumni who had made their way to London, and see if one of them could point him in the direction of someone working in football. There, he had a stroke of luck. Amit Bhatia, the co-owner of Queens Park Rangers, had attended Cornell. So had his chief executive and longstanding friend Ishan Saksena.

Anderson finagled a meeting, and Saksena – an engineer, by training – seemed interested. He invited Anderson and Sally to conduct a piece of research for the club, analysing what it needed to do to avoid relegation from the Premier League. They called the project 'What It Takes'. They presented it to Saksena and to Bhatia, who passed it along to the club's manager, Neil Warnock. His response was not what might be termed positive. 'It was along the lines of "fuck that, I'm not interested in this shit",' as Anderson remembered it. That particular avenue, it turned out, was a dead end.

Anderson pressed on. He arranged countless meetings, ricocheting around Mayfair, sitting down for cups of coffee in an endless parade of hotels – the Connaught, the Westbury, the Corinthia – and private members' clubs, his name taken at the door, registered as a guest. Managers of private equity funds are cash rich and time poor. There was no room for small talk. They deigned to hear out Anderson's elevator pitch, and that was all.

After a while, he found he had pared his proposition back to the barest of essentials: he did not want to demand too much of them too quickly, for fear of frightening them off. In its simplest form, it was this: football was a lucrative industry, but it was mired in inefficiencies, held back by outdated thinking and tangled up in moribund traditions. Clubs did things because that is what they had always done, and even owners new to the game seemed to allow themselves to be shaped by that herd mentality. He wanted to do something completely different: cutting edge and untested and, to some extent, heretical. He wanted to buy a football club, and then he wanted to use data to make it smart.

Some of the meetings ended with a hint of progress, a promise to stay in touch or direct him to a friend, an acquaintance, a contact. Often, the result of one meeting, one pitch, was the chance to go to another meeting, to make another pitch. Others concluded only with a polite admission that the project was not for them. It felt, to Anderson, like he was piecing together an 'intellectual puzzle'. Perhaps the better parallel, though, is a maze: one in which there is no way of knowing if anyone, and anything, is quite what they seem.

By the time Anderson arrived in London, English football had been in the midst of a takeover frenzy for the better part of a decade. It had started with Roman Abramovich's sudden, stealthy capture of Chelsea in 2003: his heart allegedly won by the sport while watching Real Madrid ransack Old Trafford that spring, his eyes initially captured by the sight of Tottenham's training ground. A couple of years later, the Glazer family had alighted – with hundreds of millions of dollars as baggage – at Manchester United. Liverpool had been sold in 2006, and again in 2010, first to Tom Hicks and George Gillett, and then, from the brink of bankruptcy, to John W. Henry and his Fenway Sports Group. Two rival tycoons, Stan Kroenke and Alisher Usmanov, had been jostling for control of Arsenal since 2007.

They were just the Premier League's crown jewels. Below them, almost every team either was or had been for sale. Prospective owners had been drawn in equal measure by the booming television income generated by the most glamorous league in the world's most popular sport and by the league's avowed insistence that it was entirely 'ownership neutral': it did not care where the money came from, or how it was made, as long as it kept flowing.

And it came from everywhere. There was American ownership at Aston Villa and Sunderland. An Indian consortium took charge at Blackburn. Leicester City was bought out by one of Thailand's richest men. Southampton was owned by a German and run by an Italian. West Ham had Icelandic investment. Portsmouth ricocheted between Serbia, Russia, Saudi Arabia and the United Arab Emirates. Just five years on from Abramovich's arrival, there was so much external money flowing into English football that clubs were already welcoming a second generation of foreign investors. In 2008, the former Thai Prime Minister Thaksin Shinawatra sold Manchester City to a group backed by the wealth of Abu Dhabi. It would turn a team that had been drifting for decades into one of the biggest, and best, in the world. Many, many more would follow: Italians at Watford, a Kuwaiti at Nottingham Forest, Russians at Bournemouth, Americans at Fulham.

One of those newcomers, the Liverpool owner John W. Henry, would eventually describe the sport he had invested in as a kind of 'wild west', a place where the rules did not seem to apply. The sensation, though, was more akin to a slightly different period of American history. English football, at the end of the 2000s and the end of the 2010s, was in the midst of a gold rush. And, just like with any good gold rush, there were plenty of people determined to find a way to secure a piece of the wealth for themselves.

It was that world that Anderson was drawn into as he picked his way from coffee to coffee in the hotels and private members' clubs of Mayfair: a 'shadow economy', as he put it. It was populated not just by lawyers and wealth managers but by all manner of brokers and fixers and consiglieri of opaque and occasionally dubious origin. Some of them were acting on behalf of private equity houses. Some of them had mandates from institutional investors. And some of them – most of them, in fact – were much harder to read.

Anderson had met Tareq Hawasli, an Arab-American businessman, at a conference at London Business School in the spring of 2012. Hawasli's day job was helping Middle Eastern investors find places to put their money, whether in companies or in real estate, in Europe. But he seemed intrigued when Anderson suggested he was looking to find someone to buy a football team; he might, he said, have just the sort of buyer he needed. It was over coffee, a few weeks later, that Hawasli confirmed his client's identity: Prince Abdullah bin Musaid Al Saud, owner of Al Hilal United, supporter of the San Francisco 49ers and, most importantly, one of the grandchildren of King Abdulaziz, the founder of Saudi Arabia, and as such a member – albeit not an especially prominent one – of the inconceivably wealthy, fractious and sprawling Saudi royal family. The prince, Hawasli told Anderson, wanted to buy a club. The two might be able to help each other.

The courtship that followed dragged on for months. Hawasli flew to Riyadh to talk to Prince Abdullah; Anderson heard nothing back. He chased him up. He and Sally were instructed to fly to Doha, the Qatari capital, where they might be able to make progress: the prince was due to attend an exclusive gala at the country's state-of-the-art Aspire Academy, the centrepiece of its attempts to become a pioneering force in sport. They took the flight. They visited the Museum of Islamic Art. They went to the gala. They met some Olympians. They did not speak to Abdullah. They did not make any progress. 'There were a lot of false starts,' Anderson said. And then, as the trail threatened to go cold, he got a call. The prince was coming to London, and he wanted to hear Anderson and Sally's pitch.

Anderson was new to this world. He had never moved in these circles before; he was, by his own admission, startlingly naive. It was not just that he did not 'know the difference between a hedge fund and private equity', or that he had no real idea of how to read a balance sheet. It was that he had no way of navigating these waters, or assessing the characters who inhabited them.

He had assumed that finding a buyer for a club would be a vaguely logical, coherent, professional process. If he was expecting a complication, it was with getting close enough to the money to make his pitch. He was not stupid; he knew that the super-rich were not what anyone might consider easily attainable.

What he was not prepared for was quite how opaque, how uncertain, how chaotic the ecosystem around them would be. He was not the only person hitting the streets of Mayfair trying to make a deal happen, trying to get access to just a little of the money that lay within its walls, trying to perform some complex alchemy which took something that did not yet exist – an idea, a dream, some air – and turned it into cold, hard cash.

The buying and selling of football clubs had become such big business that dozens – hundreds – of speculators and intermediaries had flocked to the industry, such as it was, all of them trying to insert themselves between the people with the money and the people with the clubs. Anderson might have had a different angle, a sincerely held belief that he could make an investment smart, but he was not the only one competing for a meeting, for some face time, for an ear. Everyone had something to sell, and everything was for sale. That was the theory. Trying to work out how much of it was real, and how much of it nothing but talk, was the problem.

Some of the brokers were clearly above board: they were slick, professional, representing some private equity house or family wealth fund, based in one of the quietly lavish Mayfair houses with the gold plaques on the door.

And some of them were not. There were 'young men in cheap suits and good haircuts,' as Anderson put it, who claimed to know the owner of one club or another, and to have an exclusive mandate to put a sale together. As the *New York Times* wrote of one of them, a 'businessman' in his mid-20s by the name of Alexander Jarvis: 'His rise shows how someone with apparently little in the way of experience or a track record of success can forge a reputation with relative ease, especially in the largely unregulated realms of international soccer.' That very internationalism was part of the complexity: there were Brits and Americans, Italians and Russians, emissaries of Chinese conglomerates and Arab sheikhs, all of them trying to find the money to buy a football team, something that in its community was a treasured institution but here, in Mayfair, was just an asset to be traded, a trophy to be acquired, a vehicle for making money. They all claimed legitimacy; they were all wary of showing their hand. Anyone could be real and, because of that, anyone could pretend to be real.

Hawasli had seemed smart, energetic, connected: far more likely to belong to the first group than the second. He was, a quick Google search would confirm, a legitimate businessman. And yet Anderson had no way of knowing for certain that he knew Prince Abdullah, or even if he did that he had the sort of sway that might be able to obtain an audience with him. He found the sensations it inspired – the long, empty periods of uncertainty, the sudden, urgent bursts of action – a little disorientating. 'There's a point at which you think: I don't know who you are,' he said. 'I don't know if this is real, or not real. I don't know if this prince is real.'

It is, perhaps, the best gauge of how much Anderson wanted his idea to work – how much he wanted the chance for his idea to work – that he jumped through the hoops anyway, regardless of the doubts in the back of his mind, the feeling that he was grasping at smoke. He and Sally put together a proposal. They found a late-night copy shop in Mayfair who could bind it together for them, to give their efforts a veneer of professionalism. And late one night, they piled into a black cab with Hawasli and drove to the Corinthia Hotel. They were greeted by members of the prince's entourage, who checked their identities, performed the necessary security. Only once they had passed were they ushered into the prince's presence, and given the chance, at long last to present their ideas, to talk him through their vision of how a football club should be run.

As far as Anderson could tell, the presentation went well. The prince seemed warm and welcoming. He listened attentively. He asked questions. At one point, when he briefly left the room, Hawasli offered an encouraging smile: it was going great, he thought. They were doing a really good job. 'In the moment, I thought it was good,' Anderson said. 'We're sitting here with this guy in this amazing place, pitching to this guy, and his right-hand man thinks it's going well.' After they said their goodbyes, Anderson felt hopeful. Hawasli had been real. The prince had been real. They had pitched their idea, and they knew their idea was good. This could be the moment it all coalesced; when all of those ideas became something.

Abdullah went on to buy Sheffield United and would eventually help take the club into the Premier League. Hawasli would sit on the board. Anderson and Sally were not involved. They never heard back from the prince.

There was just one person minding the reception desk at Bramall Lane, the home of Sheffield United, when two men walked in. It was quiet, a weekday afternoon. They were tourists, they said. They certainly looked and sounded like tourists: middle-aged, dressed casually but respectably, obvious American accents. They were in the city for a few days, it turned out, and they just loved soccer, and this was such a great club, and they knew it was a bit of an imposition, but they were wondering if they might be able to take a look around?

Anderson was not just spending his time in England trying to find someone with money. He was busy trying to work out what, when he eventually encountered them, he would advise them to buy, too. To do that, he had to get out of Mayfair, to expand his horizons beyond London, to work out what, exactly, you got when you bought a football club. 'I never felt comfortable telling someone to buy a team if I hadn't actually seen it,' he said. 'We wanted to get a feel for a place, to soak it up, to be able to talk about it knowledgeably. To feel halfway comfortable that I actually knew what I was talking about to people, I felt like I had to see these places. I had to meet people. I had to understand everything from the balance sheet to what it actually looks like, what it smells like.'

And so he did what came naturally. 'What do academics do? They research stuff,' he said. Most often with Sally, visiting from the United

States, he got in his car or hopped on a train and went to see the industry that he was desperately hoping to join, one day, eventually.

Their ruse was not especially sophisticated. They posed either as tourists, just visiting, enamoured with the sport, dazzled by the club, or as authors, writing a book about the sport, trying to get a sense of the place. Looking back, he realises it had the distinct air of an ill-conceived caper, two guys in their 40s, aimlessly wandering around England, just looking at stadiums. 'In retrospect, what we were doing was kind of stupid,' he said. But, as with so much within football's chaotic ecosystem, the ramshackle reality that lies beneath the smooth veneer, that was not a bar to success. It should not have worked. Anderson and Sally should not have just been able to wander into clubs to nose around. But they did.

'People are proud of their clubs, and people love Americans, and the English are just so nice,' Anderson said, his voice tailing off, a broad grin on his face. 'And so when someone has come a long way and seems to take an interest, they're happy to show it off.'

At both Sheffield clubs, Wednesday and United, Anderson and Sally were granted an impromptu tour of the stadium. They took a look at the dressing rooms, they wandered up into the stands, they were invited to stroll on to the pitch. At one, the receptionist decided they should see the training ground, and so drove them up there, introducing them to the women who washed the kit and the staff who prepared the food.

They tried the same trick, with the same results, elsewhere. Anderson sneaked into Villa Park, home of Aston Villa, when he noticed that an open gate offered direct access to the pitch. He managed to get a guided tour of Goodison Park by playing the tourist card. He made trips to Reading and Leyton Orient and Coventry. Occasionally, there would be a proper invite – he was given a guided tour of Finch Farm, Everton's training ground, and hosted to lunch; he remembers sitting down to eat next to Petr Cech on a day at Cobham, Chelsea's base, too – but for the most part, he relied on his chutzpah, and the warmth of club staff, to get inside.

Anderson enjoyed those trips. He was not only 'star-struck' at being around all these actual flesh-and-blood footballers, but by the clubs themselves, too. 'I'm an analytics guy, but I loved going to see these teams,' he said. 'I really love them as organic institutions. I was star-struck by the clubs, the stadiums, the feel of professional football. Just seeing that up close.'

But he was not, of course, doing it for fun. Those visits might have had the air of a caper, but this was part of Anderson and Sally's research. They were trying to identify where they might put their – or, more to the point, someone else's – money if the chance ever arose. They knew that when the chance came to pitch their idea to someone – to anyone, really – it could not have the air of a theoretical, academic exercise. A room full of time-poor millionaires did not want to listen to a hypothetical. They wanted a concrete proposal. Anderson and Sally needed to present them with a specific case for investment. And they could not do that, they believed, without seeing each club in the flesh.

They had approached their selection process as might be expected of a couple of academics, ones with a particular interest in analytics. They did not stick a pin in a map and see where it landed. Instead, they concocted formulae. They looked at the data. They drew up spreadsheets.

Sally was the driving force: he had the background in consultancy, after all. The first step was to identify a set of 'key variables', a group of characteristics that made a club more or less likely to succeed. Their conclusion was that the best investments were to be made in one of two places: either London, and the vast grey sprawl of England's south-east, or in the country's north-west. London, of course, had the advantage of being a truly global city, home to a huge accumulation of capital. It was familiar to the sort of investors Anderson and Sally were hoping to persuade; its transport connections made it convenient; its powerhouse economy meant that sponsorships and corporate partnerships would be easier to acquire.

The appeal of the north-west was a little different. The stretch of England that runs along the East Lancashire Road serves as football's equivalent to Silicon Valley; Anderson believed it to have 'co-location advantages and synergies. You don't just have big companies located there; you also have everything that goes with it that provides support for those companies to succeed. Just the sheer concentration of professional football infrastructure, people, everything else: it's right there.' Their search, they decided, would be weighted towards those two areas; any opportunity outside them would have to be much more compelling to catch their eye.

That was just the first filter they applied. Painstakingly, they screened the 92 clubs in England's four tiers of professional football, hoping to whittle down their choices. They automatically eliminated any team that had not previously spent at least one season in the top flight. They disregarded just as quickly any of the clubs that would be far too expensive to be feasible: the billion-pound heavyweights at Manchester United, Liverpool and Arsenal, the state-owned enterprise at Manchester City, the oligarch-backed project at Chelsea. As the list of candidates started to shrink, they researched teams' finances, picking through what publicly available sources they had to work out how much debt a team had, and what sort of debt, and how much that debt might be worth and when it had to be paid back. They considered the socio-economic health of the regions in which clubs were located. Any part of the country where gross domestic product was below £16,000 per capita, they determined, was not fertile ground: the local economy would not allow them to attract the sort of sponsorship they would need to finance the project.

They considered infrastructure, too. Any team with a stadium that held fewer than 18,000 fans was, they decided, too small to be 'viable in the long term at the top end of football'. They did not want to take on a project that involved major structural work; money spent on building a stadium, or even fundamentally renovating one, was money not spent on something else. They weighted the system against teams that did not own their own ground, and against those that had homes in urgent need of repair.

And then, most delicate of all, they started to think about brand. They looked at historical success: how long had a team spent in the Premier League, making it a familiar name to all the millions of fans around the world who followed English football? How had it fared in the FA Cup? Had it ever won a trophy? Was there something, in other words, to build on, something to reignite, something to restore?

Once all of those screens had been applied, Anderson and Sally found that three-quarters of the teams in England that might have attracted their attention had fallen by the wayside. There were twenty or so left. 'So we started ranking them,' Anderson said. It was not, he admits, a 'scientific' approach – these were, ultimately, judgement calls – but it was 'methodical'. They gave each one scores for its local economy, its history, the state of its finances, the size of its stadiums, the value of its brand. Some names stood out immediately: Leeds United, with its rich and storied past; Nottingham Forest, a two-time champion of Europe, marooned in the second tier; Derby County, a champion of England in Anderson's lifetime. That none of them were in London or the north-west, though, counted against them. There were cases to be made for less famous names: Reading and Southampton, say, had the advantage of at least being in the general orbit of the capital; Birmingham City, a seemingly permanently distressed asset, called a city of more than a million people home.

Once they acceded to the obvious, though, and started weighting their search in favour of London, one name stood out. Not long after they arrived in London, Anderson had dragged his wife, Kathleen, to the Valley, the home of Charlton Athletic. It was not an especially glamorous day trip: the tube out to Greenwich, and then a bus journey into the monotonous suburbs of south London. Anderson admits that it was not one of his proudest moments as a husband. It was the same ploy: charm whatever security there was and take a look around. A few weeks later, Anderson went back in a more legitimate capacity: he bought a ticket for a game. (Kathleen did not have to come that time.) And then he bought another one.

Charlton were not the biggest club he and Sally had identified as a potential target. In the early years of the twenty-first century, they had been a Premier League stalwart, occasionally flirting with qualifying for Europe, but they had been relegated in 2007 and had not looked like returning in the intervening years. They had bounced around between the Championship and League One. They had oscillated between managers. They had become something of a cautionary tale, a warning about the dangers of not knowing your station: while they were in the top flight, the club had fired Alan Curbishley, their long-serving manager, in the hope of pushing on, competing at the very summit of English football, and been condemned to irrelevance as a penance.

To Anderson, though, Charlton was an opportunity. Here was a team with a large, modern stadium – in need of a lick of paint, perhaps, but not bad at all – situated in south-east London, rapidly becoming one of the most fertile areas for young players in Europe. And unlike the rest of the city, much of this was unclaimed territory. North London was stocked with major clubs, an arc that ran from

Fulham and Chelsea in the west to West Ham in the east, taking in Arsenal and Tottenham on the way. The picture south of the river was different. Crystal Palace sat in the deep south. Millwall occupied a small corner of the city's old docklands, around Bermondsey. The rest of it, though, was up for grabs: Blackheath and Eltham and Bexleyheath all the way out to Dartford, all areas becoming more and more popular with transplants and Londoners priced out of the rest of the capital.

There were drawbacks, of course. Charlton's brand was a little 'milquetoast', in Anderson's eyes. Nobody had really strong opinions on Charlton. There was a rumbling dispute with the local council over some land adjacent to its stadium, the Valley. But that was all outweighed by the positives. The Valley held 27,000 people, and though it would probably not be described as state-of-the-art, it would certainly not look out of place in the Premier League. It was easily accessible. There was a little debt, but nothing too onerous. And, most of all, it was London. To the Americans and Russians and Gulf potentates flooding into the game, there was an appeal to the capital that did not apply to Manchester, Liverpool, Leeds or Sheffield. Or even, really, Reading. 'There was always a real premium on London,' Anderson said. 'And as soon as we put our thumb on the scale for London, Charlton made a lot of sense.' Charlton, they decided, would be the pitch. They had found the ideal club to buy. Now they just needed to find someone to pay for it.

Standing in front of Blitzer and his invited guests, that smattering of Masters of the Universe, Anderson and Sally had thirty minutes. Obtaining even that had been a small triumph for their indefatigable networking. Anderson had shared a coffee in Mayfair with someone who invited him to a glitzy event at London's Guildhall. There, he met someone who put him in touch with someone else. That pitch went nowhere – not the right sort of investment, Anderson was told – but it ended with a suggestion. Had he thought about David Blitzer?

He seemed to fit the bill nicely. Blitzer was already heavily invested in sports: he part-owned the 76ers, Philadelphia's basketball franchise. He was part of a consortium attempting to buy the New Jersey Devils of the National Hockey League, too. More importantly, he had the sort of profile Anderson and Sally required. His undergraduate thesis, at the Wharton School of Business at the University of Pennsylvania, had been on sports economics. The 76ers had adopted a data-driven approach, hoping that by making as many good decisions as possible, they would eventually create reliably good outcomes. Like John W. Henry, the principal owner of Liverpool, he had made his money in a financial industry that ran on data; like John W. Henry, he saw no reason why that would not apply in sport as it does everywhere else. Maybe he could be tempted to spread his wings across the Atlantic. Crucially, too, they had something of an in. Sally had run into Sam Hinkie, the general manager of the 76ers, at a function in New York. The two men, it turned out, had a common background: they had both spent a portion of their early careers working at Bain. Hinkie could, at least, vouch for their legitimacy to his ultimate boss. It worked: eventually, Anderson and Sally had been summoned to meet Blitzer. They pitched as hard as they had ever pitched. Blitzer peppered them with questions. At the end, though, he had been sufficiently intrigued to promise to arrange a meeting in London. He would invite twenty or thirty friends to listen to the pitch, to see if they were interested. 'We'll have a dinner, and you get the floor,' he had said.

Anderson and Sally did not want to waste their chance. The presentation they had settled on, titled 'FC 2020', opened with a grand, eye-catching claim: a graph depicting innovation over time, garlanded with the crests of those teams that had passed into folklore as trailblazers and game-changers. There was the Arsenal of the 1930s, the side that drove football's first great tactical shift. There was the Ajax of the 1970s, purveyors of Total Football. There was Barcelona, inflected by the thinking of Johan Cruyff through the teaching of his great disciple, Pep Guardiola. 'And then there was a question mark,' said Sally. 'We knew the next great change was coming. The question was who would get to claim it. We wanted it to be us. We were offering them the chance to fill the question mark.'

They knew, though, that they needed far more than a slick sales pitch. They needed details. Anderson's endless round of coffees in Mayfair's expensively appointed hotels had honed his talking points, but they fleshed them out with the sort of information that investors would need: rates of return and cash-flow projections and base cases, upsides and downsides. They had prepared slides, plotted graphs, designed graphics. They knew their stuff. This might not have been their normal audience – there would be no deference to the professor here, they knew – but it was their subject matter. They were just two numbers guys, talking to a room full of other numbers guys.

That was what they told themselves, at least, right up until Blitzer handed them the floor. Sally was, perhaps, more comfortable than Anderson in the alpha-male environment of the boardroom – he had the real-world experience from his time at Bain, after all – but even he felt a twinge of intimidation. Almost as soon as they started speaking, a forest of hands sprouted on the other side of the table. 'It was herding cats, really,' Sally said. 'We were having these parallel, overlapping conversations, Chris on one side of the table, me on the other. Everything we said was challenged.' There was, they knew, an element of sport to all this: a chance for those in attendance to show off a little to their friends and rivals. There was a hint of relish as these potential investors tried to poke holes in what they had heard.

But while their central message might have been trussed in corporate euphemism – 'our analyses expose the extent to which long-held football truths are actually fallacies' and 'time and again we have witnessed how owners, managers and staff follow traditional paths up and down their organisations' – it was, at heart, very simple. Football is stupid. We, and you, are smart. That is a competitive advantage. So let's use it.

By smart, Anderson and Sally meant doing exactly what had made all those men in the room rich, exactly what had got them an invite into the room in the first place: using data to make decisions, or, as page four of the presentation put it, 'challenging conventional wisdom with systematic analyses'. They wanted a club that could use analysis to identify which players to sign and which players to sell; they wanted a club where how the team played was defined not by some intangible philosophy, or some archaic belief deep in the manager's soul, but by how the numbers told them they should play. They wanted to try 'experimental football', to challenge convention, to 'take the road less travelled'.

Anderson and Sally, of course, were academics. Their plan was to put their ideas into action, to take their theories off the page and place them on the field. They wanted to know if what they thought should work actually did work; like all academics, they wanted to be proven correct. But that, they knew, would not win over this audience. A private equity boardroom would not be swayed by the chance to prove some theory or other; that room wanted to know how this theory could make them money.

Fortunately, they had an answer for that, too. Anderson and Sally had researched the finances of all of the clubs in English football's top two divisions over the previous decade, and they had used that information to map out every possible eventuality from investing in one specific club in one specific league. They had come up with 239 feasible outcomes, if an owner adopted a data-driven approach. In the best case, the ideal case, the case they were sure was the only relevant case: they would win promotion to the Premier League, establish the club in the richest football division in the world, and then sell up after seven years, in 2020. That, after all, is what private equity is about: getting in low, getting out high. Potential investors did not want to be saddled with a football team to run long into their retirement. They would let their money go only if they knew when they could expect that money to come back, bringing some friends with it. They buy in to get out. The worst case, one which did not entail promotion, and one in which the data made no difference at all, was hardly a disaster: the rising tide of television rights would cushion any potential loss.

Their thirty minutes up, Anderson and Sally felt the presentation had gone well. It held together. It was, they thought in retrospect, mostly convincing. There were only two things that had given them pause for thought. They had known both were coming. They had done their best to prepare for them. The first was the obvious one, the one that anyone would ask in that situation, the one that Anderson and Sally could not answer, not really, not convincingly. Why, exactly, should I entrust my money, my investment, my reputation to two academics who had no experience in football or, for that matter, business? Anderson could only grin as he replied: 'Good question.'

The second was the one that surprised them. Fun or not, this was a business proposition. To make an investment, they needed evidence that the idea was sound. Had anyone tried it before? How had it gone? These two academics claimed to have a black box, one that could crack the code, one that could give them a competitive edge in one of the most competitive fields on the planet. How did they know it would work? Where, in financiers' jargon, was their proof point?

The only way to answer that was to say there was no answer. There had been clubs who had used data in some way: Bolton Wanderers under Sam Allardyce, or Tottenham through its connection with Decision Technology. And they knew that other teams, by the spring of 2013, were starting to dip their toe in the water. But there was no forerunner of what Anderson and Sally were proposing. Nobody else – or at least, nobody as far as Anderson and Sally could tell – had ever placed data in the middle of everything a club did; nobody had ever threaded it into the double helix of a team's identity.

That was the root of the proposition, the reason for the investment. This was a chance to be the first team to be rooted in data and analytics, to stake claim to that question mark. That was the whole idea. That was, in essence, the point. Other teams might be using data when it suited them, trying to find a way to operate this new weapon in their arsenal, but what Anderson and Sally wanted to do was different. They knew that for it to work, the data had to be at the centre of everything; it could not be something you played at, something that could fall victim to the swirling internal politics that wrack any football club. It had to be at the heart of things. That, they said, was the edge.

5

ARSENAL TRY TO WALK IT IN

Hendrik Almstadt stood at the front of the plane and walked Arsène Wenger through his mistakes. As the Arsenal executives and coaching staff in the nearby seats strained to hear his voice over the dull rumble of the aircraft, he coolly, confidently, explained exactly where Wenger had gone wrong in the last couple of years. And then he asked him to sanction the spending of £2 million to prevent him doing it again.

The circumstances, Almstadt knew, were not ideal. Arsenal had spent the last couple of weeks on a whistle-stop pre-season tour of the Far East. The schedule had been sprawling, exhausting: three games in five days, ranging from Malaysia to Hong Kong, with a stop-off in China in between. It was a microcosm of why Wenger, the club's totemic manager, disliked these long-haul trips: his job was to make sure his team was ready for the start of the season, but between the travel and the fixtures – not to mention the stifling, cloying heat and the succession of public appearances – there had been scarcely any time to train. He had given the tour the green light only under sufferance: he would much rather have spent the time in some scenic retreat in the Alps, his players hidden away, but had been persuaded of the value of a bit of face-time with the club's Asian fans by Arsenal's commercial and marketing departments. It was a small mercy, from his point of view, that a fourth date – a game against the

Nigerian national team in Abuja – had been cancelled. Still, Wenger was not likely to be at his most receptive.

But as the plane ferrying the team back to Europe cruised at 35,000 feet, Ivan Gazidis, Arsenal's chief executive, strolled up the aisle and summoned Almstadt to the front. Wenger was not his direct line-manager – like Wenger, he officially answered to Gazidis – and nor was he, in theory, the arbiter of the club's business decisions. It is a measure of the power Wenger, then entering his 17th season in charge of Arsenal, wielded that he, and he alone, would have ultimate sign-off on Almstadt's idea. Nothing happened without Wenger's approval. Even Gazidis, at times, referred to him in private as 'the boss'.

Almstadt, though, was not the sort to be cowed, either by his audience or by the setting. He believed in his plan, and he believed in himself. He knew he only had a few minutes, and he knew he needed to make an impact. The approach he took was deliberately – and, in a certain light, riskily – provocative. He handed Wenger a prospectus and launched into his presentation. As Wenger flicked through the booklet, Almstadt discussed two players Arsenal had signed in previous summers: Maroaune Chamakh, a Moroccan striker picked up on a free transfer from the French side Bordeaux in 2010, and Park Chu-Young, a South Korean forward who had arrived for a nominal fee from Monaco, the club where Wenger first forged his reputation as a manager, a year later. Wenger had signed off on both.

Almstadt told him he should not have done. He had both players' performance data at their previous clubs. It showed what Almstadt believed to be 'clear red flags'. Chamakh had undeniable talent, and had scored goals consistently, but he did so in streaks, and his output outside the box – how much he was involved in play, his work-rate, his ability to fold into the team's structure – was limited. Park's metrics were not impressive enough, even for a young player, to believe that he would soon be ready to play first-team football for a club of Arsenal's scale and scope. Neither had cost a vast amount of money, not by the lavish standards of the Premier League, but both represented another player, a more fitting player, not signed. Both occupied a space in the squad. Both ate up a little of the wage bill. Both had been poor choices, and both had been entirely avoidable. Or, rather, both would have been avoidable had Arsenal used data as a matter of course in their recruitment process.

This was the root of Almstadt's idea: he wanted to help the club, and Wenger, avoid making such missteps in the future. To Almstadt, the key, immediate advantage of data was not that it would tell the manager who to sign or how to play or what to do, but that it could help a club work out the opposite. Data's most immediate use, in a football context, was to outline what not to do. 'Stupid player transactions kill clubs,' Almstadt said. 'It helps you not to do stupid stuff.'

The way to do that, Almstadt told Wenger on the plane, was to get the best information they could get. And that, Almstadt felt, was provided by an American company called StatDNA. Headed by Jaeson Rosenfeld, a former consultant with McKinsey possessed of what has been described as an 'encyclopaedic knowledge' of football, StatDNA had been consulting – on an exclusive basis – for Arsenal for a year or so, much like Decision Technology had been working for Tottenham for several seasons. Almstadt wanted to go a step further, though. He wanted to bring StatDNA in-house. That was the next step, he felt, the way to make Arsenal a global pioneer in football's gathering data revolution. He wanted Arsenal to buy the company.

In his seat, Wenger waited for Almstadt to get to the end of his presentation and tell him how much it cost: £2 million or so. He had never spent money especially easily. In recent years, as Arsenal tried to offset the cost of building the Emirates Stadium, he had developed an especially parsimonious streak. In part, that was why he had been forced to look at players like Chamakh and Park: Wenger saw his job as maintaining Arsenal's presence in the Champions League, while working on a strict budget, and enduring the regular departure of some of his finest players for richer, more extravagant rivals. He needed to find bargains. He needed, to some extent, to take risks. But he knew that meant Arsenal had little or no margin for error. He nodded his assent. Almstadt should see if there was a deal to be done. Arsenal should buy StatDNA.

The issue that concerned Sarah Rudd, most of all, was the same one that most of her fellow Arsenal fans had been fretting over for the better part of a decade. The trope had long since embedded itself in the external perception of the club's identity; it was now so familiar a refrain that it had bled into popular culture. The joke was so established that, in 2008, Graham Linehan could co-opt it for *The IT Crowd*, his cult sitcom starring Richard Ayoade and Chris O'Dowd. Attempting to pass off as 'real men', rather than socially awkward computer technicians, the two adopt a single, catch-all phrase to convince other men they know about football. 'The thing about Arsenal,' they assert, regardless of relevance or context, 'is they always try to walk it in.'

A year or so after that episode aired, Rudd was hardly alone in wanting to know whether the cliché held water. But she was better qualified than most – all, perhaps – to set about answering it.

A software engineer from Columbia, New Jersey, Rudd worked as a developer at Microsoft, based in the company's vast, sprawling campus in suburban Seattle. Her professional expertise was in big data: she worked on the company's Bing search engine, improving its contextual relevance: it was her job, in part, to make sure the results that showed up on a user's screen were best suited for where they were, and what they were interested in. If their search history showed an interest in football, for example, then a search for Barcelona would place the team, rather than the city, higher in the results.

She had never, though, quite shaken the idea that she wanted to work in football. Soon after joining Microsoft, she had been added to an email server for all of the company's employees, world-wide, interested in the sport. Most of the time, it was filled with discussions of the relative strengths and weaknesses of Manchester United and Liverpool, but there was one member, based in India, who would constantly bring up Villarreal, a mildly unfashionable Spanish team. Rudd had a soft spot for them, too: Villarreal had once been home to Giuseppe Rossi, an American-raised Italian striker. He had grown up in Clifton, not far from Rudd's home. She had kept an eye on his career ever since.

She struck up a correspondence with Ravi Ramineni, an engineer based in Microsoft's Indian headquarters. He was a Villarreal fan by inclination and by accident – he had always liked Sonny Anderson, a veteran Brazilian forward who celebrated goals by pretending his hands were pistols and spent a year at the club as his career wound down – but professionally, he worked on Microsoft's payment and subscription services. He, too, spent his time drowning in data.

They had been in touch for a couple of years when Ramineni was summoned to Seattle to work on a different project, analysing user behaviour on search engines. He would build programs to test minor changes to Bing's pages: a sample of users would see results in a marginally different font size, or some microscopic alteration to the pixellation of the pages, and he and his team would assess whether that seemed to make the experience any better. If they believed it did, they would recommend to an oversight board that a barely percepti-ble change should be made. Often, their advice went unheeded.

Rudd and Ramineni would meet for lunch every week, or every couple of weeks, as often as work allowed. They bonded over their mutual love for football, for Villarreal. But mainly, as they grew closer and their relationship blossomed, they talked about how they could get out of Microsoft and, daydreaming, into sport.

Rudd was, at that stage, closer to the exit door. It had occurred to her during the course of her work that many of the same techniques Microsoft was using to convince people – forlornly, some might say – to use Bing rather than Google could have an application in football; to someone so familiar with, so suffused by data, numbers held the promise to solve every problem. She had asked those of her colleagues who watched football whether they felt the same. The answer, every time, was that there simply was not enough data to work with.

She had heard the same from Adrian Hanauer, the owner of the Seattle Sounders, then a member of the United Soccer League, the division that effectively serves as the sport's second tier in the United States. Rudd, seeking her way out of Microsoft, had got in touch with him to enquire whether he was interested in harnessing data analysis to help his team. He was, he said: at the same time, he was in discussions with several investors, including Paul Allen, Microsoft's co-founder, with a view to taking his team into Major League Soccer. The problem, he told Rudd, was that he had no idea how to get the data needed to make such an approach work.

That had already occurred to her. There was no way, as far as she could tell, for a hobbyist to access the data provided by Opta and ProZone. The idea of gleaning usable information from television footage – what is now known as broadcast tracking – was, as recently as 2008, entirely fanciful. 'The world was not ready for it,' Rudd said. 'It would have been computationally too expensive.' Suspecting that Hanauer might be her way out, and eager to prove the principle, she set about gathering whatever data she could. Early in 2009, the *Guardian* newspaper started publishing 'chalkboards', a set of interactive graphics that allowed fans to compare players' statistical performances. To Rudd, it represented a back door to the Opta data that powered the feature. 'You could get it if you were technical enough,' she said.

Together with two more Arsenal-supporting colleagues from Microsoft, she set about writing a program that could take the data that lay beneath the chalkboards and start to use it as a source. The first thing she searched for, when it was ready, was where on the pitch the players of the Premier League took their shots from. She was trying to establish, once and for all, whether Arsenal really did try to walk it in. (They did, she concluded.)

Looking back now, Rudd is well aware of the limitations of her early work: she was used to working with 'industry standard data mining' at Microsoft, but now she was forced to scrape together what limited numbers she could find, often obtaining it in ways that were if not against the letter of the law, then probably not entirely within the spirit of it. But those first, tentative steps into football analytics served to convince her that this was something worth pursuing: that she could marry her professional expertise and personal interests. In 2010, she attended the Sloan Sports Analytics Conference in Boston. Mike Forde, then Chelsea's performance guru, was one of the handful of speakers with a football background. He told the audience that his sport was 'peppered with people who want' to use analytics to change the game. All anyone who saw data as football's next frontier had to do was to prove they were capable of doing it. Rudd decided to try. She quit her job at Microsoft, started an MBA at the University of Washington and gave herself a deadline of a year to get a job in football, or give it up for good.

* * *

EXPECTED GOALS

Jaeson Rosenfeld had no background in football. In sports at all, in fact: he had spent much of his career either employed by or acting as an advisor to McKinsey, the globe-spanning consultancy firm. He had built up a wide, eclectic portfolio of expertise: launching non-profits to teach English to children in the favelas of Rio de Janeiro, establishing micro-financing programmes in Mexico, contributing to reports about the Indian labour market and the reform of China's financial system and fluctuations in the price of oil. But then, like so many others, he read *Moneyball*, and a lightbulb went off.

Rosenfeld did not quite have the same epiphany as Damien Comolli or Daniel Finkelstein or Ram Mylvaganam, though. The more he read about the transformation of baseball in the sabermetric age, he told *Sports Pro Media* in an exceedingly rare interview, the more he tried to work out why there had not been a similar revolution in other sports. 'The real reason was that the data just was not available,' he said. 'I thought to myself: with all the billions of dollars changing hands, why don't people collect more data?' Rosenfeld set out to solve that particular problem.

Rosenfeld did not have ambitions of being football's equivalent to Billy Beane. Instead, his instincts honed at one of the bastions of global capitalism, he saw data in football as a business opportunity. He wanted to be the person selling the information Beane's equivalents would need.

In 2009, he founded StatDNA, using a business model borrowed from his time at McKinsey. A few years previously, Rosenfeld had helped to set up Digital Divide Data, a social enterprise based in the Cambodian capital Phnom Penh. Its driving ethos was simple but effective: if firms in the United States farmed out their data entry roles – typing in endless screeds of script and figures into digital files – to countries in the developing world, they would cut their costs. At the same time, locals in Cambodia, say, would have access to stable, relatively well-paid jobs that made use of the digital skills younger age-groups were rapidly acquiring. StatDNA's approach would be the same. Rosenfeld's expertise was not in analysing data, telling managers and scouts where they were going wrong. It would, instead, be in possessing better data than anyone else could offer. To get it, the company would set up an office in Laos, where staff could log games in a detail far more intense than any of its rivals; the result would be data that was cleaner than anything else on the market.

Rosenfeld dispatched a colleague – an economics graduate and former college striker called Fran Taylor – to Laos to oversee the project. StatDNA's process was 'painstaking,' Rosenfeld said. The company's office in Boston would record clients' games, or those of their forthcoming opponents, and send them digitally to a local telecom company in Laos. There, they would be downloaded onto a hard drive, something that could take hours, given the limitations of local internet speeds. Taylor would collect the drives at 5 a.m. and drive them to the office. There, staff who had been trained to 'remove any subjectivity from their analysis' were tasked with spending up to 40 hours to code and log a single game. That level of detail meant that the work had to be outsourced, to use the McKinsey parlance, to the developing world. 'If you are going to pay someone in the United States to do 25 hours of work to collect data on one game, it is going to be too expensive to be sustainable,' Taylor told *American Soccer Analysis*. Once it had been completed, Taylor would upload the data into a program that could then be shared with the client. In the evenings, and in his spare time, he played in the Laotian Premier League.

Assiduousness was not StatDNA's only advantage over the likes of Opta and ProZone. The time taken to go through each game meant that every event carried a precise time-stamp, which meant that clients could glean a level of insight unavailable elsewhere: the amount of pressure on the ball when a cross was delivered, or the position of the defence, or even how quickly a goalkeeper could cover their ground as they came to claim it. 'Time-stamps were the big difference,' Taylor said.

Initially, StatDNA's client base was small and diffuse: the company worked with the University of North Carolina's women's team, the Brazilian men's side Botafogo, a couple of agencies, a sportswear brand. Rosenfeld, though, had his sights set on further expansion: to attract more business, to make more of an impact, the company needed to be able to do more with its data, to be able to offer clubs a more rounded service. It needed to tell them what the numbers meant, not simply what they were. To do that, StatDNA needed more analysts. And to find them, it launched a research competition. In the spring of 2011, at that year's Sloan conference, StatDNA revealed that it would make available a tranche of its data – drawn from a whole season of games from Série A, the Brazilian top flight and a smaller sample of Premier League fixtures – to whoever wanted it. The challenge, for any aspirant analyst, was to show StatDNA what they could do with it.

Sarah Rudd, by that stage, was nearing the end of her self-imposed year-long deadline to find a job in football. In her spare time, she had built up a reasonable online portfolio: the work she was doing, she said, was 'pretty basic', based on the sparse – and patchy – data she could find, but it had been enough to embed her in football's burgeoning blogging community. 'A lot of the stuff was not that compelling,' she said. 'But it was still satisfying: a way of saying that we do know something, we don't just have to assume it is true.'

When she heard about StatDNA's contest, she viewed it, more than anything, as the company indulging in a little viral marketing. 'It was free advertising,' she said. 'A way of showing people what was possible with their data.'

Still, the opportunity was too good to miss. She entered, and received the data in return, a screed of information from Brazil and England. 'It was a good sample,' she said. Still, she asked for more; StatDNA said no. With what she had, she compiled a piece of research that involved breaking the pitch down into a couple of dozen zones, and then working out how each player's decision in each of those zones impacted on the chances of a goal being scored. It was similar, conceptually, to what Ian Graham and Decision Technology were already doing at Tottenham, though Rudd had no way of knowing that. She referred to it, then, as an attempt to establish the worth of a variety of 'game situations'; it might be referred to, now, by the less snappy but more insightful 'Expected Possession Value'. Like Graham before her, an idea similar to Expected Goals was a byproduct of her work.

Of all the entrants StatDNA received, her work was by far the most advanced, the most promising. It was also the most in tune with something they were already working on. Rosenfeld and his colleagues selected Rudd as their winner. Not long after – only a little more than a year after she had left Microsoft – he offered her a job. He was coy, at first, about what sort of clients the company was working with; all he would acknowledge was that StatDNA had recently taken on some consultancy work for a Premier League team. Only after she accepted did he tell her that it was Arsenal.

To the hundreds of fans who had gathered outside the Emirates Stadium as darkness fell, what mattered was that Arsenal – at last – were spending money. For years, as the club paid down the debt accrued in building its state-of-the-art home, they had watched one star after another jump ship. Cesc Fabregas had gone to Barcelona. Samir Nasri and Emmanuel Adebayor had left for Manchester City. Most painfully of all, Robin van Persie had gone to Manchester

United. Now, though, something seemed to have changed. Arsenal, at long last, had flexed their muscles in the transfer market. Arsène Wenger had just spent £43.5 million on Mesut Özil, Real Madrid's elfin playmaker. When the Sky Sports News reporter stationed among their number for the duration of transfer deadline day confirmed that the deal was done, the crowd erupted in euphoria. It mattered that Özil was, without question, a player of rare gifts. It mattered more that Arsenal had spent some money, shown some intent.

That was not quite the way Billy Beane saw it. His interest in football had only grown since those initial meetings with Damien Comolli, back in 2006. He had made his way across the Atlantic several times since, as often as his work with the Oakland A's would allow. He had met with several executives and coaches, to discuss his ideas. And he had struck up a fierce admiration for Arsène Wenger, and for Arsenal.

From Beane's office in Oakland, the decision to sign Özil did not – as it, perhaps, seemed to those fans outside the Emirates – have the air of a new direction for Arsenal. This was not proof that, finally, the club was going to loosen the purse-strings and start to build a squad of Real Madrid-style *Galácticos* for Wenger as he entered the autumn of his reign. Instead, to Beane, the German playmaker had the air of the quintessential 'Moneyball' signing.

Among the many and varied ways in which football misinterpreted the lessons of Michael Lewis' book, and Beane's life's work, was the assumption that any club adopting a data-led approach would, inevitably, not spend significant sums of money. Why would they, when the analytics they had access to would give them the ability to sign hugely talented players for a fraction of the cost? 'Moneyball' was about exploiting inefficiencies in the market; paying premium fees was the very definition of an inefficiency.

Beane, though, had always been clear: sometimes, paying the market price – even over the market price – for a player of particular abilities was the smart thing to do. A player valued at, for example, £43.5 million could still, in certain circumstances, be undervalued: they could, after all, be worth more to your team than they were to the side selling them. To Beane, Özil represented just that strain of thought. He was a world-class performer who had, unexpectedly, become available, and he provided a skill set that Arsenal were sorely lacking. He was, he said in an email at the time, very much a 'Moneyball' signing.

Though it had not yet been made public, that was in line with a new strain of thought incubating at Arsenal by 2013. Hendrik Almstadt had started work in the club's commercial department three years previously. His background was in finance – private equity, investment banking – and he was brought in to help price some of Arsenal's commercial deals. Almstadt, though, is not the sort to limit himself to one sphere of expertise. In his precise, German-accented English, he is gregarious, warm and fiercely intelligent, but he could not, it is fair to say, be described as reticent. He is not backwards in coming forwards. And so, after a few months working at the club, he started to play around with Opta's data: he was interested in football, and he had a familiarity with numbers, and he wanted to see what he could do.

It was just a hobby, at the start, but Almstadt was intrigued by what he found. When he set the parameters to pluck out midfielders who might add the zest and aggression that had been lacking from Arsenal's midfield seemingly since the departure of Patrick Vieira, he found that his homespun algorithm recommended Arturo Vidal, a dynamic Chilean midfielder with a fearsome Mohawk and a swatch of tattoos playing, at that point, for the German side Bayer Leverkusen and would go on to grace the likes of Juventus, Barcelona and Bayern Munich. That, Almstadt thought, was precisely the sort of player he was hoping he would find. It convinced him that data had a role to play in recruitment.

He was far from the only person coming to that realisation at the turn of the decade, of course. Tottenham were already running their potential recruits past Decision Technology, even if they had a habit of leaving it to the last minute. Damien Comolli, the man who had introduced the club to the company, had moved on to a similar role at Liverpool: he would, by 2011, be overseeing a data-inflected recruitment policy that delivered Stewart Downing, Andy Carroll and Jordan Henderson to Anfield. Manchester City's analysis department was growing, the club's finances functionally infinite after its takeover, two years previously, by the Abu Dhabi United Group. Mike Forde was advocating the use of data at Chelsea; the perception was that the work his team, led by Steven Houston, was doing made Arsenal's rivals the leader in the field.

Few, though, were openly discussing their work, or sharing their ideas. Almstadt, as a commercial employee of another club, was locked out from what little rumour and gossip there was. He thought he had found his team an edge to exploit, and he went to his ultimate superior – Ivan Gazidis, Arsenal's South African-born, British-educated but ultimately American chief executive – to advocate further exploration.

Gazidis had been appointed to the role a couple of years previously, having spent more than a decade serving as the deputy commissioner of Major League Soccer, the top-level professional league in the United States, and against the backdrop of a simmering boardroom struggle between two opposing factions: Stan Kroenke, an American real estate mogul, and Alisher Usmanov, an Uzbek-born Russian petrochemicals magnate. Both wanted to own Arsenal outright. Both kept increasing their shareholdings, and with it their influence.

Gazidis was not an analytics evangelist, particularly, but that his background was in sports in the United States meant that he was not instinctively opposed to the idea. 'He got it,' Almstadt said. He was aware of what had happened in baseball and, more recently, basketball, where cutting edge teams were using data to shape the way they played. With the two respective takeovers seemingly holding each other in an uneasy stalemate, he understood, too, that the club still needed to find value for money if it was to compete. He encouraged Almstadt to keep finessing his methods on the side. More importantly, he mentioned what Almstadt was doing to Arsène Wenger.

This was, to some extent, the future that Wenger had foreseen more than a decade before, when he told Comolli that ProZone would change the shape of the game. He invited Almstadt to London Colney, Arsenal's training facility on the M25, to talk through his findings. The two hit it off. Wenger comes from the Alsace, on France's border with Germany. Almstadt grew up in Bremen. They spoke in German. The key thing, though, was that Wenger could see that Almstadt was not angling for a job in scouting. 'I didn't want an office at Colney,' he said. 'I wasn't about to start giving him tactical advice.' Wenger indicated that he was on board. 'Keep doing that,' he told his colleague.

Almstadt did as he was told. He finessed his methods to parse the data. He highlighted players he thought were interesting. He looked into how Arsenal were playing. And, most of all, he tried to keep his finger on the pulse of the little that was happening publicly within football's burgeoning analytics industry. That was how he found a blog by an American company about Expected Possession Value: a way of analysing how much every pass, every decision made in a move increased or decreased the likelihood of it leading to a chance or a goal. It was a concept that was familiar to Almstadt from his days in finance. He did not know it, but the work was strikingly similar to what Sarah Rudd had carried out for her submission to the research contest. The blog had been published by StatDNA.

The mood inside the cavernous hall at the Emirates Stadium was fractious, as it always was in those days. Arsenal had not won a Premier League title for 10 years. Worse than that, in the eyes of many fans, nobody was trying to put an end to that wait. The club's accounts were in rude health, but the squad at Wenger's disposal seemed to diminish every year. The disquiet over the lack of transfer activity had long since turned toxic. Some blamed Wenger for a lack of ambition. Some blamed the board for a lack of largesse. Everyone agreed that there was blame to be apportioned. The fanbase seemed to be splintering, inexorably, into two groups, one pro- and one anti-Wenger.

The club's Annual General Meeting was the forum at which all of these complaints could be aired, when Arsenal's minority shareholders – ordinary fans who owned a handful of pieces of the club, often passed down through families for generations – could make known their grievances to the team's executives. Gazidis was always there. Often, Wenger was, too, sitting quietly on a raised table at the end of the room as his life's work was subjected to bitter criticism.

By the time the 2014 AGM rolled around, the jubilation that had greeted Özil's arrival had dissipated. Arsenal had not suddenly been transformed into title challengers: Manchester City and Liverpool had contested the previous season's championship. The club's bank balance showed that it had cash reserves of more than £200 million and yet, as David Hytner noted in the *Guardian*, it possessed just 'five senior defenders'. Worse still, in the eyes of many, Arsenal had somehow still suspended its parsimony to spend £2 million buying a company referred to on the books only as AOH-USA LLC, the official name given to StatDNA. Would that money, a succession of shareholders wanted to know, not have been better spent on a central defender? (Along with 'trying to walk it in' and lacking bite in midfield, the idea that Arsenal were undermined by a soft centre was a leitmotif of the late Wenger era.)

Gazidis' riposte was a strong one. 'The company is an expert in the field of sports data performance analysis, which is a rapidly developing area and one that I, and others, believe will be critical to Arsenal's competitive position,' he told the assembled shareholders. 'The insights produced by the company are widely used across our football operations – in scouting and talent identification, in game preparation, in post-match analysis and in gaining tactical insights.'

It was not just the club's fans who were sceptical of this new direction. Arsenal had first struck up a relationship with StatDNA in 2011. After discovering their work, Almstadt had contacted the company's founder, Jaeson Rosenfeld, and found that many of their ideas dovetailed nicely. With Gazidis' permission, he commissioned StatDNA to work on a number of projects for Arsenal, an attempt to road-test their capabilities. He was impressed by what they delivered: not just the quality of the analysis but the cleanliness of the data. 'They were light years ahead of Opta and ProZone,' Almstadt said.

Much of that was down to the way StatDNA worked. Whereas Opta, for example, effectively only analysed games in real time, the team Fran Taylor had trained in Laos worked much more slowly, and much more forensically. As a result, the data was cleaner, and the insights they could generate more perceptive.

By the start of the 2011 season, Almstadt was sufficiently convinced that he suggested to Gazidis bringing the company on board in an exclusive – to the Premier League, at least – consultancy role. The cost was minimal, by football's standards: £250,000 or so. Gazidis backed the idea, as did Wenger. The partnership worked sufficiently well that, when Rosenfeld hired Sarah Rudd on the back of her winning submission for the company's research competition that year, he told her that he intended to make StatDNA a subsidiary of Arsenal within 12 months. He wanted the club to buy the company he had built from him.

Almstadt was rapidly coming to the same conclusion. He was no longer officially attached to the club's commercial department, doing analytics work in his spare time: his job, now, was in what had started as his hobby. He liaised with StatDNA's team in London: both Fran Taylor and Sarah Rudd, among others, were installed permanently at Colney. Rosenfeld visited frequently, building an intimate, trusting relationship with Wenger. The work StatDNA were doing was growing in sophistication and complexity: mining the data not only to assess potential signings, but where Arsenal were strong and where they were weak. They were working on building a set of metrics to gauge defensive performances; they were building on the work both Rudd and the company had been doing on how every decision in a move influenced the likelihood of a goal being scored; they were assessing set-pieces, and how to approach them; they were working out where players should be encouraged to shoot, and where they should not. Data was analysed to manage the squad, too, to justify salaries and to explore when and whether players should be moved on. These, now, comprise fairly standard building-blocks of analytics at almost every club. In 2012, with only a handful of exceptions, they were almost revolutionary.

Quickly, StatDNA's data infused everything Arsenal did. Almstadt did not need much encouragement from Rosenfeld to build a business case for bringing them in-house; he was a devotee by the time he pitched the idea on the flight back from China.

Not everyone at the club was so convinced; like those fans at the AGM, there were plenty of people who felt the money might have been spent better elsewhere. Almstadt had anticipated there would be some reluctance from within the football ranks of the club at these perceived interlopers, and so organised a series of workshops, partly to assuage fears and partly to explain that analytics existed to support, rather than to replace, them. They were 'really basic,' he said. 'No data tables, nothing like that: just visualisations, and a lot of conversations. We would always use player profiles. We would pick out, say, Mikel Arteta, and say that this is what the data sees: he's good at keeping the ball circulating, and that creates a lot of value in possessions. That is the same thing you see from live scouting: the data is there to support your judgement.' He emphasised how busy the scouts were, how many players they might have to watch, and how data might help make them more efficient, more targeted.

There were other examples: Almstadt would highlight players he knew Arsenal were tracking, work through what the data said about them, and then move on to potential recruits who had similar profiles. 'We would tell them that of course they knew this striker playing in Germany,' he said. 'But then ask if they had considered this very similar player in the second division there, or this player in Austria.' As a rule, the response would be sceptical: goals scored in Austria did not mean as much as those scored in the top flight in Germany, effectively. Almstadt tried to work through that, too, indicating which elements of the data might be relevant regardless of context. A player's conversion rate, for example, was more a measure of their quality than that of their opponent.

The response was mixed. Fran Taylor, who relocated to London from Laos to work with Arsenal, recalled the analysis department becoming a place where coaches and staff came to decompress, to watch games back, to see what the data could tell them. He does not remember any sense of alienation, of an embedded resistance to analysis: this was a club, after all, that had been an early adopter of ProZone, that already had a staff of analysts, that had witnessed first-hand the benefits of sports science.

Almstadt's experience was more mixed. He found some of Wenger's technical staff receptive to new ideas. He struck up a rapport with the club's goalkeeping coach, Tony Roberts, and its first-team analyst, Ben Knapper. Steve Bould, Wenger's assistant, incorporated a lot of StatDNA's work into his defensive drills. But others were much more resistant, particularly when it came to scouting. At one point, he recommended a player at his hometown club, Werder Bremen, who StatDNA had picked out as a star in the making. Arsenal's scouting staff were not quite as convinced that Kevin De Bruyne would make it. He was, one scout told Almstadt, not dynamic enough to make it in England. The striker plying his trade in Austria who had caught Almstadt's eye was dismissed, too. Nobody was that impressed by the number of goals Sadio Mané had scored.

Every club has stories like this, of course, memories of the ones that got away; by the time he retired, Wenger would essentially have claimed to have been close to signing basically all of the world's best players. And everyone involved in recruitment clings on to the times they were right, too: Almstadt did not, it is worth noting, bring up the names of the players he suggested who did not go on to be Sadio Mané or Kevin De Bruyne. 'Mistakes are orphans,' as he put it. None of that is unique to a data-driven approach.

Indeed, to Almstadt, that was the problem. He does not believe that Arsenal's failure to take advantage of the head start the club had been granted by the arrival of StatDNA was to do with sort of implacable ideological resistance to data. It was not even, particularly, a suspicion of outsiders, a reluctance to kowtow to these people drawn from the worlds of finance and consulting and software engineering who now seemed to be wandering the halls of Colney, telling lifelong scouts who they should be signing. It was, instead, something far more mundane: self-preservation.

In *The Numbers Game*, Chris Anderson and David Sally described coaches and scouts as a group in possession of 'protected knowledge'. They alone knew the formula for either identifying or creating talented players; they knew it because of the precise and personal experiences and backgrounds. It could not be taught or shared or acquired. That knowledge gave them their value. It gave them their jobs.

It is, of course, the great advantage of data that it explodes that status quo; as Billy Beane put it, 'data leads to transparency'. It shifts the power balance on a fundamental level, away from that protected, inside group and toward anyone who has – and anyone who can interpret – the data. From the point of view of the self-selected establishment, that is not so much an advance as a threat. The data might bear out what they can gauge with their own eyes, but in doing so it reduces the value of their vision.

More than once, Almstadt was accused of 'trying to take someone's job,' he said. That was not, he always said, his intention. It made little difference. Arsenal's scouts did not object to data for ideological reasons, not really. The resistance, when it came down to it, was existential.

After all those years scraping what little data she could from wherever she could, Sarah Rudd was, all of a sudden, in paradise. In her first few months working for StatDNA, she had found that Arsenal had kept the company – then still a consultant, nothing more – at arm's length. It did not quite want to share everything it had with an external organisation, one that was, in effect, still in a probationary period. Once Almstadt made his pitch and Rosenfeld got his wish, though, that all changed. Once StatDNA was part of Arsenal, there were no secrets anymore. Rudd had all the data she could have hoped for, and more.

'That was the big bonus of the takeover,' she said. 'We had access to things like tactics, so we knew what the team was trying to do. The sports science department shared information with us on performance and injuries. We had access to a lot more information.'

Even now, she is a little coy on how exactly she and her colleagues used that wealth of information. 'As a department, we did some cool stuff,' Rudd said, refusing to go into any great detail. But, speaking to those who worked at Arsenal during that period, it seems fair to assume StatDNA not only had better data than almost anyone else – thanks, in no small part, to the fact that it was so painstakingly piecing together its own information – but that it was doing more with it. Rudd and her colleagues forensically investigated every aspect of Arsenal's style of play, trying to find out how it might be improved. They looked at set-pieces and at shot locations and, building on the work Rudd had done before joining the company and the club, how decisions made at any point in a move increased or decreased the chances of the team scoring a goal. They picked their way through defensive mistakes, working out how they might be eradicated, and analysed how individual error intersected with structural failings. They looked at defensive positions and at defensive pressure. They scoured the world for players, supporting the work of the scouting team, offering alternatives, recommending values. In the summer of 2015, when Arsenal signed a Brazilian defender called Gabriel Paulista from the Spanish side Villarreal, it was reported as the 'first' StatDNA signing, the dawn of a new age of data-driven acquisition. In reality, that was behind the curve: Almstadt recalled being involved with every signing the club made as early as 2012. Ted Knutson, founder of the data and consultancy firm StatsBomb, was surprised at how much overlap there was between Arsenal's reputed targets in those transfer windows and the players his own company was recommending to its clients.

StatDNA was, to a large extent, embedded in the fabric of the club; Arsenal had made a commitment to analytics that no other club, at the time, had yet matched. Rosenfeld kept an office at Colney; he and Wenger spent hours discussing ideas and players and concepts whenever he was over from the United States. Rudd was based in London, too, leading a team of specialist analysts, few of whom were drawn from a traditional football background; like her, for the most part, their expertise was in the data, not in the sport which produced it. As baseball had before it, football was starting to seek out talent from other fields, to realise that having played the game was not the only qualification for being able to influence it. Wenger believed in the idea, and so did Gazidis. There was the institutional support that Decision Technology had never quite enjoyed a few miles away at Tottenham. Arsenal were, at that point, at the game's absolute cutting edge.

And yet, a few years on, there is little or nothing to show for it. Data did not transform Arsenal into Premier League champions again. It did not allow Wenger the glorious, stirring send-off his long and illustrious career deserved. That is not to say it did not succeed: much like Henry Stott at Tottenham, Almstadt is inclined to believe that StatDNA's impact is better gauged by what did not happen than by what did. As counter-intuitive as it is, he believes that StatDNA did its job by ensuring the wrong players did not arrive, as much as by making sure the right players did. 'If you look at what happened afterwards, when they paid £75 million for Nicolas Pépé, that was not happening when StatDNA was at the centre of everything,' he said.

Still, though, Rudd is a little rueful at what might have been. 'We were not as successful as we could have been, given how far ahead we were,' Rudd said. 'We were ahead of the curve in a lot of ways.

Especially early on, there was a big gap between what we were doing and what most other people were. There were things that were unique to StatDNA that gave us an advantage. Now that has closed quite a bit.'

There is no one simple answer for why that is, no easy explanation for why Arsenal did not prove to be home to football's 'Moneyball' epiphany. Almstadt, given his time again, might be more 'aggressive' in staking out his territory: he would ask Ivan Gazidis to give him £10 million to play with every year, he said, just for him to spend in the transfer market, to see if he could uncover the sort of gems the team so desperately needed, to prove that his methods worked.

But he accepts, too, that perhaps the environment at Arsenal was not as conducive as it might have been. If Tottenham, half a decade earlier, had been the wrong time, perhaps the Emirates Stadium was the wrong place.

By the time StatDNA arrived, the club was already deep into the aimless, listless malaise of late-era Wenger, waiting to find out when the future might be; within a couple of years, one of the tasks set before Rosenfeld and his team was to begin to draw up a list of potential replacements for the man who had commissioned their arrival. Decisions were made in a spirit of uneasy consensus, while the parsimony of the Kroenke family, once they had complete control, meant that Arsenal could not be sure of signing the players the club really wanted. The team, the squad, the club were all meandering, labouring under the shadow cast by the knowledge that, sooner or later, Wenger would go.

Almstadt, like Stott and Anderson before him, had believed that analytics would only be given its wings if it was threaded into the core of a club; it was not something that could be played at, disregarded. But the story of StatDNA and Arsenal highlights that that approach is not without its risks, too.

One of the players Almstadt used in the workshops they held to explain the power of analytics was Mikel Arteta. In six seasons at Everton, he had established himself as a cerebral, authoritative midfielder, one so highly regarded that, occasionally, the idea that he might play for England – despite being born in San Sebastian – would float around the Football Association. It seems fair to assume that, according to Rudd's modelling, the decisions he made helped increase the chances of his team scoring. Arsenal duly signed him, late in the summer of 2011; he would end his playing career there, as the club's popular, intelligent captain.

A few years later, after spending time as an assistant to Pep Guardiola at Manchester City, he returned as manager, replacing Unai Emery, the far from unanimous choice to succeed Wenger. Arteta came back to a club that, since the Frenchman had left, had splintered and fractured and fallen apart. Nowhere was that more clear than in its use of data. Almstadt had left, taking a job at Aston Villa in 2015, and so had Rosenfeld, plucked by Wenger for a role alongside him at FIFA. But StatDNA remained, now known as Arsenal Data Analytics.

But they were not the only analytics operation within the club. In 2017, as Arsenal prepared for Wenger to leave, Sven Mislintat had been appointed to oversee the club's recruitment department. He had built his reputation as one of Europe's foremost talent-spotters at Borussia Dortmund, and he was an analytics devotee: he had developed his own platform, Matchmetrics, to provide both data and insight into potential recruits. Though Mislintat only lasted little more than a year at Arsenal – victim of a schism with the equally short-lived Director of Football, Raul Sanllehi – his influence remained; the analytics used by the club's scouting department were different from those offered by Arsenal Data Analytics. Arteta's solution to that problem was not to unify the two teams, but to throw in a third: he brought in Lee Mooney, a former colleague at Manchester City, as a consultant.

It had been one of Rudd's great frustrations at Arsenal that every signing seemed to be a 'compromise', not just economically but politically: the club would frequently move for the player that nobody objected to, rather than the one that a specific department advocated. That issue outlasted Almstadt, Rosenfeld, Wenger and even Rudd herself. She left Arsenal in 2021, proud of what she had achieved and faintly regretful at what she could not. Arsenal never quite managed to shed the tendency to overcomplicate things.

Perhaps it is understandable, then, that she is a little sceptical at the idea football has undergone a data revolution over the last decade or so. Her experience, after all, has been shaped by what did not happen as much as what did. Her instinct tells her that many of the problems, much of the resistance, have not gone away. But then she pauses, and she reconsiders, comparing the world she entered in 2011 to the one she exited, a decade later. Arsenal may not have made the most of the advantage they had, but that is not to say that StatDNA did not have an impact, either inside or, more importantly, outside the club. Football may not have known, precisely, what Rudd and her colleagues were doing, but the game heard whispers that they were doing something, and so it did what it always does: tried to find a way first to blunt, and then to match, that edge.

'There's not been a single moment, a specific year, where things have really changed,' Rudd said. 'But over the last ten years, say, there has been a fundamental shift in how a good club operates. Then, you would have been hard-pressed to find a club doing analytics. Now, it is the opposite: you do not find many clubs not doing it.'

6

HOW (NOT) TO BUY A
FOOTBALL CLUB

For one fleeting moment, David Sally found himself wondering exactly what the suave, impeccably tailored financier sitting across the desk from him might look like with long hair, a leather singlet and flares. The chairman's office at Seymour Pierce, one of London's most venerable investment banks, was filled with ego-swelling memorabilia: keepsakes and trinkets, and pictures accrued from a career spent among the City's great and good. The photo that took pride of place, though, was something of a non-sequitur: a signed image of Greg Lake, the vocalist and bassist with King Crimson and Emerson, Lake and Palmer. Keith Harris, it turned out, was not just a sharp, urbane banker. He was also a prog rock superfan.

It was not exactly what Sally and Chris Anderson had been expecting. Harris' reputation went before him. Though he had relatively undistinguished origins in Stockport and Essex, he was every inch the City archetype: bespoke suits, cut-glass accent, comprehensive contacts list. He had been the youngest director in the history of Morgan Grenfell, one of Britain's most illustrious financial institutions. He had worked at the New York trading firm Drexel Burnham when it was home to Michael Milken, the disgraced financier who would become known as the 'King of Junk Bond'. He had held one of the most senior positions at HSBC, the global banking behemoth. He was, both by taste and inclination, a creature of the City. In 2002, he was described as a 'ubiquitous fixer' by the London Evening Standard.

Most importantly in their eyes, though, he understood the contours of the football business better than anybody. By the time he invited them to meet at Seymour Pierce, he had been the game's foremost financier for more than a decade. A lifelong Manchester United fan, he had served for two years at the turn of the century as Chairman of the Football League, ending his tenure by declaring that he was 'handing the asylum back to the lunatics', but it was his role in Roman Abramovich's takeover of Chelsea on which he had built much of his business. It had been Harris who had received a call from Ken Bates, the club's former chairman, late one Thursday night in 2003, brusquely demanding that he appear at Stamford Bridge immediately. It had been Harris who had been introduced, a few hours later, to Abramovich, his associate Eugene Tenenbaum and his lawyer, Bruce Buck. And it had been Harris who helped usher the deal through so smoothly, and so quickly, that the most impactful takeover football had ever seen was ready to be announced barely four days after it had first been mooted.

That success – and that story – turned Harris, in the burgeoning world of football finance, into a star. In the years that followed, when almost every club in England seemed to be targeted by external investors, Seymour Pierce was invariably the first port of call. He advised Randy Lerner on the takeover of Aston Villa in 2006. He was involved with the purchase of Manchester City by Thaksin Shinawatra, then the Prime Minister of Thailand, a year later. Harris was a man who knew how to buy football teams. And, crucially, he was happy for everyone else to know that, too.

There was a reason for that. Harris did not court publicity purely for the sake of his own ego; he took up a post directly under the limelight because it was good for business. There was no doubt, in anyone's mind, that Harris was credible, genuine. His credentials were well documented. His references were in the public domain: he had worked on the Chelsea deal, the Villa deal, the Manchester City deal. The *Sunday Telegraph* journalist Duncan White had once described him as 'arguably the most influential man in British football'.

He was not necessarily universally popular, by any means, but nor could he be accused of being nothing but smoke and mirrors, noise and bluster. He could prove his bona fides. The financial side of football was then, as it is now, one of shadows and whispers and doubt, where nothing is quite as it seems, where the most valuable currency – perhaps beyond even dollars and pounds and euros and yen – is trust. And people could trust Harris; or, at least, they could trust that he was who he said he was. His word carried weight. His prominence was his superpower. It was not just that Harris, over the previous decade or so, had built up an enviable contacts list; it was not just that he knew everyone. Far more important was the fact that everyone knew him. He was, as Anderson put it, a 'central node'.

'That is what you would call it in the sociology,' Anderson said. 'He's kind of the central node in a network of clubs, of brokers, of owners, of sellers, in the financing of deals. We'd been learning about this world from afar, and when we'd done our work, we'd read about Keith, and it turned out that he was a central player. He's experienced. He's been involved in almost every deal there is or has been. He's smart. He's charming. So, at that time, if you wanted to buy a club or sell a club, you gave Keith a call. He gave you credibility.'

He was, in other words, exactly what they needed. If Anderson and Sally were to turn their flight of fancy into something approaching a reality, they would need not only someone to bankroll their vision, but someone to act as their Sherpa through alien, uncharted territory. Harris, more than anyone, knew the trails.

Anderson, in particular, had made a point of seeking him out; his friend was, as Sally said, a 'dogged and effective networker'. He had attended a talk Harris gave at the London Business School, lingering afterwards to seek him out backstage. He introduced himself, making no attempt to hide his true intentions. He was, he told Harris, seeking to find a way to put some money together and buy into a club, to give him and Sally the chance to test their theories in real life. Harris was sufficiently intrigued, and sufficiently well disposed to the amiable academic who had waylaid him, to invite Anderson to Seymour Pierce a few weeks later, this time with Sally in tow.

That meeting went well, too, and only partly because Sally also knew his way around Greg Lake's back catalogue. Harris was not entirely sold on the idea that data might be able to reshape the game in quite the way that Anderson and Sally saw it – he was aware of the revolution unfolding across the Atlantic, in baseball in particular, but he wondered if football might be a little too chaotic, a little unpredictable, to bear similar treatment. Still, he liked the pair enough to offer to help. He could not sell them a club, of course: he did not have one to sell, and they did not, at that stage, have any money to buy. But he would vouch for their legitimacy, should anyone ask his opinion. 'It was reciprocal utility,' Sally said. 'We thought Keith could help us, and Keith thought we might turn out to be of some use to him.'

He could not, though, quite hide his qualms. Harris had seen enough, over the course of more than a decade in football, to know that it was a strange, hostile and often impenetrable landscape to outsiders. It did not operate according to the regular rules of business. Clubs were circled day and night by hawks and vultures, all seeking to pick off their own piece of the carcass. Buying and selling them was bad enough; operating them, trying to make the industry make sense, was even worse. He felt compelled to warn Anderson and Sally about what they were letting themselves in for, even to dissuade them against going through with it. It would, he feared, prove to be an expensive folly. Keith Harris had been around football long enough to see that it could leave even the brightest minds, the sharpest operators and the most successful business people utterly stupefied. He knew everyone in football, and he was pretty sure that they would eat these two academics alive.

That day in Caffè Nero, when they had dreamed up their scheme, everything had seemed simple. Anderson and Sally needed a 'whale', someone to finance their vision, someone with enough money and faith in the power of data to act as their benefactor. Then they needed to identify the right club to buy.

The first part had proved more complex, more fragile, more laborious than they had imagined. They had wandered down countless alleys that turned out, on closer inspection, to be frustrating cul-de-sacs. They had explained their idea to countless intermediaries and fixers and financiers and rain-makers and deal-breakers, only to find that the promised call never came, or that it was not for them, thank you, or that the investors they claimed they represented did not, in the cold light of day, exist. Even when they did make headway, when they found someone willing to be involved, they ran into the Mark Cuban problem: money follows money. Even the wealthiest people on the planet would only commit if some of the other cool kids were involved, too.

It had taken a year or so, innumerable man-hours and considerable shoe leather, to finagle an introduction to the person who could introduce them to the person who could introduce them to the person who might have a way to meet David Blitzer. At last, they felt like they were making progress; a group of those present at the FC 2020 pitch had, in the following months, agreed to come on board, to explore the idea in more depth. They were getting there. Or so they thought, anyway.

There is a stigma to regarding something as cherished, as precious, as a football club as just a business. We prefer to think of them as social institutions, entities that have a profound emotional bond with their communities. Fans are not mere customers, willing to change their loyalties if better value or quality is available elsewhere, but something closer to members of a family, a part of a tribe. Their purpose runs deeper than massaging the bottom line, maximising returns. There is a reason that, whenever a new owner pitches up at a club, they have a tendency to reassure supporters that they see themselves not as proprietors but as custodians.

But beneath all those layers of meaning and connection and soul, it is a business that sits at the very core of every football club, at least in England: one that is concerned with profit and loss, one that has to submit annual reports and financial filings, one that has assets and expenses and sometimes even a human resources department. And football, elite English football, is big business, awash with money, bankrolled not just by multi-billion-dollar television contracts from across the globe but by the seemingly endless parade of corporate sponsors and betting firms and cryptocurrency exchanges of dubious provenance all willing to pay top dollar to bask in the reflected glory of a club or a league or competition.

That desperation, of course, has its roots in the fact that the Premier League, in particular, is the most popular sporting competition on the planet, the world's generator of choice of what is known in the trade as time-decayed media content: the only reliable source of entertainment that cannot be delayed or binged but has to be tracked in real time. Its worldwide expansion over the course of the twenty-first century has turned it into not just the globe's paradigmatic sports league, but one of Britain's greatest cultural exports, alongside the Royal Family and the BBC and Jaguar Land Rover (though that particular claim should be caveated by the fact that it is drawn from research carried out at the behest of the Premier League itself). The vast majority of its clubs might have turnovers more akin to an out-of-town supermarket than a blue-chip corporation, but their health is of far greater meaning than that of much larger companies. Their wellbeing is close to the hearts of millions of people across the world. Their machinations and motivations are debated by parliament. Their success or otherwise is considered a matter of governmental importance. Beyond the balance sheet, there is no business bigger.

Perhaps that is the trap that Anderson and Sally fell into: thinking the next step was to buy a business. After all, buying a business is, if not simple, then certainly regulated. There are rules and there are mechanisms. There is a process. There are mergers and acquisitions and paperwork that has to be filed with various statutory bodies. Like buying a house, it can be fraught and faintly furtive, reliant for a long time on trust and compromise, but at some point it is governed by a set of firm and fast covenants. As Harris tried to warn them, it most definitely does not quite work like that in football.

If Anderson had found the network of fixers and facilitators prowling the streets of Mayfair, panning for gold, to be arcane and opaque and almost entirely indecipherable, it was almost straightforward compared to trying to work out who had what for sale within football itself, where teams were bartered and traded and haggled over with an opportunism and a carelessness that would be considered just a little beyond the pale in a backstreet market. Sally had been a consultant at Bain. He had taught at a business school. He was, by his own estimation, a 'cynical person'. Even he, though, was a little taken aback by what he found in football.

He expected to find that every club was effectively for sale at all times. 'It's a marketplace,' he said. 'It's a thin marketplace, with a limited supply of clubs, but it's still a marketplace.' That is true in real estate, too, of course. All houses are for sale at all times: if someone turned up and offered you ten times the market value for your home, you would probably be tempted to sell, even if you were perfectly happy there, and had just redecorated the kitchen. It is just that some houses are more for sale than others: they have a sign outside, designed to drum up interest, and an estate agent has been deployed to find a buyer.

A handful of clubs are for sale in that sense: they have drawn up a lavish, glossy prospectus – a 'deck' – designed to tempt potential investors. There are dozens, at least, of these documents floating around at any given moment, circulating among finance houses and brokerage firms and legal offices around Europe, the Middle East and the United States. They can, at times, be a little light on detail – panoramic photos of stadiums and bold claims about growth targets, rather than forensic financial information – and at times their research is a touch superficial: some contain lists of players currently under contract, an attempt to highlight the value of the team's current playing assets, with price-tags drawn directly from the crowd-sourced German website Transfermarkt.

Sometimes, they prove to be a false dawn. The valuations they contain might be so unrealistic that there is no negotiation to be had. The owners who have commissioned them might be looking not so much for a successor but a partner, someone to hand over a few million pounds to cover losses or finance improvement. But they are a sign, at least, that a specific club might be receptive to an approach, might be willing to start a conversation.

What Sally had not expected, so much, was the labyrinthine world of rumour and whisper that surrounds clubs who are not, officially, for sale. Football does not have an equivalent of an estate agent, not really. Instead, that role is played by a cast of 'lawyers, brokers, investment bankers, known middlemen', as Sally put it. 'It's an old boy network.'

It was to plug themselves into that network which convinced Anderson and Sally they needed to recruit Harris as a sort of referee; even with his assistance, though, they found it opaque and cryptic and, at times, wholly baffling. They were invited to buy whole clubs over canapés at society events. They received unsolicited prospectuses – the financial world's deck pics – in great reams. They met agents, more usually associated with trading players, who were hawking clubs on the side, fixers claiming an exclusive, intimate relationship with a certain owner, who insisted they and they alone had the mandate to sell a team. They encountered executives who promised to finesse a deal as long as they received a cut. They found chairmen who were little more than frontmen, willing to pose as a custodian for the highest bidder. There were the friends and the acquaintances and the idle fantasists, the slick men in sharp suits hoping to find someone with money first, and then worry about how they would use it later, attempting to conjure a deal, any deal, from a clear blue sky, hopeful that they could generate an offer sufficiently lucrative to tempt someone – anyone – to sell up, and allow them to make a killing.

To take the final step, Anderson and Sally had to pick their way through that morass. They had their investors. They had identified, in Charlton, the club that they wanted to buy. And yet still they found themselves caught in a warren of blind alleys and false dawns and endless, relentless misinformation. It would have been naive to think that the clubs would be treated as social institutions, but they were not even afforded the same care as businesses. They were, instead, handled like patches of land in a gold rush: picked clean with a rapacious glee. 'It's not exactly surprising,' Sally said, 'but it turns out there are quite a lot of charlatans in football.'

Those who do deals for a living have a specific language to discuss their work. Much of it, as should probably be expected, is borrowed from sport. After all, negotiation is, in some lights, a little like a contest: the back and forth, the to and the fro, a denouement in which there will, or at least there might, be a winner and a loser. 'Hanging around the hoop', for example, refers to the point at which one deal might be in danger of falling apart, allowing another investor to swoop in and pick up the pieces, like waiting for a rebound on the basketball court.

Some of the jargon, though, has a slightly different inspiration, one that casts negotiation not as a sport but as a flirtation. The stage after 'hanging around the hoop', for example, is generally known as 'showing some leg', when one side or another will offer just a little encouragement to their counter-party. The faint thrill of suggestiveness is not accidental. To those who regard themselves as deal-makers, who make their money by getting the better of a negotiation, there is a subtle eroticism to the process.

Occasionally, the flirtation is consummated quickly. The takeover that opened football's floodgates to outside investors – Roman Abramovich's purchase of Chelsea – took place over the course of little more than a weekend. But the circumstances in that case were so favourable as to be almost unique. Chelsea were publicly listed. Anyone could buy the club, so long as they could satisfy the club's shareholders. They did not need to perform due diligence. They did not need to worry about offering proof of funds, gathering together loans and bankers' drafts and reassurances, because to buy a publicly traded company you need to have the money in the bank. And Abramovich, of course, not only had plenty of money in the bank, he was also not desperately concerned by the need to get the best price he could. His motivations for investing in Chelsea, it is fair to say, were not purely financial. Most deals, though, are not like that. Most deals to buy football clubs take so long that they border on tantric.

In part, of course, that is because these are complex, incredibly valuable transactions, the sort that should not be made lightly or hastily. Prospective buyers must make an indicative offer – a sort of ball-park figure of what they think a club is worth – in order to obtain a period of exclusivity, in which they will be granted access to what is known as the 'data room', a set of documents which lay out in detail the reality of a club's financial situation: its debts and its liens and its wage bill and all the rest of it. At the same time, they will conduct surveys into the team's bricks and mortar infrastructure, checking on the state of its stadium and training ground. Once they have seen exactly what they are buying, they will be able to go back with a more concrete idea of what they should pay, and start to negotiate accordingly. All of that can take weeks, or months, depending on what the due diligence finds, to reach an end.

But the particular, peculiar climate that surrounds football means it can take just as long, or longer, simply to get to the start of that process. Chelsea's sale to Abramovich was an outlier; for most, those early exchanges are a form of halting, anticipatory dance. Buyers attempt to look serious, but not too serious; rich, but not too rich; interested, but not too interested. Sellers, even those who have gone to the trouble of engaging an investment bank or commissioning a brochure, grow cool on the idea. In one of the most public industries imaginable, everything must be done in the utmost secrecy: the owner in situ does not want a deal to collapse in public, leaving them with a restive fanbase and a weakened bargaining position; the prospective purchasers do not, under any circumstances, want to alert potential rivals to the fact that there is a deal to be done. After all the eyelash-fluttering, nobody wants to blink.

That, certainly, was what the group Anderson and Sally had helped bring together found. The first target was the one all of their research had identified: Charlton Athletic, the club that Anderson truly believed data could transform into the 'Tottenham of south London'. The experience was as valuable an education as any as to the nature of the world, its curiosity and its chaos, they were all hoping to enter.

First of all, there was one factor that had not been included in all of the spreadsheets the academics had drawn up: it was not immediately obvious who they needed to talk to. Charlton's chairman was a lawyer, Michael Slater, but who stood behind him was a matter of some debate. At the time, the person trying to sell the club was a property developer called Tony Jimenez, a one-time steward at Chelsea who had gone on to play a behind-the-scenes role in Mike Ashley's regime at Newcastle. An enigmatic businessman, Kevin Cash, though, was also often described as a 'co-owner'. So mystifying and so complex was the web of trusts and shell companies through which the club was held that, years later, the High Court would declare that neither of them technically owned Charlton. Even the pinnacle of the British justice system could not determine, exactly, who did.

That was not the only issue. The club had options. That summer, while in London for a pre-season tournament, Aurelio De Laurentiis, the bombastic film producer and owner of the Italian side Napoli, had pinpointed Charlton and Leyton Orient as he mulled over buying an English team. Roland Duchatelet, a Belgian entrepreneur who ran a network of teams around Europe, had expressed an interest; so, too, had a Thai consortium.

Sally, in particular, had been hoping to be part of the team that negotiated the purchase, but neither he nor Anderson were involved in the cautious, circuitous talks with the club. 'It was frustrating,'

Sally said. 'I teach this stuff. I know this stuff. But I get it, too: these are guys who do deals for a living. They don't feel they need an academic to tell them how to do it.' For months, they waited as the two parties circled each other nervously. 'Delaying the talks, adding extra conditions, typical things for a negotiation,' as Sally said. Things progressed far enough for the group to be granted the right to examine Charlton's books; they seemed to be homing in on a price that might satisfy both buyer and seller. Anderson and Sally felt, for a while, as though they were close to getting exactly the right club to run their grand experiment.

And then, in an instant, everything evaporated. There was a gap, and when it did not close, it was deemed insurmountable. The Blitzer group walked away. Sally's read was that the deal was scuppered, as much as anything, by a 'cultural misunderstanding. These are private equity guys. They aren't afraid to talk about numbers.' Charlton had been too reluctant to reveal their hand, to state what they wanted, what they needed, to do a deal. Private equity does not, as a rule, have limitless patience.

That divergent approach should not have been a problem for the next opportunity that arose. Once the Charlton deal had collapsed, the offers now came thick and fast. Reading was for sale. Everton was searching for investment. The most compelling case, though, came from one of the first wave of American owners to have landed on English shores.

When he arrived at Aston Villa in 2006, Randy Lerner had seemed precisely the sort of outsider that fans dreamed about. He was fabulously wealthy, having inherited the chairmanship of the MBNA credit card company from his father, Al, and then sold the business to Bank of America for $35 billion. Unlike the other early investors from across the Atlantic – the Glazer family at Manchester United and Tom Hicks and George Gillett at Liverpool – he had not borrowed a cent to fund his takeover of the club. He had experience in sport: he had run the Cleveland Browns of the NFL for the previous four years, having inherited the ownership of that team from his father, too. Lerner was no data evangelist, but he believed he, too, had an edge that could restore Villa to their former glories. American sport, and particularly the NFL, was light years ahead of football when it came to merchandise, ticket sales, corporate revenue, television rights. Lerner was convinced he could leverage that wisdom to improve the club's fortunes.

He also, crucially, possessed a genuine interest in football, and a sincere passion for Villa. He had fallen in love with the game while studying at Cambridge University; he had adopted Villa as one of the three clubs he followed when he moved back to the United States. He spoke in hushed tones about the history of his new team; he dutifully insisted on calling himself a custodian, rather than an owner. He saw parallels between Villa and the Browns, teams with proud pasts and deep-rooted bonds to their local communities. One of his first priorities, upon taking control at Villa Park, had been to start work on restoring the Holte Hotel, the pub that sits outside the iconic Archibald Leitch-designed stand that houses the team's most ardent supporters.

For the first few years, Lerner had been one of the more popular owners in English football. He ploughed money into the squad – between 2006 and 2010, only Roman Abramovich and the Abu Dhabi-backed group behind Manchester City spent more on transfers – to give his manager, Martin O'Neill, the best possible chance of breaking the stranglehold Chelsea, Arsenal, Manchester United and Liverpool had on the Premier League's four slots in the lucrative Champions League. Consistently, Villa came close, finishing sixth three seasons in a row. The final leap, though, continued to elude them.

Lerner, according to those who know him, had been confident that the expertise he had gleaned in American sport would translate relatively easily to football; when it did not, when he found that there was no simple formula for success, he grew increasingly frustrated. He did not want to continue throwing good money after bad. The funds started to dry up; Villa grew more parsimonious in the transfer market. O'Neill left, replaced by the experienced French manager Gerard Houllier; when he departed, Lerner turned to Alex McLeish, the coach of the club's hated rival, Birmingham City. Writing in the *Guardian*, the journalist Stuart James called it an 'unfathomable' decision. The club began an inexorable descent, first into mid-table and then down towards the tension and the fear of the relegation zone. His popularity waned. The atmosphere at Villa Park turned sour, toxic.

The decline pained Lerner; his affection for the team never dimmed. Rumour had it he had a tattoo of the club's crest etched on his body. One executive who worked with him closely at Villa remembers that he often struggled to watch the team's games, particularly when results were poor, because he was so emotionally invested in their fortunes. Slowly, Lerner realised that he was engaged in a Sisyphean task; he could no longer take the stress or the abuse that came with overseeing a failing team. Quietly, in the spring of 2014, word filtered through to the offices of Inner Circle Sports in New York, a boutique investment bank that had become the first port of call for Americans looking to buy into European football, that he would be prepared to listen to offers.

Villa were a very different sort of proposition to Charlton: not only a Premier League club, but a former English and European champion. They had been, at the advent of the Premier League in 1992, considered one of England's 'Big Six', alongside Manchester United, Arsenal, Tottenham and the two Merseyside teams. They would be significantly more expensive, and likely much more resistant to the sort of change that Anderson and Sally envisaged. The business case, though, was compelling. Villa had a rich history, a large fanbase, and no shortage of room to improve. Through Inner Circle, Blitzer's group opened a line of communication to Lerner.

This time, the sailing seemed much smoother. There were no doubts about who owned Aston Villa. There was no need to try to persuade Lerner to sell; all he wanted was to hand it off to a group that he felt had its best interests at heart. He inhabited the same, relatively close, New York financial world as Blitzer. They had a shared set of expectations as to how the process of acquisition should work. The price, meanwhile, would not be a problem. Blitzer had been a part-owner of the Philadelphia 76ers, the NBA team, since 2011. In the summer of 2013, he acquired a slice of the New Jersey Devils, the NHL franchise, too. In both ventures, he had partnered with the private equity investor Josh Harris, one of the founders of Apollo Global Management, an investment management firm that ranks as one of the most powerful on the planet. Apollo had hundreds of billions of dollars of assets under its control; Harris' personal fortune at the time stood somewhere in the region of $4 billion. After closing the purchase of the Devils, he decided he wanted to extend his reach into football. He would be part of what would later be described, by the Crystal Palace chairman Steve Parish, as a 'serious' bid for Villa.

This time, everything seemed to be aligned. Though reports did not surface in the media about Blitzer's and Harris' interest until June 2014, discussions had started long before that. The two sides were close to reaching an agreement. Then, one day in training, Christian Benteke heard a crack. Benteke was the jewel in Villa's crown, the club's leading scorer for the previous three seasons, by some distance its most valuable asset. He assumed, at first, that he had been tackled; only after a beat did he realise there was nobody near him. His teammates, standing on the halfway line, had heard the noise, too. The

Belgian striker's Achilles tendon had snapped. He would not play again for six months.

Football clubs are delicate things; all it took to derail a takeover worth hundreds of millions of dollars was one injury to one player. Or, more accurately: that one injury to that one player. 'We had a couple of sleepless nights reading the medical literature on the Achilles tendon,' Sally said. There was, they discovered, no guarantee that Benteke would be as effective when he recovered from the injury, if he recovered fully at all. And, as difficult as it was, that would have to be reflected in the deal; the group had no choice but to try to insert a contingency clause. If Benteke did not come back from the injury, the price would have to be lower.

Lerner was not prepared to tolerate that. According to one executive who worked with him on the sale, he saw it as proof that Blitzer's group did not have the club's best interests at heart, as he did. He would not agree to the contingency. Once again, Anderson and Sally watched from afar as the deal fell apart. Once again, after months of exploratory talks and painstaking negotiations, the road had led to a dead end. Yet again, there was no takeover. Everything was for sale in football. But, as far as Anderson and Sally could tell, there seemed nothing to buy.

Kathleen O'Connor was in Ithaca when Chris Anderson called and told her he was done. They were spending much of their time apart. Their sabbatical periods had expired after their first year in London. He had decided to take an unpaid leave of absence , hoping the extra time would see his dream come to fruition. Kathleen had not had that privilege. Someone, after all, had to earn some money. She had returned to upstate New York, to teaching, spending months at a time away not just from her husband but her sons, too. She would spend six-week stints sleeping on friends' couches or in their converted garages, and then she would catch the red-eye back to London to spend some time, in spite of the jet lag, with her children. She was exhausted. Anderson was painfully aware that not only was it all, at root, his doing, but that there was a very real possibility that the whole exercise would lead nowhere.

He had been waiting for months for a deal to buy Charlton to come off. He had felt, at times, as though it was so close that he could almost touch it; at others, football appeared to be so oblique and arcane and incomprehensible that the idea that he might be able to find a doorway into it seemed unimaginable.

There were times when that voice won out. 'I'd been in London for a year and this dream is just kind of fading away,' he said. 'I was pretty sure it wasn't going to work. It was a stupid idea. What am I doing with my family? This isn't right. It isn't going to work. I want to go home.' That was when he had called Kathleen, an ocean away, and told her he was ready to give up, to stop putting his fanciful dream ahead of their family's happiness. 'I told her I was done. It was dumb. We'd met a lot of interesting people, and it had been fun, but that was it. Let's go home to Ithaca. We have a beautiful house, two good jobs at an Ivy League University. Let's move on.'

She did not agree. She urged him to stick it out for another year. The boys were settled in schools nearby. They both liked London. They had developed a little ritual, every Saturday morning, of Anderson walking them down to Regent's Park to play football; Eli, in particular, was showing genuine promise as a left-winger. 'I was really reluctant,' Anderson said. 'But she thought it was too early to call it off.' They decided to stay, and try to see it through.

It was not without its costs. Anderson could not remain on a leave of absence from his job in perpetuity. He had to make a call. He decided to quit, to surrender the post and the title and the status that he had worked all his life to achieve, all in pursuit of his quixotic ambition. 'I found it hard,' he said. 'Really, really hard.' Unable to keep commuting, his wife tendered her resignation, too. He worried about how they would earn money, how they would cope. His and Sally's consulting business, Anderson Sally, had made a little money, but it was an unreliable, piecemeal source of income. His family was totally reliant on Kathleen as the breadwinner. He had overturned their lives for this idea. He had given up his job and his home, and he still had nothing firm, nothing concrete, to show for it.

The prospect of the group he and Sally had brought together buying Villa staved off those doubts, for a while; when that, too, disappeared in a puff of smoke, their patience started to wither. Anderson Sally had developed something of a speciality in what they called a 'football audit'. When a group was interested in buying a club, they would go in and cast an eye over the squad, the management team, the youth academy, the facilities. Other consultancies offered something similar, but for Anderson Sally, it had always been a means to an end. 'The idea was always that the prospective owners might like what we did, and retain us once a deal had gone through,' Sally said.

As they waited for another opportunity to emerge, they kept their options open. Sally worked on a couple of audits for groups exploring deals for Nottingham Forest and Everton; neither of them was successful. Anderson did a little work for agents, seeking to use data as supporting evidence for their players' demands in salary negotiations. They were stuck in a holding pattern, left with nothing to do but wait until, one day, Keith Harris reappeared.

Harris had been acting for Lerner in the talks to sell Villa to Blitzer's group; he had not become the 'central node' in football finance by failing to spot an opportunity. He had connections with both Blitzer and Josh Harris: the former was a near neighbour in Chelsea, the latter was, like him, an alumnus of Drexel Burnham.

When Steve Parish, the chairman of Crystal Palace, called him in the summer of 2014 to say that his club needed access to greater financial firepower in order to solidify the club's place in the Premier League, he immediately thought of them.

Once again, just as their reserves were dwindling, Anderson and Sally had another glimmer of hope. Buying Palace, though, was laborious. Parish was not a sole owner; a potential deal had to satisfy not just him, but his quieter partners in the club, too. Everything had to be agreed not only with the multiple parties involved in the American consortium, but with the multiple parties already in power at Selhurst Park. He was not offering to sell up; he wanted Blitzer and Harris' group to dilute the current ownership, rather than replace it. There were, as a financier who worked on the sale said, 'quite a lot of variables'. Once again, all Anderson and Sally could do was wait. Not for weeks, but for months.

Increasingly, though, Anderson felt he could not wait forever. He had run into Joy Seppala, the chief executive of an investment management firm called SISU Capital, as he made his rounds of Mayfair. They had got along well; he found her bright, sharp, engaging. She had invited him to do a little bit of consultancy work for her in her role as the ultimate owner of Coventry City. Under her aegis, Coventry had become one of English football's great problem children. The club was at war with, variously, the local council, the group that part-owned its stadium, the fans, the city's media and, at times, itself. Having been a mainstay of the top flight only a little more than a decade before, it was now mired in the third division, living on a shoestring, backed by an owner accused of cutting it loose. It existed under permanent threat of being evicted from the city it called home. It was hard to think of a less attractive place to work.

But when Seppala suggested to Anderson that he might make a suitable chief executive, he was tempted. The job would not offer him the sort of complete control – the financial leverage – he had long thought necessary to pursue his vision, but over the previous two years both he and Sally had drifted closer and closer to the conclusion that their original idea was no more. 'You can imagine someone handing over a £20 million Championship club to a couple of academics,' Sally said. 'Just about, anyway. You cannot imagine someone doing that with a £200 million Premier League team.' Perhaps, Anderson thought, Coventry represented a way to get under the skin of the game, to see how a club worked from the inside, to put at least some of his ideas into practice. Just as importantly, it was a chance to do something other than wait. The experiences of Charlton and Villa indicated to him that there was no guarantee a deal for Palace could be done; there were too many variables, too many obstacles. For all the heat and light being expended on a daily basis in Mayfair, the hawking and the horse-trading of these precious institutions, the mechanism by which someone might successfully buy a football club remained wholly inscrutable to Anderson. The fact that it would mean he would finally be earning money again, generating a reliable income for his family, was not insignificant.

He ran the idea by Sally, who told him to leap at the chance. He floated the prospect by Blitzer and the rest of the consortium. They were supportive. It would be a great learning curve, they said. It could function, in effect, as a sort of loan spell: he could learn the ropes and then come back to Palace when the deal was done, armed with the sort of knowledge only real-life experience could bring. Coventry would be his apprenticeship. They happily gave him their blessing.

That should, of course, have been welcome – Anderson, certainly, was appreciative of the support, the cordiality, the warm handshake and the sincere expression of thanks – but it left him in a bind. All the time he had been in London, pounding the streets of Mayfair, pitching to investors, assessing clubs, making contacts, researching opportunities, he had never quite lost sight of why he was there in the first place. Even as the negotiations dragged on, even as it seemed as though what mattered, more than anything, was getting a deal done, front and centre in his mind had been the mission that had convinced him to give up his job, to leave his home, to move his family in the first place. He was only involved in football because he believed, deep down at his core, that the sport could operate more smoothly, more smartly if data was placed at its heart; the team that cracked that would have a considerable competitive advantage.

But to do that, he knew, data could not be reduced to an option; it had to be the priority. To have any chance of succeeding, he had to be an emissary of an ownership that believed, as he did, in the transformative power of analytics. That had, in his mind, always meant controlling the club. And, for all that he appreciated Seppala's interest and support, that was not on offer at Coventry. In taking the job he would be subverting his own logic; he would be taking a different approach to the one that he had spent years advocating. He would be accepting, on some fundamental level, that reality had intruded on his dream. He would be waking up. It felt, to him, 'very sensible, so practical, so rational, but also very dry, very cold'.

Not long before Christmas, 2015, after all that time spent hanging around the hoop, Blitzer, Harris and several other members of the group that had gathered together in Mayfair more than two years earlier to listen to Anderson and Sally's pitch took what amounted – collectively – to a majority stake in Crystal Palace. They had, after all they had been through, done a deal. They had bought a club. Anderson, by that stage, was not involved. A month earlier, he had told Seppala he would take the job. He had been presented as the new chief executive of Coventry City in November. He had waited long enough. At last, he had found his way in. It was not the one he had envisaged, perhaps, but it was a way in, nonetheless.

7

POSITION OF MAXIMUM OPPORTUNITY

The watershed moment lasted no more than a couple of seconds. Nobody mentioned it or referred to it or even gave the impression of acknowledging it. It would have been possible not to notice it at all: it appeared in the bottom left corner, against a bright yellow backdrop, part of a succession of facts from the game: the percentage of possession each team had enjoyed, the number of shots they had taken, the number of corners won. It was soundtracked by a subdued Antonio Conte reflecting on his Chelsea team's defeat at home to Burnley on the opening day of the Premier League's 2017/18 season. It was a blink and you'll miss it sort of thing. To most, it was nothing, but to some, it was everything. No matter how fleetingly, Expected Goals had appeared on *Match of the Day*, and in that instant, the world changed, just a little.

A surprising amount of time and effort had gone into those few seconds. It was not a decision that had been taken lightly. Richard Hughes, the programme's editor, had been aware of Expected Goals for some time; he had been talking to Opta about perhaps including it in his show's coverage for a couple of years. He saw it as a way to add 'an extra layer' to analysis, to help *Match of the Day* expand its audience appeal, to approach the game in a different light. Once he had decided that the time was right, he had invited a couple of Opta representatives to the BBC's studios in Salford to explain to *Match of the Day*'s pundits precisely what it meant. Later, he would email all of his regular pundits the video Opta had produced to introduce the concept. The reaction was not universally positive. One replied that he had been 'bored shitless' after the first minute.

Hughes was well aware that the idea would have to be introduced delicately, with the lightest of touches. There was a practical reason for that: the show's format allows only for a couple of minutes' dissection of each of its featured games; there was simply no room for a long, drawn-out explanation of precisely what Expected Goals means. He was concerned, too, that if he foisted it on a cast of hesitant pundits, it might be rejected before it had a chance to establish itself. Opta had the same worry: seeing their measure derided on television would have been a substantial setback.

There was, after all, a precedent. In the early 2000s, when the BBC had lost the rights to show the highlights of the Premier League to its commercial rival, ITV, the new show had included a feature called 'The Tactics Truck', in which Andy Townsend picked apart a game's tactical rhythms from – for some reason – a van stationed outside a stadium. The idea was to look at a game as the clubs did through the ProZone technology that was growing in popularity. 'It was an innovative idea,' Hughes remembered. 'A lot of the people who worked on that went on to work for a lot of the data companies in football. But the reaction to it was quite negative.' The Tactics Truck became something of a running joke, and Hughes did not want a repeat.

The best way, he decided, would be to include Expected Goals, nonchalantly, among the portfolio of statistics *Match of the Day* provides after each match, as the respective managers are invited to give their thoughts on what has just happened. No alert, no fanfare, no dramatic introduction. *Match of the Day*'s audience is, after all, a 'broad church', as Steve Houghton, the producer of *Match of the Day 2*, put it.

Its viewership stretches from devout fans watching the action for the second time that day to those who keep only the most cursory eye on the sport; it has to cater for people rolling home from the pub and for children who want to watch on a Sunday morning; there are those who demand searing analysis in the couple of minutes afforded to each game, there are those who would rather there was no talking at all; there are those who pay attention for the first 20 minutes but then find themselves unwillingly and inexorably drifting off to sleep, their eyes heavy either thanks to or despite Jermaine Jenas' discussion of Everton's marking at set-pieces. *Match of the Day*'s job is to be all things to all people.

'We could not beat people over the head with it,' Houghton said. 'If you knew what it meant and you were interested, it was there,' Houghton said. 'If you didn't know or didn't care, you could ignore it.'

Match of the Day was not the only show to be wrestling with the same conundrum. That season, *Monday Night Football*, Sky Sports' flagship discussion show, had also made the decision to include Expected Goals in its coverage. Attitudes had shifted among the network's producers and pundits since the day, more than a decade beforehand, that Andy Gray had bristled at Henry Stott's pitch for Decision Technology's metrics to be included in the broadcaster's coverage.

David Jones and Jamie Carragher – Sky's touchstone presenter and one of its star pundits – were a little more open-minded to new forms of thinking. Sky, like every other broadcaster, had long included the basic facts of a game in its coverage. Expected Goals was a step beyond: it was not simply a measure of what had happened, but a look at what might have happened. It implied a value judgement about the result, whether it was merited or not. Carragher, though, was enthused. Expected Goals was 'the simplest thing in the world to understand,' he felt, a measure that was intuitively comprehensible to any football fan: a way of putting a number on how many chances a team had managed to create. And besides, if the Premier League's clubs were paying attention to Expected Goals, he said, then it was *Monday Night Football*'s duty to reflect that. 'The last thing I ever want is to be accused of being old-school,' Carragher said.

Timing meant that *Match of the Day* – broadcast on a Saturday – had first bite. In a way, that was fitting. To many, *Match of the Day* was the big one. The BBC's late-night highlights show was a national institution; for all that the Premier League's international renown had been built on the billions of pounds lavished on the division by Sky, in particular, *Match of the Day* remained the way that the vast majority of football fans consumed the sport. For those who had devoted their professional lives to helping football embrace analytics, even seeing Expected Goals flash up for a couple of seconds on the screen during a broadcast represented something between vindication and victory.

For a decade, they had been working to convince their colleagues, their peers and in many cases their employers that this was the sport's next frontier. They had been forced to overcome the sceptical orthodoxy that football was too fluid, too dynamic to bear analytical assessment: this was not baseball, they were told, there were too many variables. Many of them had been ignored; those that had not, those that had won some influence within their clubs or their organisations, had invariably faced criticism and occasionally outright mockery. Football held its traditions tight; those who considered themselves the game's spiritual guardians did not welcome interlopers, with their bright ideas and their new ways of doing things. For all of them, it had been a struggle.

Their reward was no more than a slender yellow bar in the corner of the screen as Conte, defeated, complained about an early red card. It did not look like much, but it felt like everything. The moment Expected Goals appeared on *Match of the Day* was the moment it all felt worth it. Analytics, in some small way, had made it into the mainstream. The revolution had, at last, been televised.

Expected Goals did not change the world straightaway. By 2017, when it first appeared on screen, it was not even particularly cutting edge. Charles Reep had divined a system that calculated something similar decades beforehand. A more updated version of the concept had been floating around in analytics circles for almost ten years. Both Decision Technology, at Tottenham, and StatDNA, at Arsenal, had been working with models that included the idea of Expected Goals, though the omertà under which both companies operated meant that neither ever had the chance to win any public acclaim. It was only when Opta, a data provider with a vested interest in as many people as possible having access to and then, ideally, paying for its work, produced its own model that the idea started to gain traction, gaining popularity on social media and, later, winning a little niche attention in the press. Even that had been in 2012: it had still taken five years to bleed into football's broader discourse.

Opta's motivation for developing Expected Goals – what would come to be known as xG – was not especially ideological. From its earliest days, when it functioned essentially as an advertising gimmick for a consultancy firm, the company had always been primarily concerned with selling data to the media. Its business model did not, particularly, extend to analysing the reams of information it had at its disposal. 'It collected it, parcelled it up and used it to tell stories,' said Sam Green. Opta had never tried to work out what all of its data meant. Green's job was to change that.

A maths and physics graduate from Bristol University, Green was not a particularly devoted football fan; cricket had always been his sport of choice, though he had dabbled with baseball in his student days, spending long nights haunting various forums tracking that sport's analytics revolution. He had started his career in the gambling industry, using his twin interests in sport and statistics first at a company that provided tipping advice to bettors, and then taking a job at the betting integrity firm Sportradar.

He arrived at Opta in 2011. His job title was chief statistician: chief in the sense that he was in charge of a department of one. The company had decided on a change of tack. For years, football's two primary data providers had effectively stayed out of each other's way: Opta focused on the media, ProZone dealt with the clubs.

At the turn of the decade, though, Opta had decided that it wanted to park its tanks on its old rival's lawn. It started a sub-brand, OptaPro, targeted specifically at producing performance insights for clubs; the name was designed to reassure potential clients that there was a firewall between the information they might be seeking and the arm of the company that dealt with the media.

Green was hired with an 'open brief' to trawl through Opta's data and find those insights, whatever they might be. 'The idea was to claw back some of the club market,' Green said. Many in the professional game saw Opta as little more than a purveyor of trivia; few had contemplated using its information for anything more in-depth. 'They tended to see Opta as somehow not as serious as ProZone,' Green said. 'But we had all this data. We just needed to develop it.'

That was where he came in. His job was to help change perceptions of the company: he travelled the country, visiting various training grounds and describing to clubs what sort of services Opta might be able to offer; he helped produce 'analytics-led statistics' for a promotional calendar that could be sent out to prospective clients:

numbers that meant something, rather than quirks of history. Most of all, though, he needed to change what Opta did, rather than how it was seen. He had to find out what its data said. And to do that, he needed a system which would allow him – just like Decision Technology and Sarah Rudd before him – to give a value to each and every action on a football pitch.

To Green, that task did not seem quite as gargantuan as it might have done to others. He saw it as a series of building blocks: start with the purpose of the game, scoring goals, and work back from there. This was, in effect, precisely what the sabermetric pioneers in baseball had done, years before: broken down the point of that sport, scoring runs, and worked out what led to them. Green needed to find out how goals were most likely to happen. It was, in his mind, the obvious first step in a journey that would end with a complete picture of what was happening on the pitch. 'You need something like that to describe football,' he said.

Green had his question; finding an answer, or something approximating an answer, took about two weeks. He had all of the data he required: hundreds of thousands of shots from Opta's years of records of the Premier League. In the coding language R, he built a program that could pick through those shots for all sorts of 'features': things like distance and angle and whether they were taken with the foot or the head, whether they came at the end of a sweeping counter-attack or from a set-piece, anything at all that could be established and might be relevant to making the shot a success or not. He 'threw it all in' and then tested his thesis until he could prove it worked.

There was a simplicity to his approach, one that would help it strike a chord with Jamie Carragher on Sky Sports years later. His program assigned every shot a value somewhere between 0 and 1. A striker on the goal-line, the ball at their feet, would score 99 per cent of the time. That chance would have an 'expected' value of

0.99 goals. A lumbering centre-half, taking a desperate shot from the halfway line as a game slipped away, might score (being kind) in one out of a hundred attempts. That effort would have an expected value of 0.01 goals. Every other chance would fall somewhere in between. 'It was pretty easy to test,' he said. 'I was confident in the football sense of it.'

In its purest, simplest form, Green had designed a system that gave a relatively – though not purely – objective way to measure whether a team had created good chances or not, something a step further than merely noting down how many shots they had enjoyed. Now, it would be possible to know if they were good shots or not; if a player should have scored or might have been expected to miss; if a manager, rueing a narrow defeat, was accurate in declaring that their team had the opportunities to win.

Green does not regard himself as the inventor of Expected Goals. He did not know, while he was building his system, of the work being done by StatDNA and Decision Technology, but he recognises now that they were all thinking along similar lines. There was a reason, he said, that when he was out pitching Opta's services to clubs, he did not spend much time in north London. Among his peers at clubs and consultancies, there were a handful of people developing metrics that did much the same thing, after all. His version, though, would be the one that caught the imagination, the one that popularised the idea, the one that would be presented to the Royal Statistical Society, the one that would, in time, germinate so broadly that it appeared on *Match of the Day*. Green was in the right place at the right time to give football what would turn out to be its breakthrough metric, the one that would take analytics if not into the mainstream, then certainly into one of its tributaries. Football has Green to thank for the – belated, eventual – arrival of xG.

* * *

Simon Wilson knew that it was, at least partially, his own fault. He had been in Boston, Massachusetts, for a few days, attending the MIT Sloan Sports Analytics Conference. They had been long days, too: attending countless panels and lectures at the conference hall, and then nights spent networking with executives from all manner of baseball and basketball teams. Now, sitting on stage, the audience eagerly awaiting his pearls of wisdom as part of a discussion on 'Emerging Analytics', he was not feeling quite at the top of his game.

But that was not the only issue. The deeper the conversation went, the more Wilson felt like he did not belong. His background ought to have given him an authority: a semi-professional playing career, foreshortened by injury; a sports science degree from Liverpool John Moores University; years spent working as an analyst for ProZone, rising to become Head of Performance Analysis first at Southampton and then at Manchester City; in his time at the Etihad Stadium, he had been promoted to an even broader role, one which involved helping to build out both the club's analytics team and its capability. Within football, City had become a trailblazer; it was held up regularly as a prime example of a club devoting a portion of its considerable resources to the data revolution. That he was on the stage in Boston alongside another pioneer of data in football, Mike Forde, was testament to how senior, how respected, he had become in his field.

The problem was that, all of a sudden, Wilson had the distinct impression he was out of his depth. He listened, intently, as a third guest – an executive at the San Francisco 49ers – talked in detail about the way that team was interpreting data, and he realised that football, in comparison, was grasping at shadows. When the questions from the audience started, he feared his answers were anything but convincing. 'All I could do was bullshit, really,' he said.

EXPECTED GOALS

On stage in Boston, Wilson had come to the same realisation that many in football were reaching at the start of the 2010s. The sport was suffused with data. Forde, for example, would tell the *Financial Times* a year after that conference, in 2011, that his team had now logged somewhere in the region of '32 million data points from 12,000 or 13,000 games'. What nobody had worked out, at that stage, was what any of it meant. Football was searching for what Omar Chaudhuri – who started out in the sport as, in effect, ProZone's answer to Sam Green, trawling its vast tranche of data for insight – would come to call the 'So what?'

Wilson was in a position to accelerate that search. At his instigation, City had spent the previous few years investing heavily in its analysis department. Even before the club was bought by the Abu Dhabi United Group, making it at a stroke the richest team in the world, Wilson had successfully not only installed a 'technical scout', using data to assess players, but persuaded the club to employ not just one analyst for the first team, as was broadly standard at the time, but four: one focused on preparing for games, one on parsing them, one on training and one attached to the recruitment department. 'We kind of had two responses from the analytics community,' Wilson said. 'One was positive, a sense that this was the way things were going. The other was that it was complete overkill.'

That was just the start. Once the club's new owners arrived, money was no longer an object; Wilson could have access to any information he deemed valuable. City subscribed to everything Opta and ProZone could offer them. They built up databases of players, spent time trying to find a signal in the endless noise. There was, he said, an ambition within the club that it should be a leader in this field and a belief that, with City's wealth now all but guaranteeing it would be overcharged in the transfer market, developing a method to do some form of due diligence was crucial.

He had always been conscious of the limits of his – and his colleagues' – expertise, of the unavoidable fact that, for all their experience within the nascent field of football analytics, none of them were data scientists; to interrogate the data properly, they would need outside assistance. His trip to Boston convinced him. And so, upon his return, he came up with a plan to obtain just that.

Football had always treated data like a state secret. Clubs were so fearful of giving anything at all away that, for years, the Premier League's teams could not even agree to create a standardised, shared set of data between themselves; the division's smaller members, as a rule, felt that allowing their richer peers to see their information was effectively being complicit in their own defeat. Those teams that had yet to pursue data to any great extent, in particular, saw no benefit in helping others learn more about them. That contrasted sharply with the approach that had helped analytics grow in sports in the United States, where the data belonged to the league, and could be accessed by any of its members.

The chances of the general public being given a glimpse, then, were vanishingly small. The clubs would not share what they knew. The data providers would not give away what they had, because their businesses relied on people paying for it. That locked out the growing community of amateurs, academics and enthusiasts, the bedroom Bill Jameses, who wanted to help the game develop, just as their counterparts had in baseball and basketball. 'A lot of that is proprietary,' Chelsea's Forde told the *Financial Times* in 2011. 'The club has been very supportive of this space, so we want to hold some of it back.'

Wilson's plan was to do the opposite. He was going to release City's data into the wild. But he was not going to do it purely out of the goodness of his heart.

'I was reading analytics blogs and you could see that a lot of the stuff that was being done on the outside was much more sophisticated than we were managing on the inside,' he said. 'We felt like we were at the cutting edge, though perhaps teams like Bolton and Tottenham were ahead of us, but we felt we needed a new breed of person, someone with a curious mind and certain skills, ones that we just didn't have in our team. We weren't maths purists.'

Going public was an unorthodox – bordering on heretical – step, but Wilson and his colleague, Gavin Fleig, pitched the idea hard to City's executives. It would help the club identify talent that it might be able to hire, for a start; even if it did not, it might inspire some ideas that the team might be able to, well, let's say borrow; the worst-case scenario was that it proved to be nothing more than a cheap marketing ploy, a way to place the club as a progressive, innovative sort of place; in the best case, they would find someone or something that would help City gain an edge. With the support of Opta, he got a green light.

City's data went live in the summer of 2012, the club offering the event data – the things that happened on the ball – from the preceding season to anyone who was interested: every single pass and kick and shot, right up to the Sergio Agüero strike that won City's first English title for 44 years. 'We hope it will lead to a new culture of open data in football,' the accompanying press release read, as it outlined City's excitement at the chance to 'engage directly with the resulting community to see where this collaboration can take us all'.

In one sense, of course, what became known as #mcfcanalytics failed. Football did not suddenly adopt the crowdsourced approach that had helped accelerate the rise of analytics in baseball; clubs remained steadfastly opposed to revealing what they had to their opponents, and to the public at large, City among them. This was still a business, after all.

But in another, it was something of a Big Bang moment. 'It was a course-changing move,' said Ravi Ramineni, a member of the community that coalesced around the release. Ramineni had been first a colleague of Sarah Rudd's at Microsoft, and would eventually become her partner; he, too, had harboured ambitions of leaving Redwood for a career in sports. He had dabbled with journalism as well as launching a podcast. He had attended Sloan, too, to see if he could find a more sustainable entry point to the industry. 'A group formed around it, sharing insights, updating each other on what we had done,' he said. 'You could use it to analyse City's opponents, too, remember. A lot of the stuff at the start was fairly obvious: whether there was a causal relationship between the number of passes in the final third and the success of the team. But it still felt like there were Eureka moments every couple of months, the more we dug into it.'

Manchester City never really planned for the release of its data to be an act of pure altruism; Wilson is happy to admit that the club was hoping for something back. The plan duly delivered: City would appoint Lee Mooney, a former Barclays employee who specialised in the visualisation of data, as its head of recruitment analysis on the back of the research he did as part of the project. But its real impact was far more diffuse, far less distinct: by granting the broader analytics community the chance to flex its muscles, the club gave the first public demonstration not just of what could be done with data in football, but what might be done in the future. It showed that there was something precious there, waiting to be mined. And by doing it so openly, it ensured the game as a whole would take notice.

The years after Manchester City's data release represent the blooming of football's digital age. It was not, by any means, the only factor behind that transformation – the release of the film version of *Moneyball* was significant; so, too, was the awareness of Arsenal's acquisition of StatDNA – but the timing suggests it did have some effect. Certainly, in its wake came a raft of appointments that suggested that most major clubs, at least in England, were now alert to the possibilities that data held; or, at least, had recognised that they had to be seen to be alert to those possibilities.

Those recruits tended to share one of two backgrounds. Some, like Hendrik Almstadt, who was headhunted by Aston Villa from Arsenal in 2015, and Simon Wilson, who left Manchester City for a more senior role at Sunderland a year later, represented sports' traditional response to pioneers. Just as the success of the Oakland A's had led a host of Major League Baseball teams to staff their own front offices with Billy Beane alumni, football saw teams like Arsenal and Manchester City pushing the boundaries in analytics and hired people they hoped were capable of repeating the trick.

Others, though, went down a different trail, one that had also been blazed in the United States. Teams across the major leagues had hired a swathe of statistical and mathematical specialists from Ivy League universities and technology firms; they had even borrowed the term 'quants' from Wall Street to describe them.

Football was no different. The outsiders included people like Daniel Altman, a Harvard economist appointed as an advisor to Swansea City in 2016, and Green, who made the jump from Opta to Villa a year earlier. Those clubs that could either could not afford or were not inclined to set up their own data analysis departments fell back on the suite of data-driven consultancies being established to provide outside advice on recruitment and strategy: firms like 21st Group, set up by Omar Chaudhuri and the Opta alumnus Blake Wooster, and Ted Knutson's Statsbomb.

For the first time, too, analytics was starting to take root in continental Europe. For a combination of reasons, much of the early progress in the field had been made in England. First and foremost, that is where the money was, but it was also where American investors first landed, drawn not just by the shared language and the

Premier League's hegemony but by the proximity to London, Europe's financial centre and a city that, in many cases, they knew well.

English football had long looked to American sport for inspiration: as Joshua Robinson and Jon Clegg discuss in *The Club*, their history of the growth of the Premier League, many of the pioneering executives who built the competition had borrowed ideas from the National Football League, in particular. Two decades later, then, England was more receptive than most of its peers to the stream of analytical ideas emanating from across the Atlantic, first from baseball and then basketball.

By the mid-2010s, that was starting to change. In Germany, the Bundesliga had been far quicker to generate and disseminate the performance data of its clubs, reaching an agreement under which all 36 teams in its two divisions would receive every shred of information the league had long before the Premier League's clubs decided to do the same. In the Dutch Eredivisie, an American connection had placed AZ Alkmaar at the vanguard: Robert Eenhorn, who had played in Major League Baseball, was appointed as director of the Dutch team AZ Alkmaar in 2014; the following year, he recruited Billy Beane into an advisory role. Not long after that, Luke Bornn, an assistant Professor of Statistics at Harvard who had once specialised in tracking the location of herds of bison, took a role at AS Roma, then owned by the Boston-born Jim Pallotta.

But there was a native acceptance, too, particularly in the Netherlands – where Ajax would start to build a world-leading analytics section – and in Germany. Consultancies like Metrica and SciSports emerged from the former, while Impect developed from an idea hatched by two stalwarts of Bayer Leverkusen and the Bundesliga.

There was change occurring inside teams, too. Jonas Boldt had always been fascinated by statistics: as a child, he would listen to games on the radio, noting down the number of corners and yellow cards, creating his own database of what had happened in each game. Despite not boasting a playing career of any sort, he would go on to work as a scout for Bayer Leverkusen, and eventually rise as high as the club's sporting director. He was one of the first in Germany to adopt and advocate video-scouting services like Wyscout, which he saw as a way of making recruitment more efficient; his unorthodox background meant that he was always open both to the idea of using data as a tool and to seeking expertise from outside the sport.

That reputation meant that he received countless pitches from companies and consultants who promised they, and they alone, possessed the numbers or the insight to help him recruit. Not all of them lived up to their billing: he recalled one metric which he discovered that rated David Alaba, the Bayern Munich left-back widely regarded as the finest in the world, as only the 27th best player in his position. 'There were people I had never heard of above him,' Boldt said. 'So I said that maybe the data is not quite right.'

But others seemed valuable. He was captivated by a niche website called Spielverlagerung and impressed by the work of one of its young bloggers, René Marić, in particular. Boldt invited him to come to a meeting, along with Leverkusen's coach at the time, Roger Schmidt. Marić drove all the way from Vienna in blistering heat, and arrived at the meeting 'with sweat all over his clothes,' Boldt said. To test his mettle, they set him a project: Leverkusen's team was creating plenty of chances but needed a specific type of forward to finish them off. Who would Marić recommend?

'We were looking for a killer,' Boldt said. 'We had a player in mind: Chicharito Hernández, who was at Manchester United at the time. We did not mention that. He went away, did his analysis, and came back saying that he had found one obvious name, but he was worried he would be too expensive. It was Chicharito.' In 2015, Leverkusen ended up signing both Marić and Hernández. The latter played upfront. The former was tasked, largely, with running opposition analysis. Later, Schmidt would recommend Marić for a job at his former club, Red Bull Salzburg, working alongside one of the youth coaches, a former player by the name of Marco Rose. The two of them would go on to work together at senior level at not just Salzburg, but at Borussia Mönchengladbach and Borussia Dortmund, too.

There were others. Sven Mislintat, Dortmund's head of recruitment, had been working on his own analysis platform, Matchmetrics, as early as 2012, though he had initially failed to convince the club to adopt it. In *Football Hackers*, the German journalist Christoph Biermann relates how, when he first pitched the idea to Dortmund's executives, the program cited Lasse Sobiech, a journeyman defender in the second division, as one of the finest players in Germany that season; just as Boldt had when he saw Alaba relegated to being just the 27th best left-back on the planet, Dortmund presumed that the product was not yet ready. After all, that was demonstrably not true. Mislintat, though, continued to finesse the data he was using, incorporating it into a scouting system that, for a time, seemed to represent a Platonic ideal of football's vision of 'Moneyball', tapping a rich seam of rough diamonds.

The Red Bull clubs were comparatively early adopters, too. In 2016, Johannes Spors, the head of recruitment at the energy drinks firm's Leipzig branch, ran into Bastian Quentmeier, a softly spoken sports science graduate with a background in mechanical engineering, at a conference in Munich. Quentmeier, a highly regarded high school hockey player, was working for a video analysis platform at the time. His job was to work out which leagues were worth covering. 'We were paying for all of these games from all of these leagues,' he said. 'But the clubs who were paying for the product were not watching all of them. We had viewing figures for each game, so we used that to work out which ones were valuable, and which were not.'

Quentmeier thought nothing more of the conversation until a few months later, when Spors got back in touch. Would he like to come to Leipzig and work for the club part time, partly in recruitment and partly doing opposition analysis? Quentmeier packed up his home in Munich and headed east. At a club famed for its innovation, part of a network that prided itself on being at football's absolute cutting edge, Quentmeier soon found that he would be starting from scratch. 'There was no data being used at all,' he said. Spors and Ralf Rangnick, the godfather of the Red Bull football empire, wanted to change that; within a few months, impressed by his work, they decided that Quentmeier was the man to do it.

He spent much of his first year as a permanent employee not just speaking to football's data providers – Opta, the Russian firm InStat, the Italian company Wyscout – but seeking intelligence from outside the field, too. 'I met anyone who was working in any part of data analysis,' he said. 'I went to FIFA, but I also spoke to people in engineering, too.' His conclusion was that he did not just need a comprehensive spread of information – giving himself access to the aggregate, rather than relying on one provider – but to create his own system for analysing it. 'I wanted to ask the right questions of it,' he said. 'We had to be able to change it depending on the profile of player that a coach was looking for, or to be able to read it in such a way that we knew which bits of our match plan had worked, and which parts had not.' Rangnick and Spors trusted him to do it. 'There is always an advantage in having more information,' Rangnick said. He had long been interested in physical data: he knew, for example, that there was a correlation between how many high-intensity sprints a team made and how likely they were to win; the style of football he preached and popularised, first across Germany and then in England, was founded on that basic principle. But the system Quentmeier had built, he realised, was different. He was, in Rangnick's words, effectively Germany's first data scout. 'He had something really good,' he said. 'Really good and unique.'

In hindsight, it was not what you would call an auspicious start. Sam Green had travelled to Birmingham a few days before he was due to start work at Aston Villa, appointed as the club's inaugural Head of Research. It was not a leap he had ever imagined making; in his years at Opta, he had never really considered what it might be like to work on the inside. He was not, after all, an ardent football fan; the data had always been enough for him.

Still, when Villa approached him, he knew instinctively he could not say no. He had got to know staff at the club while presenting Opta's research to them; he knew that they were interested in adopting a more analytics-led approach. It was a risk, but it was also too good an opportunity to miss. 'How can you not want to try it?' he said.

When he arrived in Birmingham to take care of life's administration – setting up home, getting to grips with his surroundings – he was excited. This was a chance to see if all of the theories he had developed, the building blocks of a way of understanding football that he had established, actually worked. And then, a couple of days before his first day, Paul Lambert, the manager who had consented to his arrival, was fired. Tim Sherwood was appointed in his place. He and Green effectively started at the same time. This would prove to be a problem.

Reasonably slowly and moderately begrudgingly, football had started to accept data by the time in February 2015 that Green took on his role at Villa. In theory, at least. Social media was awash with various Expected Goals models, though his remained the one that was most prominent in the legacy media. Platforms like Wyscout, Scout 7 and InStat were growing exponentially. Consultancies found their services increasingly in demand. A host of specialist websites were growing to meet fans' hunger for concrete information. Broadcasters were using ever-more sophisticated measures during games: only a couple of decades after it became common to see the number of shots each team had managed flashed up on screen, it was already widely accepted that the percentage of possession was a broadly meaningless number. That may represent a curious growth, but it is a growth nonetheless.

Far more significant, though, was that some of the principles of analytics were starting to bleed into the way the game was played. The clearest example, perhaps, is in the decline of the long-range shot. In 2010, Premier League teams took just under half their shots from outside the penalty area. According to the gospel of Expected Goals, of course, that is less than ideal; as a rule, and other than in exceptional circumstances, long-range efforts carry with them a fairly minimal chance of scoring. They are low percentage efforts; scant reward for all of the energy expended in building an attack.

Since then, though, England's teams have turned their backs on the speculative shot. The number of efforts from distance has been declining since 2014, and the number of goals scored from range along with it. Some of that, of course, can be attributed to the rise of teams playing a Pep Guardiola-inflected passing style; but the concept of Expected Goals, the idea that some shots are worth more than others, is central, too. It is an idea that football as a whole has internalised, though it has done so largely silently. Managers rarely talk about discouraging their players from trying their luck from range. Unlike in the NBA – where analytics led to the converse, and some teams began to focus on three-pointers, traditionally seen as something of a gamble – there has not been substantive, public acknowledgement that football is following the data. In this case, there does not need to be. The numbers are incontrovertible. The lack of actions speaks far louder than the absence of words.

Theory and practice, though, are two different things. Even as ideas drawn from analytics started surreptitiously to seep into football, as fans and players and coaches began to be shaped by what the data told them, that did not immediately translate into either authority or success for those on the frontline.

The experience of Green and Almstadt at Aston Villa provides as good an example as any. Talking to Green, it is easy to wonder if he was just too nice for the fickle, political and unreservedly cut-throat world of a Premier League club. He is passionate about his work and firm in his belief in its value, but he is also softly spoken, measured, self-deprecating. He found almost everyone he encountered at Villa to be 'friendly'; he is reluctant to criticise or badmouth even those who were not. 'There were young guys who were open-minded,' he said. 'And a lot of the more old-school people loved football so much that they were happy to talk, whatever perspective you were coming from.'

He can admit that he 'whiffed' on a few of the players he suggested the club sign, but his list of successes, or even near misses, is impressive. The recruitment models he built pointed him to Hakim Ziyech, who would end up at Chelsea, and Joe Gomez, who would later join Liverpool; he highlighted a Dutch striker, Vincent Janssen, to the club; a year later, he would sign for Tottenham. Perhaps his biggest regret was a simple choice. Green had identified two midfielders in France as worthy targets. Both had similar profiles: busy, energetic, tactically intelligent players who could help break up play and build attacks. The one Villa signed was Idrissa Gueye. He would go on to be considered one of the best players in a poor Villa team; Green remembers him fondly, not least because of his enthusiasm for his own performance data. His career would take him to Everton, fleetingly, and then on to Paris Saint-Germain, where he would help the team make the Champions League final. He was a good signing. The only caveat is that the alternative, the player who was the club's other option, was N'Golo Kanté.

The players that Green did help the club sign were not exactly resounding successes. Part of that was down to the situation that the club found itself in. In Green's first summer transfer window, Villa lost their powerhouse centre-forward when Liverpool paid the release clause inserted in Christian Benteke's contract. A few weeks later, on the eve of the season, the industrious midfielder Fabian Delph declared that he wanted to leave for Manchester City. Micah Richards, who had joined on a free transfer that summer, felt from that point on that the club was going to have a serious problem; the club needed experience, nous, and had bought a raft of young players.

But part of it, too, was down to the manager. Green is circumspect about Tim Sherwood. He will admit that their relationship was 'strained', and that essentially Sherwood did not 'believe' in the club's focus on data, but he is adamant that the manager was always cordial with him. Another colleague from that time, Almstadt, is not quite so encumbered by politeness. 'We did not get on,' he said. Blame for that should not squarely be laid at Sherwood's door: Almstadt is a naturally assertive sort, and his role at the club was ill-defined. In a struggling team and an unhappy club, that is a recipe for finger-pointing and backbiting. But the way Almstadt remembers it, Sherwood was not especially interested in helping all of the club's signings succeed: he refused an entreaty to get a translator for the first few months to help the young, primarily Francophone new arrivals settle in. 'He told us,' Almstadt said, 'to fuck off.'

Neither Green nor Almstadt stayed the course at Villa: Almstadt lasted less than a year; Green made it only as far as 18 months. In some lights, there might be some solace in knowing that both survived longer than Sherwood – sacked after just eight months in charge – and that many of the players both advocated went on to vindicate their judgement, and their approach. Jordan Amavi, a young French left-back, would emerge later as one of Marseille's finest players. Jordan Veretout went on to play for Fiorentina and Roma. Adama Traoré, a raw, unfiltered talent that much of Europe had been watching, would become an occasionally devastating attacking force at Wolves. The problem was that none of them succeeded at Villa. They were the right players, just at the wrong time. That sort of nuance, though, gets lost in the emotionality and the immediacy of football's existence. In 2016, Villa were relegated from the top flight for the first time in almost three decades. The squad that had taken them to the abyss, and the methods that had brought them to the club, were written off as failures.

It is that, as much as the residual hostility of those who consider themselves native to the game, that acted as a roadblock to the adoption and acceptance of analytics. To succeed, a new idea needs not only fertile ground – a club willing to embrace it, a manager willing to accept it, executives happy to support it – and germane circumstances, but a longer-term perspective. Analytics, in whatever form, was never going to provide an overnight transformation. It required time and patience and a little indulgence, even, to bear fruit. These are not characteristics that elite football has in abundance, and that proved a problem even when things went well.

Luke Bornn had been headhunted by Roma, a faded Italian giant under new American ownership, specifically to make the club more 'data-driven'. He had the backing of the club's owner, the fast-talking, somewhat hot-headed Bostonian Jim Pallotta, and his astute, powerful right-hand man, an Italian American called Alex Zecca. Bornn had never particularly wanted to work in sports in general, or football in particular; he had always assumed he would gradually turn into a 'crotchety old professor', haunting some ivy-strewn campus and gently intimidating his undergraduates. But thanks to his academic background and his eidetic memory, he had gradually drifted into the world of 'quant gambling', as he put it, using data to make significant money in the betting markets, and that brought him to Zecca's attention.

In Rome, he was empowered, encouraged. Like Quentmeier at Leipzig, he set about building a data infrastructure. He used data harvested from the GPS vests that players wear to construct models to help predict players' fitness and fatigue levels, allowing the club to modify their training loads. He investigated whether there was a more scientific way to make selection decisions. And he worked heavily on recruitment, the sphere in which football had most readily accepted data, and the place where he felt it could be most effective. 'That was the biggest point of influence,' Bornn said. 'And it has the biggest impact on a team's performance.'

Bornn spent a year at Roma. In that time, the recruitment process he helped to influence brought Alisson Becker, a goalkeeper playing for Internacional in his native Brazil, to the club. It also encouraged Roma to pursue permanent deals for Antonio Rüdiger, a German international defender, and a spry, quick-witted winger called Mohamed Salah. Rüdiger and Salah left the club in 2017, both sold at vast profits. Alisson followed a year later, for what was briefly a world-record fee for a goalkeeper, not long after Roma had reached the semi-finals of the European Cup for the first time in 34 years (where they were knocked out by a Liverpool team inspired by, as it happens, Salah.) Bornn was not around to enjoy it. He had left Roma in 2017, drawn back by the desire to spend more time with his young family and the offer of a job from the NBA's Sacramento Kings.

He does not seek to monopolise credit for that success by any means. Zecca's strength, he said, was in ensuring there was a 'variety of voices at the table' when the club was signing players. It was, in his mind, very much a collective effort: his data blending with the expertise of the club's more traditional scouts and coaching staff and all the rest of it.

But it is hard to escape the thought that this, perhaps, should have been seen as proof of data's potency to help transform a club, football's first real 'Moneyball' moment. Maybe it would have been, had Bornn still been there, or if he had been more willing to shout his corner from afar. But he was not, and so the credit was spread elsewhere: deservedly, to Rudi Garcia, the club's French coach, and more curiously, to Monchi, the celebrated Spanish sporting director who joined just before Bornn left but after the core of the team that came within a couple of goals of the biggest game in European football had been signed. Bornn was rarely mentioned. There were, after all, plenty of people happy to highlight their role in Roma's success and, in absentia and by proxy, diminish his.

Monchi's arrival in Rome heralded something else, too: the end of the club's dalliance with data, and the start of a different approach to recruitment. Football is a shark. It always moves forward. It thinks only in the here and the now. It forgets quickly and reflects rarely. Roma had toyed with data for a while, and then moved on, just as Villa and countless others had.

The consequence was that, by 2017, even as Expected Goals appeared on *Match of the Day* and *Monday Night Football*, even as more and more fans were either starting to be familiar with the precise metrics of analytics or to adopt and understand many of the principles of play that they inspired, the sense remained that – five years after the release of *Moneyball* on film, five years after the invention of a public xG model, five years after Arsenal had bought

StatDNA – data was struggling to gain much of a foothold in the game.

In November of that year, in the aftermath of a 3–0 defeat to Manchester City, Arsène Wenger mentioned that this team's Expected Goals for the game had been rather better than the scoreline suggested. The comment was met, in certain quarters, with unrestrained glee. 'It has to be the most useless stat in the history of football,' one presenter on Sky Sports said. 'He's the first person I've ever heard take any notice of it.'

That was not the case, of course; far from it. More and more people inside football were starting to pay heed to the suite of new metrics analytics was creating, with xG at its head. But to claim its place in the sport more firmly, analytics needed to find a more permanent home. Not a club, like Roma or Villa, where it might be seen as an optional extra, something to be quietly dropped when things were not going well; not even a team like Manchester City, where it was just one weapon among many, but a place that would put analytics front and centre, that had analytics at the very core of its being. It needed a team that used analytics to win, and win again. In the autumn of 2017, that team was just getting started.

8

ALIEN

Chris Anderson had barely had time to take his seat before he heard a knock at the door. He was still feeling a little overwhelmed, a touch untethered. Coventry City's training ground just outside the village of Ryton, on the outskirts of the city itself, was hardly intimidating. It had a grand name – Sky Blue Lodge – but it was a modest, cheek-by-jowl sort of a place, extending to no more than a couple of pitches and a single, two-storey building, the ground floor of which had been given over to the first team: changing room, gym, medical facilities, canteen. The first functioned as the administrative block. Most of the club's staff shared a lone, open-plan room. Only the manager, the head of human resources and the managing director had private offices.

It was not quite what Anderson had envisaged, back when he was daydreaming what it would be like to run an actual football club, but he liked it all the more for it. He had to walk past the players and the coaches and the ground staff to get to his office. His window looked out directly onto the training pitches. The whole club was crammed together under one roof. He had spent years thinking about football in the abstract: first, back in Ithaca, as a series of data points, of quantifiable actions; then, in those long months on the streets of Mayfair, as a sequence of figures on a spreadsheet, all of them measured in dollars and cents. At Coventry, he suddenly found himself presented

207

with football lifted off the page and presented in three dimensions and vivid colour: a living, breathing thing. He could see it and feel it and smell it – the sweat and the liniment and the ambition and the fear – all around him.

It was that, more than anything, that Anderson found disconcerting that first day: the tightness of the quarters only served to accentuate the unfamiliarity of his surroundings. Anderson is self-assured, confident, a little debonair, not naturally given to self-doubt. He wears it lightly enough, but he has a keen sense of his own intelligence. He accepted the offer to become Coventry's chief executive because, deep down, he believed he could do it. But he knew, too, that not only did he not have any experience whatsoever running a football club, he had precious little experience running a business, either. The project he had uprooted his life to pursue was centred on the idea that he might be able to teach the game something. He was sharply aware, that day, of quite how much he had to learn.

It became very clear, very quickly, that he would have to do so on the fly. He had been in his office for only a few minutes when that first knock on the door came. It was the first of many that day, a steady stream of supplicants all beating a path to the new chief executive, all seeking the same thing: money. Not vast sums of it – not millions for a new central midfielder, or hundreds of thousands for a new contract – but just a little, here and there, to help the club keep ticking over. The groundskeeper wanted to restock his supply of fertiliser. The cook needed more equipment for the kitchen. The coaching staff wanted more balls, more bibs, to replace the old and weathered ones they had been using for months and years.

Anderson was not entirely naive. He knew, of course, that this is what happens whenever a new boss arrives at any business: everyone tries to use it to their advantage, to make sure the change at the top works in their favour, to jump the queue ever so slightly. But all of the requests seemed perfectly reasonable, solicited in good faith. They wanted to do their jobs to the best of their ability. So did he. They wanted the club to succeed. So did he. For both of those things to happen, he realised that they probably did need things like more balls and bibs and fertiliser and pots and pans. With a sincere, disarming smile, he told everyone who came to his office on that first day the same thing: he was not quite sure if they had the money – hey, he'd only just got here – but that he would look into it, and see what he could do.

The answer, it turned out, was nothing. He had not gone into the job blind. He had done his research before accepting. He knew that money was tight. Beyond tight, really. Coventry had 'no discretion-ary cash'. There was no pot of money under his aegis that he could bestow on the departments he felt were most in need. He could not just go out and buy some extra fertiliser. More significantly, he knew that relations between the club – as a sporting entity – and its owners were febrile to the point of toxic. SISU, the financial firm that had been in charge of Coventry for almost a decade at that point, long since seemed to have decreed their investment nothing more than a money pit. Joy Seppala, SISU's chair, had made it clear that she would not increase the budget. Coventry, in her mind, had more than enough money to meet its target; it just needed to spend it more wisely. That stance had hardly ingratiated Seppala, or her company, with Coventry's fans. The club's supporters loathed its owners. So did the city council, and the trust that part-owned the team's stadium, though none of those three factions were necessarily natural allies. The one thing they all agreed on was their belief that SISU appeared to be starving the club of the funds it needed, whether it was out of inclination or out of spite.

Anderson knew all of that, but he also knew that Seppala, when he had met her in Mayfair, was bright and engaging and eminently reasonable. They had talked on several occasions, before she offered him and he accepted the job as chief executive, about how a club should be run, about how making smart decisions could help money travel further. She did not seem to him to be a woman happy to write off her investment, or to cut the club loose. She just wanted to make sure she was not throwing good money after bad. That, in his mind, was not an unintelligible position to take.

He did as he had promised: he put all of the requests that had been made of him by the cooks and the groundskeepers and the coaches to the club's owners, explaining the relative merits of each one. He would, in time, spend 'hours and hours working like an idiot' to put together a business case for injecting just a little cash into the business, raising the budget by the most slender margin. He calculated every cost and then indicated every reward that they might bring. That was, in his mind, his job. He was there to advocate for the club; he was, in that sense, no different from the people who had knocked on his door the very first day he arrived and made the case for their departments to see some sort of windfall, however slight.

SISU did not budge. Word came back to Anderson that there would be no extra money. There would be no more fertiliser or bibs. Indeed, he was told, the simple act of asking for money indicated that he had misunderstood the nature of his job. The money at the club's disposal was the budget. There was no room for manoeuvre. He would either succeed with what he had, or he would fail. That was the choice.

Anderson had been in situ for a couple of months or so when, one morning, Tony Mowbray arrived in his office, unannounced, closed the door, took a seat and started to talk. Anderson did not, in truth, always find the club's manager the easiest to follow. Mowbray spoke with a thick, occasionally impenetrable Teesside brogue – he had grown up in the picturesque seaside town of Saltburn – that Anderson had spent considerable time and effort in learning to interpret. Still, whether he caught every word Mowbray said, on this occasion, was secondary. What mattered was that he was there, talking, at all.

Until that point, the two most senior figures on the club's football staff – Mowbray and Mark Venus, Coventry's technical director and recruitment guru – had circled Anderson warily. They had never been less than polite; they had offered him a cautious, but courteous, welcome when he first arrived, and he felt they had established a good working relationship.

He knew, though, that they did not quite know what to make of him. His accent alone marked him out as someone who was not of their world. Mowbray had been involved in football for almost four decades: two as a player with Middlesbrough, Celtic and Ipswich, and two more as a coach with Hibernian, West Bromwich Albion and Middlesbrough again. He and Venus – who had spent most of his playing career at Wolves – had met while they were both at Ipswich. Mowbray had given Venus his break as a coach while he was at Hibernian. The two had worked together ever since. They were, in Anderson's estimation, 'proper football people'. They had spent their entire working lives in the sport. They had taken part in hundreds, thousands, of matches. They understood its rhythms and its requirements instinctively. They knew everyone, and everyone knew them. They were comfortable in this world; it was, after all, theirs. They were creatures of the game in a way that he was not. 'They had seen success, and they were proud of what they had done,' Anderson said. 'And then this guy with a PhD shows up, and they were like: "What the hell?" I'd have been that way, too.' All he could do, he knew, was to hope that slowly, surely, he could persuade them to 'trust an alien'.

That was not the only issue. That Anderson's interest in football lay in data might, in some circumstances, have been an issue, too;

Mowbray and Venus might have regarded this interloper who thought he could teach them to be better at their jobs, that he had obtained some secret knowledge from his life in academia that they had somehow missed, with thinly veiled hostility. At Coventry, though, that was not the most pressing concern. Anderson had been appointed at the express command of the club's owners; those who worked at Coventry were long since past the point of assuming such decisions were necessarily made in good faith. Neither Mowbray nor Venus could quite be sure, at the start, of Anderson's intentions. 'There was a suspicion that I was there to spy on them,' he said. 'I was not my own person.' There was a risk, to them, that he was nothing more than a plant.

Anderson knew that winning their trust would be a delicate process. For all that he had spent years trying to prise his way into football, he never harboured any particular desire to use a club to play a real-life version of *Football Manager*; he did not see Coventry as set dressing for a little middle-aged LARPing. Venus, in charge of recruitment, would perhaps have had more reason than most to fear a newcomer with big ideas and a reformer's zeal, but Anderson quickly recognised that he had neither the expertise nor the need to get involved.

The network Venus had established in his decades in the game was extensive. He had a keen eye for talent. He had, on the tightest of budgets, forged a gifted, well-balanced, competitive squad, with a cadre of wizened old-stagers – Sam Ricketts, Marcus Tudgay, Peter Ramage – swaddling a core of bright young things. Venus had managed to bring in Adam Armstrong from Newcastle, Ryan Kent from Liverpool, Norwich City's Jacob Murphy and the Southampton defender Jack Stephens, all on loan. All four would go on to top-flight careers, either in England or Scotland. The midfield was built around

John Fleck, the Scottish midfielder who had signed for Coventry on a free transfer a couple of years earlier; he would be part of the Sheffield United team that played in the Premier League a few years later. The jewel in the crown, though, was a teenaged playmaker who was starting to emerge from the club's academy, one destined to play both for Leicester City and (fleetingly) England: James Maddison. Anderson left him to it.

He took the same tack with his manager. He did not try to impose a new way of working on Mowbray; he did not waltz in and instruct an experienced coach on where, precisely, he had been going wrong all these years. Though Mowbray was habitually inquisitive about every aspect of the club's health – 'he was always asking questions, about everything,' Anderson said – it was when they talked about subjects away from the team's form, the transfer budget, the club's future, that he felt the ice begin to break. Anderson spotted that Mowbray was reading *Pep Confidential*, the Spanish journalist Martí Perarnau's account of Pep Guardiola's first season at Bayern Munich; they bonded over that. 'He just loved talking about football,' Anderson said. 'Not money or the stadium or the local press, but football itself: the teams and the players and the ideas. He figured out, after a while, that I knew a little bit about it, too, and that was enough. He just had so much love for the game.' Eventually, after a couple of months, Mowbray had seen enough to decide that Anderson was not such an alien, after all.

As much as that moment meant to him – the outsider being validated by the acceptance of the insider – it did not herald a sea-change in how Anderson approached his job. His decision to empower Mowbray and Venus was made partly out of inclination, but partly out of necessity, too. He would not have had time to meddle even if he had the desire to do so. Taking the post at Coventry was supposed to bring him one step closer to seeing if his ideas might work in the real world; he had realised, in just a matter of weeks, that only a 'small part' of his job was directly related to the game itself.

Even there, his significance was mild, at best. His role in transfers was largely administrative; Venus identified the targets and made the initial contact and did most of the negotiating. Anderson came in at the last to sign off on the paperwork. It was not, after all, like there was any room in the recruitment budget to allow him to start experimenting.

The club's finances were so tight that all it could do was take advantage of the rare opportunities that came its way. Venus, in October, had been advised that the former England midfielder Joe Cole, in the autumn of his career and trying to find his way back from injury, might not be averse to the idea of regaining his fitness in League One. For a club like Coventry, it was a no-brainer. 'He would be a good influence on the squad, he was a good character, and we might sell a few more shirts and a few more tickets,' Anderson said. Cole arrived on a free transfer, at a vastly reduced wage. So, too, did Stephen Hunt, the Irish winger who had played in the Premier League for Reading. 'He was living locally and asked if he could come down to train,' Anderson said. 'He did, and we could see straightaway he was still more than good enough.' They added him to the roster, too.

Anderson was more involved when it came to selling players, but there, too, his decisions were more often driven by necessity than inclination. By January, it was clear that Coventry would struggle to keep hold of Maddison; his performances had caught the gimlet eyes of teams higher up the food chain, and they knew that Coventry's financial situation made them distressed sellers. Liverpool and Southampton, among a number of Premier League teams, sent scouts to the Ricoh Arena to follow his development. Liverpool tabled an offer but pulled out of the deal when word of their interest leaked. Southampton seemed close, too, dispatching a delegation to watch him in action before discussing a purchase with Anderson. They had, they disclosed, just one doubt: Maddison's gait as he ran was slightly unusual. They feared that might make him more susceptible to injury. Anderson assumed it was a gambit, an attempt to reduce the price; it made little sense to him otherwise. It did not work. Norwich City had also kept a close eye on Maddison, and agreed a deal while Southampton were still prevaricating. Maddison signed for Norwich on the final day of the transfer window, on the proviso that he immediately be loaned back to Coventry for the rest of the season. Anderson closed the sale at 10.55 p.m., five minutes or so before the deadline.

The bulk of his time, instead, was devoted to almost every other aspect of the club. Coventry's operation might charitably be described as lean; certainly, Anderson could not delegate even relatively menial tasks to one of countless staff at his disposal. He was managing director and executive vice-chairman, of course, but the grandiose titles belied the nature of his work. Anderson had to find local firms to sponsor the club; easier said than done at a time when much of the local community made no secret of its loathing for Coventry's owners. He had to attend meetings of fan groups, to explain why things were getting better, and why they might like to come back to watch their team again. He had to talk to the city's Chamber of Commerce, and to start to negotiate a new lease on the stadium, and to host events honouring former players on match days. He had to make the long journey to away games, and to exchange pleasantries with the owners of opposing teams. He had to spend countless hours on the phone to the sports editor of the local newspaper, the *Coventry Telegraph*, hoping for just a little easing of the continuous (and not wholly unwarranted) stream of criticism that came the club's way. There were times when it fell to him to try to find mascots to accompany the team onto the field. 'I was stealing time, mainly time I should have been asleep, to try to do all of it as it was,' Anderson said. Running a football club, he had learned very quickly indeed, only rarely had much to do with actual football.

Everyone was crammed into the canteen at the Sky Blue Lodge. Not just Mowbray, Venus and Coventry's players, the usual denizens of the building's ground floor, but the employees who did their work behind the scenes, too: the receptionists and the cleaners and the people from the ticket office. Even the kitchen staff were there, given the rare chance to see what the room was like on the other side of the serving hatch.

Coventry had not had a Christmas party for some time. A club without the money to buy new bibs and extra fertiliser is not likely, after all, to have spare cash lying around to pay for a few turkeys with all of the trimmings. Anderson wanted his first festive season at the club to be different. Rather than the players simply taking themselves off for a night out in London or Manchester, he wanted the whole club to sit down and have dinner together, right there at the training ground. To make sure everyone felt part of the celebrations, he brought in an outside catering firm; it would not just mean more work – and perhaps a little overtime – for the cooks. He would pay for it all out of his own pocket.

The mood, that evening, was jolly. The season so far had been more successful than anyone had anticipated. Despite operating under intense financial strictures, Coventry were flying. Mowbray's team had gone top of the table with a 4–1 win against Gillingham late in November; at the very least, the club was starting to contemplate the possibility that it might claim a play-off place. A Christmas party, even if it was just at the training ground, was suitable reward for everyone's efforts. As Anderson looked around at the players and the staff, smiling and celebrating, he felt less like an alien than he had for some time. 'I was starting to feel part of something,' he said. 'It was really nice. Those are the moments that are just really nice.'

He knew, though, that sensation would not last, not for long. He had never completely lost sight of why he had taken the job – more than that, why he had uprooted his family, why he had left his career behind, why he had spent so long trying to pick his way into football, why he was now running a team in League One – in the first place. Football itself might only have taken up a fraction of his time; he might have been inundated with other things to do just to keep the club ticking over. But, still, he found – or, rather, made – time to pursue the idea that had brought his life to this point: that a football club's fortunes would be improved by incorporating data into every decision it makes.

It had hardly been a sweeping revolution. Anderson could not devote hours and days to his passion project; it had been clear to him very early in his tenure that whatever he did on data would be extra-curricular. There were too many other pressing matters to attend to. Nor did he have a budget at his disposal to construct, from scratch, a bespoke analytics department. He would have to make do with a couple of hires. Scott Johnson, an economics student from nearby Aston University, was brought in to work as a data analyst. He was not even full-time. He worked at the club for 10 hours a week, fitting the job in around his studies. He was joined by another amateur enthusiast, Ben Mayhew, whose work had impressed Anderson. Still, they did what they could.

Still, they did what they could. Between them, they produced a weekly report, reflecting on Coventry's results, analysing their performances, working out where the team was doing well and where it might improve. Johnson worked closely with Mowbray's video analysts, making sure that the clips they were bringing to the attention of the staff and the players dovetailed with what the numbers said. Anderson tried to make the approach they took to assessing both team and individual displays more 'systematic', making sure that the briefings before and after games looked at the same criteria, all of it backed up by data. What they had, at the time, was unusually advanced for a club of their station – 'we had an xG model, which was probably not the case for most League One teams then,' Anderson said – but he did not pretend that Coventry was at the cutting edge of anything. He was tinkering around the edges, doing what he could, trying slowly and subtly to help the club get the most out of its resources. 'That general principle, that making better decisions should make a team improve, that should work regardless of the level you're at,' he said. 'I tried to ask how we fit analytics into the things we are already doing. But that all depends on what personnel you have, what data sources you have available, what dials you can turn. The reality was not always conducive to it.'

That was not, though, necessarily rooted in the sort of implacable ideological opposition to the basic idea that he had anticipated. In *The Numbers Game*, he and Sally had warned that the greatest challenge to the use of data in football was not – despite received wisdom running to the contrary – that the game was too fluid to be quantified, but that it was occupied by a group of traditionalists and conservatives who would see the empirical truths offered by the numbers as a threat to their power. Football had always passed its ideas of best practice down from one generation to the next, as players learned at the knee of the great managers, creating a hereditary in-group that had access to what Anderson and Sally described as a form of 'protected knowledge'. Only those who had been in the game, the lore ran, could truly understand it; the opinions of those on the outside could safely be disregarded. The rise of analytics was an existential threat to that belief. You did not need to have played 350 games in the Championship to have access to Opta's data. Data democratised knowledge, and in doing so might democratise opportunity.

At Coventry, though, Anderson did not discern any hostility to the concept of using data to try to improve performance. Mowbray and Venus, in particular, did not dismiss that intrusion into their territory as an act of aggression. Neither was, necessarily, an ardent believer in analytics, but nor were they instinctively cynical about it. Instead, Anderson realised, the problem was not one of taste so much as time. 'On the outside, you have time to consider all these things,' he said. It had been possible for him to spend hours poring through the numbers, finding truths that might otherwise have slipped by unnoticed, understanding what teams should and should not be doing, pursing his lips and tutting at the irrationality of it all. 'But on the inside,' he said, 'everyone is just in the trenches, trying to hold on.'

Mowbray was not 'asking for analytics', not because he did not see the value or because he did not believe it could have a value. He was happy to welcome Johnson into the fold, to see if an extra pair of hands might help, but it was not his most immediate concern. 'The manager is worried about the fact he doesn't have a left-back for Tuesday, and he doesn't know who is going to play there,' said Anderson. Anything less pressing can seem, in that sort of light, somehow remote and theoretical.

That realisation struck him with full force as the halfway point of the season came into view. Anderson had prepared a more extensive report on the team's performance to mark the turn of the campaign, an attempt to put their achievements thus far into some sort of context. It was the conclusion of that research that punctured his enjoyment, just a little, of the Christmas party. The message from the data was clear: Coventry's position in the table was not exactly an accurate depiction of their performances so far. Their results might have them competing for promotion, but beneath that, their underlying numbers – the amount of chances they were creating and conceding, the quality of those chances, how sustainable it was all likely to be – suggested that, in truth, this was a team that belonged further down the league. 'It was solid mid-table, really,' Anderson said. That was no great shame, of course: that is precisely where a team with Coventry's sort of budget should find itself. Possessing that knowledge left Anderson, though, in an awkward position. 'I had to find a way to say to the coaches that we are not as good as we appear to be,' he said. 'That unless something really magical happens, we are going to regress. And nobody wants to hear that.'

Particularly not a manager whose club is performing way beyond expectations. Anderson might have become, over the previous few years, something of a zealot for the power of data, but his academic career had been spent, essentially, studying people: their behaviour, their biases, their motivations, their needs and their wants. In a couple of dozen weeks at Coventry, he had come to realise that his former existence was, if anything, more relevant to the task at hand than his current one.

A football team was as much a sociological phenomenon as a statistical one. Data, interpreted the right way, could offer a glimpse of an objective truth. But that objective truth was not the only consideration. 'The manager's job is to keep everyone going, to keep the energy up, to make sure everyone is enthusiastic,' Anderson said. His report, the cold, hard, irrefutable evidence of his data, would make that much more difficult; it would, most likely, simply accelerate the bursting of the bubble. It is not to reject science to recognise that sport, brimming with emotion and ambition and desperation, bears a greater resemblance to art. 'I didn't want to kill that joy, to be the guy who rained on the parade,' Anderson said. That was not simply out of a desire not to play doom-monger, to make the people who he sat alongside in the canteen, toasting how far they had come, unhappy. It was an acknowledgement that there is a value in the intangible, in the parts of the game that are not reflected in, but may be affected by, the stark reality of the data. 'If the manager and the players believe they can get promoted, then that can be a positive,' Anderson said. That was, perhaps, as important as understanding exactly where Coventry's limitations might be. 'People want to believe in magic,' he said.

He had come to Coventry driven by the belief that football could be distilled and understood through the raw data that every match, every season created; there was a truth in that, and it was one that football had ignored for far too long. His experiences at Coventry did not disabuse him of that belief; his conviction never wavered. Instead, it taught him that it is fundamentally something else, too. Having the best data in the world, generated and analysed by the brightest minds in the sport, is of little or no advantage if the signals it can send are not communicated well to the managers, the coaches, the scouts and the players who can benefit from it. 'That is the only way to relate to numbers,' he said. 'Through the people who communicate them.' What matters, more than anything, is the interface: the point at which the data behind the game and the individuals who define it meet. Anderson arrived at Coventry convinced that football is a numbers game. But while he was there, he came to realise that it is, first and foremost, a game about hope, and faith, and people.

It is the quiet moments, the breaks in all of the noise, that Anderson remembers most fondly from his time at Coventry. Every so often, in the morning, he would find himself staring out of his office window, looking down on Mowbray and his staff putting the players through their paces. Finding himself that close, that central, to football never lost its allure. He could see Joe Cole perform some impossible piece of skill or Jacob Murphy leave an opponent in the dust or James Maddison take his teammates' breath away, and he would be hit again by how privileged he was to have this glimpse of the game from behind the curtain.

He tried to keep sight of that, even when his job did not feel like much of a privilege at all. Just as he had predicted, Coventry's form had tailed off in the second half of the season. The team had won just twice between the middle of January and early April; it had slumped from contention for an automatic promotion slot, down through the play-off spaces and out the other side, slipping as low as 13th at one point. A late-season rally lifted the club into a respectable eighth-place finish – as Anderson could see from the data, that represented no little success, given the financial limitations in place – but still: it was an anticlimax, given how high expectations had been just a few months before. He took precisely no solace whatsoever in the fact that his data-driven assessment had been proven correct. 'I saw it coming, and it was depressing and predictable,' he said. 'You could say the data was vindicated, but what good is that sort of vindication?'

Once the season was over, Anderson, Venus, Mowbray and a select few staff gathered to chew over what had happened, to work out what had gone well and what had gone badly, and to start to put a plan in place to improve the following year. Coventry had missed the play-offs by half a dozen points; a sliver, really, in a 46-game season. There was a consensus that it had been a campaign of considerable growth; there was, they were all sure, plenty of reason for optimism for the season ahead.

Anderson believed that on a collective level; on a personal one, he was not quite so sure. Deep down, he had known from the moment he walked into the Sky Blue Lodge, slipped his coat from his shoulder, dropped his bag on the floor and heard the first of many knocks on his door that Coventry would not be the place where he discovered if the ideas he espoused worked in practice. Trying to engineer a data-driven club is not something that can be done on the cheap, or outside working hours, or with half an eye on something else. He and Sally had worked that out from their early interactions with the sport. They had seen how the relatively few analysts they encountered at leading clubs were either ignored entirely or ground down by the relentless jostling for influence between departments. They had heard, at the Sloan conferences, the litany of complaints from those same analysts at how their work was disregarded or their contributions discarded. Those testimonies had been enough to convince them that the only way, really, to find out whether data had the sort of transformational power they believed was to own a club outright, to place analytics at the front and centre of everything the club did.

Anderson had known 'within the first five minutes' that he would not be able to do that as managing director of Coventry; he did not have the budget or the staff or the remit or the time to institute anything that constituted real change. He had added a little data to the mix of what the club did, but he knew that he would never be able to do any more. He would only ever be able to play at it. He could not become Billy Beane in the West Midlands. Nobody could, not at any club of that level, where all that mattered was getting through to the next day, the next game, the next season. Everyone was just trying to survive.

There had been times, over the course of that season, when he had wondered whether it was all a waste of time. He had confided in his wife, Kathleen, more than once that he feared he had taken the job rashly. 'I felt like there was no real point to it,' he said. 'It just sort of occurred to me to ask what I was doing. The club was understaffed.

There was no way of doing anything I wanted to, and it had probably been quite silly of me to think that I could do it anyway.'

She encouraged him to stick it out, as she always did; she asked him, more than once, what precisely he had to lose, what else he had going on that was compelling enough to make him walk away. He demurred, kept going, stuck at it, driven not only by an unwillingness to countenance failure but also by a mounting sense of responsibility: to the club as both an institution and as a group of people; to Mowbray and Venus, whose work ethic he admired; to the fans and the former players he had encountered, to the community that coalesced around Coventry City. 'I tried to own it, I suppose,' he said. When he spoke at fan forums, trying to persuade supporters that things really were different now, that they did not need to fear for the future of their club quite so much, he did so with a sincere passion. He could tell how much the club meant to them, and to the city. He felt a keen sense of responsibility for its general health. He cared deeply about the results. He was no dispassionate observer of the team; he was consumed by the desire to make Coventry as successful as possible, to make sure neither he nor the team failed. 'There are a lot of highs and lows,' he said. 'And there are a lot more lows than highs.' That year, Coventry won 19 of its 46 league games: just over 40 per cent. 'So the highs have to be really high for it to be worth it,' Anderson said. 'They are.'

By the end of the season, though, he had started to notice the toll it was taking. He was barely sleeping, shuttling back and forth from London in order to spend time with his family. He was eating badly. He felt intensely fatigued at almost all times. 'It is a privilege to work in football, obviously,' he said. 'But I don't know if you could call it a pleasant existence.' There was one night, heading back to London along the M40, when he found himself so overcome with tiredness that he struggled to keep his eyes open, and his car on the road. It occurred to him, all of a sudden, that it was within the realms of possibility that the job might actually kill him. As he contemplated another season of the same workload, the same emotional roller-coaster, the same fatigue, the same pitch of frenzied intensity, he was not entirely sure he had the energy to endure it. He felt a commitment – to the club, to his family, to himself – but the prospect of steeling himself for another year of struggle and strain with no clear reward was a dispiriting one. He knew that those knocks on the door would keep coming, those requests for just a little slack in the budget, just a little money, and he knew that he would keep having to say no. He knew he would have to spend much of his time haggling over whether Coventry would be allowed to remain in its stadium, the Ricoh Arena, for the long term, or whether it would have to move out, once again, a team exiled from its home. He knew that there would be no sudden data revolution. He knew that nothing would change. And just a few weeks into the new season, he knew he could not do any of it any longer. 'I think of myself as quite a high-functioning person,' he said. 'I should have been able to handle it. But I was so ragged. There was such a physical toll, and at some point you have to ask if it is worth it.'

In the middle of September 2016, he called SISU and tendered his resignation. A couple of weeks later, Mowbray left, too. Venus held on until the following March, but within six months, all three of them had gone. Anderson does not know whether his departure had any impact on their futures, but it indicates, at least, that they had not objected to his presence; they had, after all, grown to trust the alien who landed in their midst. If that represented a minor personal success, his overall impression was one of 'failure. I'm an ambitious guy. I know a thing or two. I've succeeded at most things I've done professionally. But I'd failed to convince the owner to do the things I thought we needed to do, and I felt like I'd failed the fans.' What Kathleen jokingly called his 'poorly paid internship' was over, and so, too, it seemed, was the dream that he had convulsed his entire life to follow.

Anderson did a little consulting work after leaving Coventry; he became a port of call for American investors looking to get involved in football. He had become a familiar enough face within the sport to function as a sort of node, just like Keith Harris, the man he had sought out, right at the start, as he sought to find investors to take over a club. He did not find the work quite as stimulating as he once had. Perhaps that was no surprise: he had been sufficiently exposed to football over the previous five years or so to feel that he was, most likely, howling into a void, that much of what he was doing would likely prove to be almost entirely futile. But the world had also changed around him to no small degree; there was, put simply, not quite as much call for his expertise. Not because the game was no longer interested, but because it was more interested than ever.

For several years, as Anderson had focused on trying to buy and then trying to run a club, the landscape of football analytics had shifted markedly. Most clubs, now, not only had access to far more data than they might ever have expected but had finally started to hire the sort of people who might be able to interpret it for them. A couple, at least, were fulfilling the vision of the future Anderson had hoped would be his: away from the game's very brightest lights, they were running their teams on strict analytical principles, and enjoying no little success as they did so. More significantly, perhaps, one of the game's most famous names was on the cusp of becoming the stand-ard bearer for football's long-awaited digital age, of obliterating the suspicion and the stigma around data that had served as received wisdom for decades, of proving that analytics could be a central ingredient in the pursuit of the biggest trophies of them all. The war Anderson had been fighting had been won, even if it felt like his personal battle had been lost.

In 2018, he applied for a post at the University of Warwick – its campus, ironically, located in Coventry – as a Professor of Politics and Economics, as well as the Director of the university's Philosophy, Politics and Economics department. He took the role. On the university's website, his academic curriculum vitae was listed in granular detail: the papers he had published, the conferences at which he had presented, the schools at which he had taught. The previous seven years of his career, the ones between publishing *The Numbers Game* and arriving at Warwick, were boiled down into a single phrase. It read, simply, enigmatically: 'Anderson has extensive experience in the football industry.'

9

MERSEYBALL

John W. Henry arrived at Dilke House at 9 a.m. sharp, one Thursday morning in late November. It was little more than a month since he had bought Liverpool, the victor in a long and fractious court battle – played out in both London and Houston, Texas – with the club's previous proprietors. As fans celebrated on the steps of the High Court, Henry had been busy assuring them that he had a lot of listening, and a lot of learning, to do. That is how he had spent the weeks since. Dilke House was his next port of call.

For all that Henry did not know Liverpool, not in detail, and was not overly familiar with football, he had a very clear idea of what he wanted the club to become. The 61-year-old had been something of a blank slate when he arrived in England. Little, beyond the broadest outline, was known about him or the New England Sports Ventures consortium – later rebranded Fenway Sports Group – he represented. Henry was a billionaire who had made his money trading futures. His most prominent partner, the producer and executive Tom Werner, had brought the world a string of major television shows, including *Roseanne* and *The Cosby Show* among them. The most salient fact, though, was that between them they already owned the Boston Red Sox, a team they had restored to the pinnacle of baseball through the wholehearted embrace of data.

When the group that would become Fenway bought the Red Sox in 2002, the year before Billy Beane's Oakland A's went on their analytics-inspired, record-breaking streak, the team was entering an 85th year without a World Series title. That enduring failure was attributed to the Curse of the Bambino, a hex placed on the Red Sox as punishment for trading the legendary Babe Ruth to their fiercest rival, the New York Yankees, in 1918. Henry, though, was not the sort to believe in ghosts.

A longstanding admirer of the work of Bill James, the writer and academic who had pioneered the use of the statistics that became known as sabermetrics to analyse baseball, Henry was a data evangelist to his core. He set about transforming the Red Sox into a cutting-edge operation, one centred on data. He tried to lure Beane away from Oakland – an encounter that earned him a place in the film *Moneyball* – and when that did not work, he hired a 28-year-old Yale graduate, Theo Epstein, and made him the youngest general manager in the history of Major League Baseball. Within two years, the Red Sox had won the World Series. Another would follow in 2007.

His plan for Liverpool ran along much the same lines. If data could provide a competitive edge not just in the trading of corn and soybean and orange juice futures – the industries in which Henry had made his fortune – but in baseball, too, he saw no reason why the idea should not hold in football. His very purchase of Liverpool was soaked in the principles of 'Moneyball': the club was a distressed asset, bled dry by the previous regime, and available for what Fenway perceived as a fraction of its true value. Henry and his fellow investors were convinced that data, still in its infancy in football, was the key to restoring it to its former glories.

Fenway had been in charge at Liverpool for just two weeks when the group made its first major appointment, hiring Damien Comolli, formerly of Arsenal and Tottenham, as the club's Director of Football Strategy. Comolli looked like a natural fit. He was one of just a handful of people within football who seemed to believe in data's power. The fact he had been a close confidant of Beane ever since their road trip at the 2006 World Cup did not hurt, either.

By the standards of the time, the move bordered on the radical. An equivalent to Comolli's post had long been fairly standard on continental Europe – where most clubs had one or more technical directors, sporting directors or directors of football – but in late 2010, it remained a relative rarity in the Premier League.

English football believed fervently in the idea of the all-powerful manager, the sporting equivalent of the Great Man Theory of History. The best, and possibly only, way to achieve success, tradition had it, was to hand absolute control to a visionary coach, to allow him to shape a club and a team in his own image. That was the legend and the legacy of the likes of Don Revie, Brian Clough, Alex Ferguson and Arsène Wenger, the men who had shaped the English conception of the game not only on the pitch, but off it, too. Technical directors and the like were seen as a hindrance, rather than a help, to any coach worth their salt. The post smacked of bureaucracy, of interference and, worst of all, irrevocable foreignness. Fenway, though, were not afraid of running against the grain. Adopting new ideas had helped them revive the Red Sox, after all. They were more than happy to do the same at Liverpool.

Comolli, though, was just the first step. For all his conviction that data could provide a competitive edge, the Frenchman did not pretend to be an equivalent to Epstein, or to Beane, or to James himself. He knew that, to use data properly, Liverpool would need specialists: data scientists who might be able to find, model and parse the millions of pieces of information generated by every game and every player around the world. Liverpool needed what were known, in baseball, as quants. It was that search which brought Henry, with Comolli by his side, to a quiet street in Bloomsbury one Thursday morning in late November.

Dilke House was home to the headquarters of Decision Technology, the firm Henry Stott had established a few years earlier and which, through its work with Tottenham Hotspur, had been among the earliest pioneers of football's analytics age. Comolli had been sufficiently impressed by their work in his time at Spurs to feel certain that they were exactly what Liverpool needed if the club was to harness the power of data; nobody, as far as he knew, was doing work quite as sophisticated as Stott and his team. He had been in situ at Anfield for just a few days when he called Stott, and suggested they meet. Stott was more than happy to talk.

The meeting was supposed to last just an hour and a half, but it ran sufficiently long that at one point Stott sent a colleague out to pick up a plate of sandwiches from one of the several branches of Pret A Manger nearby. Henry described his career, from his early days playing poker in Las Vegas to his time trading futures in Chicago. He outlined his vision for Liverpool, his absolute conviction that the club had to adopt a more rigorous statistical approach to its work. Stott, meanwhile, walked him through how Decision Technology modelled football, described some of the work it was doing, and offered a few general thoughts on Liverpool. Henry, though, was not there for small talk. After a while, with the mood cordial and warm, he showed his hand.

Henry wanted to buy Decision Technology, lock, stock and barrel, bringing it in-house at Liverpool, placing it at the heart of the club's attempt to become a beacon for the use of data in football. The problem, Stott told him, was that the firm was under contract with Tottenham. That could not simply be broken. Henry idly floated the possibility of allowing the company to complete its commitment to Spurs while under Liverpool's aegis, but the idea made Stott a little uneasy. It might have been legally possible, but he felt it was not in keeping with the spirit of the deal he had agreed at White Hart Lane.

As the meeting closed, the two men agreed to explore ways in which they might be able to work together. Stott went away and investigated whether it might be possible either to curtail the contract with Tottenham, or to add Liverpool as a separate client. He did not find any of the options especially palatable; all of them involved, in some way, reneging just a little on the terms of his contract with Tottenham. His and Henry's mutual appreciation, it seemed, would have to remain unrequited.

Liverpool did not quite see it that way. Henry was not ready to give up, not quite yet. He wanted data to do for Liverpool what it had already done for the Red Sox, and for that he needed Decision Technology. Or, rather, he needed the knowledge and the expertise that Decision Technology had built up over the previous decade. That was what mattered: not the body, but the brains.

Rasmus Ankersen was well aware of the snickering. He had expected it, really. In some ways, he almost understood it. A couple of years earlier, the Danish club he served as chairman, FC Midtjylland, had been crowned champions for the first time in its history. Now, though, late in 2016, it was in something of a slump, cut adrift by the runaway league leaders, FC Copenhagen. The pressure was mounting on Midtjylland's coach, Jess Thorup. Speculation that he was to be sacked was widespread; among the club's fans, his departure would have been little mourned.

Ankersen, though, refused to blink. He made it clear that Thorup would not be removed from his post. It was an admirable, if unusual, position for a chairman to take, and it would doubtless have remained that way had Ankersen not revealed why. If you looked at the league table, yes, Midtjylland was enduring a disappointing season. But he was not looking at the league table. Not the one that everyone else was looking at, anyway.

Instead, Ankersen revealed that the club gave rather more weight to a league table it had devised on its own. This one did not just tally up games won and lost, and points accrued, but took into account all sorts of data: the number of chances a team was creating, the quality of those chances, the amount and the nature of opportunities it was conceding. And in that league table, Midtjylland was flying. The club's models showed that Midtjylland was the best team in Denmark. Thorup's team should, by rights, have had 15 more points than it had mustered in reality. That it did not just meant that it had been a little unlucky, a little profligate. None of that was cause for concern, and none of it was Thorup's fault. He was doing a good job. What the club called its Table of Justice proved it.

Ankersen knew the name was just a touch overblown, as though it had been lifted straight from a comic book. He could see why people might get a kick out of the situation, too: a club devising a table that just so happened to prove how great they were. And he could see that – dressed up in what some might have seen as the sophistry of data and analytics and presented by Ankersen, all designer stubble and blond ponytail and Scandinavian hipster vibe – there might be more than a little residual resistance to the very idea of it. He brushed all of it off. As far as he was concerned, the data was clear. And at Midtjylland, what the data says is close to sacrosanct.

If football has a 'Moneyball' club – a team that, like Billy Beane's Oakland A's, has arranged itself according to the truths it can elicit from data, that seeks and overturns inefficiencies in tradition, that looks in its analysis for a better, smarter way to play – then Midtjylland is one of three compelling candidates. It shares an owner,

Matthew Benham, with another of that triumvirate, Brentford. He, in turn, has a distant and not entirely easy connection with the third and final member, Brighton.

All three are almost exactly what the early pioneers of and advocates for the use of data in football might have envisaged at the turn of the century. They recruit players from undervalued markets or with underappreciated skill sets. They spot talent where others see none. They play a style of football that has been shaped and honed by the study of vast tracts of data. Their approach has enabled them all to surpass teams with far greater revenues and much deeper pockets. They are the trailblazers of what football might look like, how it might work, in the digital age.

That it is those clubs who have taken that role can be traced directly to their owners. Much of the early academic work that would form the intellectual foundation for analytics in football was drawn from, and geared towards, gambling. Henry Stott, the founder of Decision Technology, had used the Dixon–Coles model – named after the two academics who designed it, Mark Dixon and Stuart Coles – as the basis for the slightly jerry-rigged system he used to assess the 2002 World Cup. What Dixon and Coles had designed was, essentially, a system for predicting the likeliest results of games. Its purpose, though, as the initial paper in which it was published in *Applied Statistics* made clear, was exploiting 'inefficiencies in the football betting market'.

To gamblers, particularly those who enjoy substantially more than the occasional flutter, the idea of analysing data to find an edge in the market has long been second nature. Information, after all, is power: the better, more accurate and more relevant your information, the more likely you are to win more often than you lose. Two men realised that approach could be used to succeed in football, rather than simply make money by betting on it. One was Benham. The other was his one-time employer turned, by all accounts, fierce rival: Tony Bloom, owner of Brighton.

Both men are, generally, described as 'professional gamblers', although they are gamblers in the same way as Amazon is a bookshop. The scale, the volume and the nature of their work is designed to strip away as much of the risk as possible; as *Business Insider Australia* once put it, Bloom's firm, Starlizard, 'treats gambling as hedge funds treat stocks'. Benham's consultancy, SmartOdds, does much the same. Both have staffs that run into the hundreds assessing every single factor that might have some impact on the outcome of a game: not just form but anything from the weather to the distance the visiting team has had to travel. Both spend hundreds of man hours generating, sifting through and analysing performance data. Both developed metrics that effectively measured Expected Goals – the quality of chances a team was creating, regardless of results – long before it was commonplace in football to do so. Both use complex mathematical models to work out the probabilities of certain events occurring: this team winning, that player scoring, all the rest of it. Both were sufficiently inspired by the Dixon–Coles system to continue working with its original authors: Dixon was central to Starlizard's system, while Benham hired Coles after leaving Bloom's tutelage and establishing SmartOdds. Both make their money by using the probabilities determined by those algorithms to spot areas where the open market is either over or undervaluing a team or a player, and passing that advice on to – and placing bets for – high-rolling clients, who can now gamble safe in the knowledge that the odds have been tilted, however slightly, in their favour.

If that sounds like an unsatisfactorily vague description of their business models, there is a reason for that. Neither Starlizard nor SmartOdds are especially keen to tell people precisely how they operate; doing so would only risk blunting the edges they have found.

Bloom, in particular, jealousy guards his privacy. He rarely grants interviews to anyone other than the local media in Sussex. His employees are required to sign non-disclosure agreements. It is possible only to sketch the broadest outline of his life. He was educated at private Lancing College, inherited a love of betting from his grandfather and enjoyed a brief career at the accountancy firm Ernst & Young before turning his passion for gambling into his business. He worked for Victor Chandler, the bookmakers, specialising in Asian handicaps – in which the favourite team for any given game must score a certain number of goals or more for a bet on their victory to pay out – before setting up a series of early online gambling portals in the first decade of the 2000s. He appeared, infrequently, on the international poker circuit; he was described by the *Guardian* as a brilliant, if deliberately 'low-key' player. He set up Starlizard in 2006; officially, it regards itself as a consultancy, available to any client with the money and the appetite for its advice. It is believed that its central customer, though, is Bloom's own syndicate, believed to be the biggest in Britain. He bought Brighton, his boyhood team, three years later, rescuing it from seemingly perennial financial strife and launching it on an upward trajectory that would transform it, within a decade, into a mainstay of the Premier League.

The success of those two ventures is not unrelated. While it is not clear what access, if any, Brighton have to Starlizard's proprietary data, it is clear they share a raft of basic principles. Starlizard's data makes the firm an 'excellent judge of talent', as one long-time employee put it. The firm has a trove of detailed information on tens of thousands of players around the world: not just the rudimentary information most hobbyist gamblers would use but in-depth, complex performance analysis. They need that, after all, to make their predictions and their probabilities as accurate as possible. A glance at Brighton's transfer activity under Bloom's ownership suggests it has adopted the same idea. The club has made a habit of recruiting players from leagues where other teams are too wary to shop – competitions where data is deemed unreliable or incomplete, or where the quality of competition varies so wildly that it can be hard to draw any concrete conclusions – or signing talent that might have slipped by unnoticed by rivals.

One such example is the German forward Pascal Gross, who had spent much of his career marooned in his homeland's lower divisions before being relegated from the Bundesliga, in 2017, with tiny, unfashionable Ingolstadt. Few would have picked out Gross as an obvious target on the back of that campaign, but Brighton did. They knew that the quality of chance he was creating for his teammates was among the best in the league; they knew that it was not his fault if his teammates lacked the quality to convert them. He arrived at Brighton, played in every single game in the club's debut season in the Premier League, and scored seven goals. He was every inch the 'Moneyball' signing of cliché.

That sort of data analysis in the transfer market is part of Brentford and Midtjylland's approach, too, though Benham – a little more open than Bloom, though still hardly what anyone would call indiscreet – has, in the past, rejected the idea that either of his clubs are 'Moneyball' teams; the term, he has said, is too easily misconstrued. 'The label can be confusing, because people think it is using any statistics, rather than trying to use them in a scientific way,' he said in a speech at the Emirates Stadium in 2015. 'Moneyball's idea wasn't about using any old statistics, but statistics as an academic and scientific exercise to see which ones actually helped predict things.'

Since buying Brentford in 2012, and Midtjylland two years later, Benham has always been clear, though, that data is not the only tool at his teams' disposal. Ankersen, for a long time his trusted consigliere at both clubs, speaks frequently about what he calls football's 'end of history illusion', the idea that the game as we see it now, the one broadcast around the world every three days in ultra high definition, is the highest and ultimate form of the game. We fall into it, he believes, because when we review footage of old games – even if, in this case, 'old' goes back no further than the 1990s – the players seem so much slower, so much less athletic, and the systems and formations feel so rudimentary. We look at how far we have come and we assume that there can be nowhere else to go.

Ankersen, certainly, has little time for that idea. 'We think the players can't get thinner or fitter or run more or work harder, so this must be it,' he said. 'But there are always edges.' Midtjylland and Brentford see it as their task to find those edges. They might, as Ankersen said, be in terms of nutrition, or injury prevention and recovery, or even in sleep, disciplines in which football's interest is still young. They might be structural: it is telling, for example, that in 2016 Brentford took the unorthodox decision to scrap its academy. It ran entirely counter to convention: teams needed youth systems, after all, in order to generate their own talent. The decision, particularly when made by a club run, in the popular imagination, by a group of people in thrall to the power of algorithms, was seen as a betrayal of the promising young footballers of west London.

In Brentford's interpretation, it was the exact opposite. The club had realised that, under England's youth development rules, it was essentially nurturing players so that bigger, richer teams could come and poach them for a pittance. Not only did it make no economic sense, it followed no sporting logic. Instead, the club chose to establish a so-called 'B team', largely stocked by players aged between 17 and 20: often, the ones who had been cut loose from other sides' academy systems. Rather than being a rival destined to lose out to Chelsea, Arsenal and Tottenham, Brentford saw this as a chance to be something closer to a partner. In the years that followed, the B team would provide the club with a steady supply of first-teamers, players who had developed late or improved rapidly or needed a change of environment. It had found, in other words, an inefficiency in the system, and exploited it.

Ankersen was just as moved to try and find edges in the way the game was played. He saw Midtjylland as a kind of 'laboratory' to test out new ideas before they were even transferred to Brentford. 'Interesting ideas don't come out of top leagues,' he said. 'The clubs there have to be more risk averse, because the consequences of taking risks can be relegation.' In a place like Denmark, on the other hand, taking risks not only came with much smaller penalties for failure, but far greater rewards for success. He and his staff set out to make the club play more 'efficiently'.

That term, of course, has a pejorative sense within football; it carries with it a distinctly Reepian connotation. But just as Beane found a strand of data that allowed him to change the way his team tried to win baseball games, and just as analytics encouraged teams in the NBA to prioritise high-risk, high-reward three-point shots rather than safer two-point efforts, Ankersen was determined to find out if football could be played more smartly. One area they identified quickly was set-pieces: a considerable proportion of goals in football come from free-kicks and corners. It made sense, then, to be good at them. Midtjylland would, in time, design what was in effect a set-piece manual, a playbook of more than 60 routines that were drilled into the players. The result was eye-catching. Midtjylland are now regularly the most effective team at set-pieces not just in Denmark, but in Europe as a whole. 'Midtjylland is further ahead of the team in second than the team in second is ahead of the team in 73rd,' Ankersen said.

That was just the start. Ankersen and his staff realised that crossing the ball is not especially efficient; in training, the club's coaches started to declare the corners of the pitch out of bounds for players, compelling them to take a more difficult, but more likely, way to goal. They realised that they lost possession from throw-ins with alarming regularity, so they hired a throw-in coach to help them improve both their technique and their strategy. 'There is a lot that has been disregarded,' Ankersen said, whole areas of the game that nobody has ever really tried to improve. When we spoke, late in 2020, he even had his eye on kick-offs.

Central to all of that, of course, has been data. Midtjylland – and Brentford – run on data; everything is checked and assessed and verified according to the data: the players they sign, the way they play, the decisions they make. Half-time team-talks are influenced by text messages sent to the coaching staff, detailing how the team is performing according to a prescribed series of performance indicators. In Denmark, they are now even trying to apply the same approach to one area that would seem immune to it: the psychology of players. Midtjylland have partnered with a university to study whether there are any common characteristics among players who have succeeded at the club, to ask what sort of traits they should be searching for when recruiting.

Not long ago, all of this would have been greeted with the same sort of giggling that Ankersen heard when he first mentioned that the club had its own system for looking not just at points gained but performances registered. That it has not is proof of the ultimate triumph of the three clubs who have become the standard-bearers of football's digital age. Jess Thorup wasn't sacked that season. The next year, he led Midtjylland to a league title. They won it again in 2020. There is, now, a regular feature in one of Denmark's leading newspapers. It is a league table based on underlying performance. They call it the Table of Justice.

In a way, that should have been enough. The story of the rise of data in English – and European – football would simply be that of

Brighton, Brentford and Midtjylland, the three teams who gave themselves over to analytics and reaped the rewards: a place in the Premier League, or a suite of Danish titles. But football does not quite work like baseball. Billy Beane managed to inspire a revolution in his sport despite not, in actual fact, winning anything other than the American League (West). That is all it took for the sport to take notice. Football is rather more brutal. It has a zero-sum approach. Vindication of any idea requires undisputed success, not relative achievement. It is a sport that wants to see medals before it buys into a theory. It is not to diminish anything Brentford, Brighton and Midtjylland have achieved to suggest that, had they been alone, football would have continued to see analytics as the preserve of minor outliers, a niche method used by a particular subset of teams. For data to go mainstream, for it to be accepted as best practice and universally applicable, its triumph had to be unquestioned, absolute. And for that, it needed a giant.

Liverpool's transfer committee had reached a stalemate. In the summer of 2015, the club was united in its belief that it had to sign a new striker. Luis Suárez, the controversial, irrepressible whirlwind who had come within a whisker of single-handedly leading the team to the Premier League title a season earlier, had left the previous year. The miscellany of players signed to replace him – the veteran Rickie Lambert, the enigmatic Mario Balotelli, the porcelain winger Lazar Markovic – had disappeared without trace. Reinforcements were needed. Everyone could agree on that.

The sticking point was their identity. Michael Edwards, the club's technical director, advocated bringing in a Brazilian forward, Roberto Firmino, from the German team Hoffenheim. Firmino had a curious sort of profile. At 25, he fitted Liverpool's preferred age bracket, and he had already made a smattering of appearances for his national team. Though his technique was flawless and his work-rate admirable, he was hardly a classical number nine. He was not reliably prolific: in four seasons in the Bundesliga, his goals tally had only once stretched into double figures. He was not especially quick, or fearsomely strong, or particularly dominant in the air. Brendan Rodgers, the club's manager, could see that he was a gifted player, but worried that he might not be cut out for the Premier League.

Instead, he lobbied for the club to sign a player who he regarded as more of a sure thing. Christian Benteke had recovered from the Achilles injury that prematurely ended his second season in England – and, unbeknown to him, scuppering a prospective takeover of Aston Villa – and returned to something approaching his best. For the third year in a row, he had been Villa's leading scorer, claiming an impressive 15 goals for a team that had only just avoided relegation from the Premier League. Rodgers was so convinced that Benteke would instantly give his team the firepower it sorely lacked that, when Edwards floated the idea of signing Romelu Lukaku as a compromise candidate, he would not countenance it. The two sides found themselves at an impasse that seemed to encapsulate the folly of Fenway's Liverpool.

The failure to recruit Decision Technology had not deterred John Henry. His belief that the key to Liverpool's future lay in data was unwavering. Quietly, painstakingly, the club was being reshaped behind the scenes with that in mind. First of all, in 2011, Comolli approached Edwards, then working for Tottenham, with a view to becoming Liverpool's director of performance and analysis. Though the two had not worked together at White Hart Lane, Comolli knew of Edwards' reputation as a smart, forward-thinking operator. Edwards, for his part, was ready for the move. The prospect of working for Liverpool was tempting enough; the fact that his wife had been offered a job in the north made it a practical choice, too. He accepted.

Edwards was not, in the strictest sense, a numbers man. He had a degree in Informatics – the study of how human behaviour interacts with digital information – from Sheffield University, but though he would later be cast by the *Daily Mail* as a 'laptop guru' sitting in an 'air-conditioned office', he was more or less native to football. He had been a player in his youth, at Southampton and Norwich and Peterborough, only for his career to be curtailed by injury. He had completed his studies and been considering a career in teaching when a friend suggested he apply for a role with ProZone. He had never harboured any great ambition to spend his life analysing sport, but it seemed more interesting than most other jobs. He thought it was worth a try. Teaching could be a back-up.

ProZone sent him to Portsmouth as an analyst. Outgoing, razor-sharp, unafraid to speak his mind, he was a popular figure. The manager, Harry Redknapp, liked Edwards immensely; he appreciated his tendency to take notes during team talks, both before and after games, and then tailor his Monday morning video analysis sessions accordingly. He left out the abstract and focused instead on practical problems and solutions. He had the art of making complex information seem comprehensible, relevant. When Redknapp took a job at Tottenham, he invited the man he affectionately called 'Eddie' to join him, tasking him with reshaping the club's approach to analysis.

But while Edwards had become an analyst, he was not necessarily a convert. He found that players simply did not respond to the statistics that ProZone provided; managers and coaches were, for the most part, only really interested in seeing their squad's physical output, a way of holding anyone suspected of shirking to account. Beyond that, he felt that many of the statistics fell somewhere between trivial and actively harmful. He was hardly a data zealot.

That had started to change when he arrived at Tottenham and started working with Decision Technology. Though his initial meetings with the company had been forthright to the point of provocative – something that Edwards, not exactly a shrinking violet, doubtless relished – he had soon been won over. Stott and his team, he realised, were working at a far higher level of meaning than ProZone and Opta. He liked their ability to strip emotion and bias from the game, to see it objectively, for what it really was. He started to quiz them to find out exactly how their models worked, why they came to the conclusions they did. He did not always agree with their findings, but he appreciated the cold rationality behind them. By the time he arrived at Liverpool, he understood both the value of data in general, and the work of Decision Technology in particular.

It did not take long for Edwards to realise the scale of the task in front of him. When Comolli approached him, he had been enthused by the idea of working for Fenway. He knew all about the group's progressive reputation, acquired through its success in turning the Red Sox into a byword for modernity. What he found at Liverpool, though, was a shock. A year or so into Fenway's reign, the club had neither a data department nor an advanced analysis one. Far from being at the cutting edge of football's brave new world, it was some way behind his previous employer, Tottenham. He had been hired, he realised, to bring it up to speed.

In those first few months, as he tried to bring some order to the chaos, Edwards held countless meetings. He met with data providers and data analysts and representatives of anyone and everyone who claimed they might be able to help. None of them, though, seemed to him to be a patch on Decision Technology. They, he was convinced, were the market leaders. They were the people Liverpool needed. They were also, as Henry had discovered, unavailable. Edwards, though, had a way around that. It was the firm's data scientist, Ian

Graham, who had built the models and designed the approach that worked so well at Tottenham. He was the part of Decision Technology that they needed. The club could not buy the company, so why not just offer him a job? Best of all, Edwards knew Graham well enough to know he stood a chance. Graham, after all, was a boyhood Liverpool fan.

Edwards' intuition was partly right. Graham had never really considered going to work for a club, but he had grown a little tired of life as a consultant. No matter how good the work he produced might have been, he was always reliant on the whims of a client – whether that was Tottenham or someone else – as to whether his advice was taken. He had started to wonder whether he might be able to have a more direct, quantifiable impact if he was on the inside looking out. As a fan, he had been delighted when Fenway bought Liverpool; as a professional, he had been a little disappointed. Decision Technology's contract with Tottenham meant he would not be able to work for the sort of group who would place exactly that kind of emphasis on his work. The fact he was a fan was secondary.

Edwards first raised the prospect of bringing him in-house while the two of them were flying to the Sloan Sports Analytics Conference in Boston. Graham was sorely tempted. Still, he did not find it an easy decision. He enjoyed working with Stott and did not want to let him down. He chewed it over for weeks, before eventually concluding that he had to take the plunge, risking Stott's wrath in the process. In the summer of 2012, nearly two years after Fenway had taken charge, the two key figures in the reinvigoration of Liverpool were in place.

Like Edwards, Graham knew that he needed time. Liverpool were effectively starting from scratch. He told the club's owners not to expect to hear from him for the first six months; he would need that time, he said, to acquire the data and build the models that would allow the club to take a more data-driven approach to recruitment. To help, he hired a friend, a software engineer, who was looking for work, and borrowed someone from the club's IT department to build the back-end of the system, writing the code he needed and establish the pipelines that would feed data into his models. Only by the start of 2013 or so could the club hope to have something that resembled a functioning data department.

The deliberate, mechanical approach behind the scenes, though, stood in stark contrast to what was playing out in public. The first few years of Fenway's tenure were volatile, to say the least. Comolli, the group's first appointment, had lasted just 18 months in his post, relieved of his duties on the eve of an FA Cup semi-final against Everton in April 2012, before Graham had even started work.

From the outside, his data-driven approach seemed to have failed. He had broken the club's transfer record twice in the same day in his first transfer window, signing Suárez and then the Newcastle striker Andy Carroll as replacements for the departing Fernando Torres. The following summer, he plucked Jordan Henderson from Sunderland and Stewart Downing from Middlesbrough. There was, it was suggested, a hard, objective logic to all of this: Henderson and Downing were among the most proficient players in England at delivering the ball into dangerous areas; Carroll, with his aerial prowess and unreconstructed physicality, was the ideal player to capitalise on their work. The conclusions of the spreadsheets, though, failed to translate onto the pitch. Liverpool struggled, finishing sixth in Comolli's first season, and then slipping to eighth after his dismissal. The experiment, Fenway were told, had failed.

Henry's response to the setback was not, though, to submit to received wisdom, to give the keys to the kingdom to a manager and let them take control. Instead, they doubled down. Comolli had been working alongside Kenny Dalglish, the beloved former player and manager who had returned as coach not long after Comolli arrived. Dalglish's status both inside Liverpool's corridors of power and among the club's fans gave him an unmatched authority; he had been able to command the kind of team he wanted to build, thereby shaping the sorts of targets Comolli pursued. There had been little pushback. Dalglish, after all, was the embodiment of a visionary coach. At Liverpool, he was every inch one of the Great Men of History.

Fenway did not want to repeat that mistake. Dalglish left not long after Comolli, the club deciding to appoint a much younger coach, one less likely – in theory – to expect to be able to act unilaterally. Henry interviewed both Roberto Martínez and Brendan Rodgers in Miami. The latter got the job. He was told that he would be working within a new structure, one in which recruitment decisions would not be made by the manager alone, as convention dictated, but by a more collective approach. Rodgers would be one of five members of a group who decided which targets the club should pursue, along with Ian Ayre, the chief executive, the head of recruitment, Dave Fallows, the chief scout, Barry Hunter, as well as Edwards, now the club's director of technical performance. To many outside the club, Edwards' presence served as proof that Liverpool had not really changed its ways. The club was still going to try to introduce 'Moneyball' to football.

The idea was not, in truth, an especially novel one. Most clubs had long operated in a similar way. Signing a single player can cost a Premier League club tens of millions of pounds in transfer fees and wages; the biggest deals can account for a considerable percentage of a team's annual revenue. It is hardly outrageous that a chief executive might solicit a range of views to make sure the signing is the right one; it is not unreasonable that they might expect to have a little input into the final decision, too. All Liverpool hoped to do was to make sure signings were vetted as much as possible, to implement a system to guarantee the club was thinking long term, as well as short.

The mistake Liverpool made was giving it a name. Jen Chang, an American journalist who had been drafted into the club's communications department, suggested it be known as Liverpool's 'transfer committee'. When the term leaked, it was met with a mixture of fury and hilarity. To traditionalists, this was somehow worse than having a technical director. It was another new-fangled idea that would constrain a manager by allowing a faceless, unaccountable quango to foist players on him. It was, received wisdom had it, a recipe for precisely the sort of conflict sparked by the schism over Firmino and Benteke.

In the end, the two sides found an uneasy accord. Rodgers would acquiesce to the signing of Firmino as long as the club also moved for Benteke. Having consulted with Fenway, Edwards agreed. There were, however, two provisos. The first was that both players must be given a fair crack of the whip; at £29 million, Liverpool were not signing Firmino to soothe their egos. The second was that, in keeping with the principle of the committee approach, credit and blame must be shared equally. Edwards would take responsibility if Benteke did not work out, just as Rodgers would be on the hook if Firmino was not a success. That settled it. The club's chief executive, Ian Ayre, was dispatched to South America to complete a deal for Firmino, where he was competing in the Copa América with Brazil. A month or so later, Liverpool submitted a £32.5 million offer for Benteke, matching the release clause contained in his contract. Everyone had got what they wanted.

The truce did not last. Though Rodgers was always complimentary about Firmino in public, behind the scenes there was a mounting belief that he was not quite living up to his end of the bargain. Firmino was frequently a substitute; when he did play, he was marooned on the right wing, a position for which he was not especially suited, and where he struggled to justify his inclusion. To the club's hierarchy, it seemed as though Rodgers was not giving Firmino a chance.

The manager, though, had more immediate problems. Liverpool had collapsed the previous season – their final game had been a 6–1 defeat at Stoke City – and, though they started the new campaign with two narrow wins, the team's form had nosedived. Rodgers' side were beaten heavily at home by West Ham, and comfortably away by Manchester United. The day before a Merseyside derby with Everton, Fenway decided it had to act. Rodgers was relieved of his duties barely an hour after a 1–1 draw at Goodison Park.

Once again, after five years of trying to turn Liverpool into a flagship for how data might work in football, Fenway found themselves at a crossroads. The popular perception was that the club's slavish devotion to the idea of analytics was sabotaging its chances of success. The *Mail* pointed the finger of blame for Rodgers' demise at the failures of the collective approach. 'They have yet to explain how they reached a figure of £29 million for Roberto Firmino,' the newspaper fumed. The transfer committee, it said, was now 'notorious'. The *Independent* described the flawed model as the single greatest obstacle any new Liverpool manager must overcome. First Comolli, then the transfer committee: Liverpool's owners must have learned their lesson by now, the thinking ran.

That was precisely the response inside the club. Liverpool had indeed learned a lesson, just not the one that everyone assumed. The problem, as they saw it, was not that the model got in the way of the manager, but that the manager had been getting in the way of the model. A collective approach did not work without ultimate buy-in from the person who made the final call. Graham had spent three years, by that stage, building and fine-tuning his models, feeding all of the relevant data he could acquire into his systems to help the club better judge prospective recruits. Liverpool were confident that not only did they have a complete picture of a player's ability, but they had the expertise to analyse it accurately, too. Everything the club knew pointed them towards Firmino. He was the right choice. That he had not worked out – yet – was more likely to be down to a lack of opportunity than the lack of suitability. Fenway resolved not to make that mistake again. Whoever replaced Rodgers would have to be happy to work in and with the structure, rather than just pay lip-service to it. Managers would come and go, but the model would remain. Liverpool were, at last, ready to go all in.

In one sense, Ian Graham was a little disturbed by the reaction. In the spring of 2015, he and Michael Edwards had been invited to Frankfurt to give a presentation to a selection of sporting directors and analysts from various Bundesliga teams. They would not, they knew, exactly be among friends, but they felt sure they would encounter a few like-minded individuals. Germany, after all, might have been behind England in terms of the application of data – the country's clubs were yet to scratch the surface of what all of that information might be able to do – but it had long been ahead of the Premier League in terms of awareness of it.

In Graham's first couple of years at Liverpool, England's teams had still been reluctant to share their data with their rivals; when the league's clubs were asked to vote on it, a slender majority rejected the idea of doing anything that might benefit their opponents. In Germany, it was different. In Germany, the Bundesliga had been producing and disseminating performance data for years. This was friendly territory.

The focus of their talk was Borussia Dortmund. Germany's second club had endured a torrid campaign. Just a couple of years after reaching the Champions League final, Jürgen Klopp's team – admittedly shorn, now, of the likes of Mario Götze, Mats Hummels and Robert Lewandowski – had reached the halfway stage of the season in danger of relegation. Dortmund had rallied, a little, as winter faded into spring, but the consensus held that whatever magic Klopp had wrought to turn Dortmund into champions in 2011 and 2012 had long since evaporated.

Graham, in particular, did not see it like that. He walked his audience through Dortmund's underlying numbers for the season: the quality of chances they had made, the quality of shots they had conceded, the points they should have gained and the ones they should not have dropped. They showed conclusively, he said, that there was nothing inherently wrong with Dortmund: the league table was lying. They had just been a little more profligate, a little more generous and a lot more unlucky. They were not markedly worse than they had been the previous year, when Klopp guided them to an impressive second-placed finish.

The shoal of sporting directors, men who well understood the relevance of data, were unmoved. They dismissed Graham's conclusions as a form of sophistry, effectively, as though he was making the numbers say whatever he wanted them to say. The idea that Dortmund had not drastically declined, he and Edwards were unceremoniously informed, was 'bullshit'.

As frustrated as Graham was at the easy, casual rejection of his work – and as enervating as he found football's wilful refusal even to try to understand these ideas – he knew, too, that being ignored was in his, and in Liverpool's, interests. Neither he nor Edwards could know for sure which other teams were starting to make progress on the use of data. Arsenal, thanks to StatDNA, would have access to sophisticated modelling. Chelsea, too, had been an early adopter, thanks to Mike Forde and Steven Houston. Several of Liverpool's recruitment staff had worked at Manchester City; they had invested plenty of money into the development of their data department. Spurs remained under contract with Decision Technology. But how advanced their work was, how much their analysts and data scientists were being heard was veiled in secrecy; even among the relatively tight-knit analytics community, clubs held their cards close to their chests. It was only on occasions like these, when a quorum of sporting directors from a major league told him that what he knew to be true was wrong, could he gauge how far ahead of the crowd Liverpool might be, or glean an insight into the breadth of the club's competitive edge. That day in Frankfurt suggested it was still a chasm. That suited him just fine.

Liverpool paid little heed to the cynicism. After Rodgers' departure in the autumn that year, Fenway considered two candidates to replace him: Carlo Ancelotti and Klopp. On paper, perhaps, Ancelotti would have been the favourite. He had won the Champions League with Real Madrid just a year earlier, yet another trophy on what was the most garlanded résumé of his generation. Klopp, by contrast, was on a sabbatical after leaving Dortmund, his reputation just slightly diminished by the travails of his final season.

Liverpool, though, had no doubts. Klopp and his agent, Marc Kosicke, met with Henry, Werner and Mike Gordon, Fenway's president and the man charged with the day-to-day running of Liverpool, at a lawyers' office on Lexington Avenue in New York. The rapport between them was immediate. Klopp got the job. What had happened in that final year did not give Liverpool a moment's pause. The club knew, after all, that the league table had been lying.

Though Gordon, in particular, had discerned at their first meeting a strong streak of 'analytical thinking' in the German – as he said in Raphael Honigstein's biography of Klopp, *Bring the Noise* –Klopp would not necessarily have regarded himself as a data enthusiast.

Sven Mislintat, his chief scout at Dortmund, had made some analytics part of his recruitment process, but little of that made its way to Klopp's desk. That he did not have any particular expertise in the field did not matter to Liverpool. The club did not need him to be a convert, or a zealot. It simply needed him to be open-minded.

The story that surrounds his first meeting with Graham has, over the years, taken on a faintly apocryphal air, slipping from anecdote to fable and on the way to something approaching a myth. It is easy to feel as though some of its details have been allowed to become slightly exaggerated in the constant retelling. It goes, in its current form, like this. Three weeks or so after Klopp took charge at Anfield, Graham walked into his office at the club's training facility at Melwood. The two had not met before, and Graham was determined to make a good impression. The printouts contained the data from all of Dortmund's games in Klopp's final campaign; Graham wanted to prove to him that he and his research department could see the game for what it was, regardless of the end result, so as to convince him to trust in their work.

He told Klopp how unlucky his team had been to lose to Mainz and to Hannover that year, because in both games they had created by far the better chances. Klopp agreed: they had been unlucky, yes. 'You saw it?' he asked. Then comes the punchline, perfectly scripted: No, Graham replied, he had not seen any of those games. But he knew the truth of them, because he had read and interpreted the numbers. He walked out, the story has it, with his new coach converted.

The reality is, in all likelihood, a little less dramatic. Part of what appealed to Liverpool's hierarchy about Klopp was that he was used to working in a collaborative structure. At Dortmund, Mislintat had handled the scouting, the sporting director Michael Zorc had taken care of the construction of the squad and the chief executive

Hans-Joachim Watzke had tied everything together. He was not cast from the British mould of believing in the infallibility of the manager; he was not likely to chafe at the perceived interference of Edwards, in particular, as his predecessor had. It helped, of course, that they had similar tastes: unlike Rodgers, Klopp had been impressed when Liverpool signed Roberto Firmino earlier that summer. At £29 million, he thought the Brazilian was something of a snip.

More than that, he was a natural delegator. 'That's what leadership is,' Klopp would later say. 'Having strong people around you, with better knowledge than you in different departments, [and] not acting liking you know everything, being ready to admit: "I have no clue at the moment."'

That was no posture. Klopp took much the same approach at Liverpool as had been adopted in rather less pressurised, scrutinised surroundings at Midtjylland and Brentford. He deliberately chose to surround himself with people who knew far more than him in their chosen fields in the hope of finding whatever edge, whatever advantage, he could find.

Among his first appointments was not just Andreas Kornmayer, a fitness expert, but Mona Nemmer, a nutritionist who had worked for Bayern Munich and the German national team. Most teams, he felt, did not pay enough heed to what their players were eating; he empowered Nemmer to conjure a menu that would help Liverpool's squad perform to their best. In 2016, Klopp joked that he and Nemmer had talked about turning her work into a cookbook. A 'wild dream,' he called it. The book came out in 2021.

It was not just in the canteen that Klopp sought what are, in sport, generally known as marginal gains. He raided Brentford for the club's throw-in coach, Thomas Gronnemark, to make his squad as efficient as possible at retaining or regaining possession. One pre-season, he invited Sebastian Steudtner, a big wave surfer, to address his players, talking to them about how he handled stress. During another, the squad was given the chance to work with Neuro 11, a German start-up that works on mental strength, to improve their penalty and free-kick technique; in early 2022, after winning the Carabao Cup on penalties against Chelsea, he made sure to credit the company for its impact.

It would, then, have been deeply out of character for him to chase Graham from his office, or to sweep the stack of paper from his hands, declaring that it was not possible to measure the size of a midfielder's heart. Klopp may not have immediately grasped what, precisely, Graham and his research department were doing, but he was predisposed to give them a chance to prove their worth, to welcome whatever help they could provide. By that stage, after all, he knew that the club had not lost faith in him when his final season at Dortmund had proved so anti-climactic; he knew that both Edwards and Graham had championed his cause, even when they were told their belief was 'bullshit', because they trusted their data. For that support, he would always remain grateful. 'The department there, in the back of the building,' he told the *New York Times* in 2019. 'They're the reason I'm here.'

Ian Graham does not, as a rule, work from his office at Liverpool's gleaming, glass-fronted training facility in the satellite town of Kirkby. Even before the coronavirus pandemic forced the club to minimise the number of staff on site, much of his role could be fulfilled from his home in the south-west of England. When he is present, though, he and the rest of his Research Department make a point of arriving early enough to ensure they can savour the delights of a Mona Nemmer breakfast.

They are not the only civilians in there – members of other departments also find the lure of free food difficult to resist – and Klopp is an ardent believer in the idea that the team, the club, extends beyond the couple of dozen professionals out on the training pitch. Still, Graham and his colleagues are conscious that the canteen is generally regarded as an extension of the players' sanctum sanctorum: it is their space, and they do not wish to disturb it. Respectfully, they make a point of maintaining a degree of distance, forming a distinct, tight knot: Graham, the polymer physicist; Will Spearman, the Harvard graduate recruited directly from CERN; Dafydd Steele, one of Graham's earliest hires, a champion chess player; and Tim Waskett, an astrophysicist.

Any sense of separation – of jocks and nerds, them and us – ends as soon as the breakfast plates are cleared away. Data is not confined to a silo at the Liverpool of Klopp and Edwards and Gordon. There is no delineation between the sport and the science, between them and us. There is no battle to be heard, no struggle for acceptance, no tectonic shifts in the politics of influence. It is that which, Graham and his staff believe, has allowed Liverpool to be so successful: the club's key advantage is not the sophistication of their work, but the efficacy of the way it is communicated. The practical staff are receptive to the ideas and the findings of what, for want of a better word, can be described as their theoretical colleagues. The work of Graham and his team is hard-baked into everything Liverpool do. It influences the recruitment and retention of players. It is factored into medical diagnoses and coaching sessions and pre-match analysis. Increasingly, in small and subtle ways, it is starting to shape the way the team plays. Over the last decade, Liverpool have been able to do what no other club of their size has tried or dared or managed, and laced the use of data and analytics into their very fabric.

It is an identity that the club wears lightly. Partly that is because it would be incorrect to claim that data is the sole root of all the success that Liverpool has had since Klopp's arrival. It is hard to gauge whether it has been more or less important than the German's charisma, his tactical nous, his percussive style of play, his gradual, gentle nurturing of a fearsome team spirit. Even those at Liverpool who have spearheaded much of their work in the sphere do not want to be seen to strip credit from all of the other things that have helped: the marginal gains in throw-ins and mental strength and nutrition; the expertise of the club's fitness coaching; the increase in revenue that has enabled the club, for the first time in the Premier League and Champions League era, to pay premium fees for premium players; and, of course, the talent and determination and ambition of the players themselves. Liverpool's story would have been different without the club's belief in data, but that does not mean it is just a data story.

And partly it is strategic, too. Liverpool do not want to evangelise their use of data too much because it is not, ultimately, in their competitive interests to do so. Indeed, after more than a decade in his post, it is only comparatively recently that Graham has started to reveal a little – and by no means all – of his methods; he is still sufficiently guarded that he did not want to be interviewed for this book. In excerpts from other interviews and conference speeches and lectures, though, it is possible to piece together a general impression of the work he and his team are doing.

'We have done one-off, bespoke pieces of work where they're concerned about a particular area of play, or want to know something about travel before a game and whether that affects performance,' he told the club's website in 2020. Some of their time is spent on the theoretical: Spearman, in particular, has been working on 'pitch control' models, working on which areas of the field are controlled by which team at any one time, and which actions can help to shift that balance in Liverpool's favour.

But the central focus of everything the Research Department does, the bedrock, is in Expected Possession Value. Using both the kind of event data that is recorded by Opta and tracking data – working out where everyone is on the pitch at any one time, using a similar sort of camera system to the one pioneered by ProZone – Graham's models calculate a team's chances of scoring a goal at any given moment during a game. The technology they use was originally designed as part of a missile-tracking system, Graham has said. Every time a player makes a decision – plays a pass, or makes a tackle, or dribbles past an opponent – they can establish whether that has increased or decreased their team's chances of scoring. That knowledge opens up a whole world of possibilities. It can tell Liverpool which approaches are most valuable, which decisions are optimal in which phase of the game, which type of attacks are most profitable. It informs Spearman's work on pitch control. Most of all, it means Liverpool know which players add the most value to their team's results.

It is still, at this stage, in recruitment that much of the work of Graham and his department is brought to bear. That is not just the greatest area of expense for any club, it is the arena in which data can make the biggest, most meaningful difference: a club that gets more transfer decisions right than it does wrong immediately has an advantage over most of its rivals. The club's hierarchy do not wish to put too much emphasis on the role data plays in the signing and the retention of players: they are insistent that nobody is being signed from a spreadsheet. For all that Mel Johnson, one of the club's former scouts, complained to *The Athletic* that a load of interlopers with 'computers' who had 'come straight from university' were now running Liverpool's transfer strategy, Edwards and his staff have always placed considerable emphasis on the central pillar of old-fashioned scouting: going to see a player to establish if they are worth the trouble.

But it is noteworthy how many of the players who would go on to become the cornerstones of Liverpool's success have been either suggested or at least approved by Graham's models. He pitched the idea of signing Mohamed Salah, a little-known Egyptian winger, from Basel in 2013, only for Chelsea to beat Liverpool to the punch. He continued to advocate his hiring even after his spell in London proved a little disappointing; by 2017, his data suggested that Salah would combine easily and effectively with Roberto Firmino. His admiration was so ardent that, in 2017, Edwards was prepared to state Salah's case to Klopp, who had initially hoped to bring in the German midfielder Julian Brandt. It is a measure of Klopp's collective approach, a stark contrast to his predecessor, that he happily bowed to Edwards' wishes. Salah joined Liverpool. It worked out quite nicely.

Naby Keita was a similar long-term project – though one, perhaps, without quite the same impact as Salah – after Graham first spotted him playing for Red Bull Salzburg. Sadio Mané had caught his eye there, too. Liverpool waited patiently for Virgil van Dijk, eventually signing him six months later than intended and enduring the embarrassment of his former team, Southampton, filing a formal complaint against them for the nature of his pursuit, at least in part because he stood out so clearly on Graham's models.

None of those players came cheap, of course: Liverpool tend to be selective in the market, but they are unafraid to commit large fees and even larger salaries – the club's wage bill runs at more than £300 million every year – if the club deems it worthwhile. That approach, too, is vindicated by the data. As Billy Beane has said, there is no tension in the idea that the right player can be simultaneously expensive and undervalued; few, now, would quibble with the world-record fees paid for Van Dijk and Alisson Becker, much less the £37 million that procured Salah. It was always a misconception that the concept of 'Moneyball' meant scouring the market for low-priced gems; it is better understood, certainly in the context of football, as a way of accurately determine the worth of a player to a specific team. Simon Kuper and Stefan Szymański proved in *Soccernomics*, meanwhile, that there is a meaningful correlation between how high a team's wage bill is and its likely position in the league. That does not justify paying average players too much; it does, however, indicate that premium players, those who command premium salaries, are worth the investment.

That, certainly, has been Liverpool's experience. On his first day at Anfield, Jürgen Klopp outlined his ambition to win at least one major title within five years. He surpassed that: Liverpool reached the Champions League final in 2018 and returned to win the competition the following year. There was another final appearance in 2022. In 2020, Klopp led the club to a first Premier League title, ending Liverpool's 30-year wait to be crowned champions of England once more. He has added a Club World Cup, a European Super Cup, an FA Cup and two League Cups to the club's honour roll, too.

In doing so, he has not just restored Liverpool to the pinnacle of the game, returning a club that had been cut adrift for much of the 1990s and 2000s to what it regards as its rightful place among Europe's great powers; he has done more than simply fulfil John Henry's vision of turning Liverpool into football's equivalent of the Red Sox, a smart and sleek super club that can compete with rivals able to draw on functionally bottomless reserves of wealth.

For years, Liverpool gazed at Manchester United, in particular, and envied its old rival's commercial clout, its global reach, its financial power. As United opened superstores and branched out into the United States and Japan and China, Liverpool always felt old-fashioned, parochial, quaint by comparison. The morning after Rafael Benítez had won the Champions League in Istanbul, with hundreds of thousands of fans on the streets of Liverpool, the club shop remained firmly shuttered. Liverpool had flown all of the staff out to Turkey to be part of the greatest day in the club's modern history. It was an admirable, sentimental decision, but hardly the action of a ruthlessly capitalistic enterprise. Nobody would ever have said it out loud, but some small part of Liverpool knew it had to be more like Manchester United.

Under Klopp, Edwards and Fenway, the roles have been reversed. Liverpool no longer looks longingly elsewhere and wonders what lessons might be learned; instead, others look at Liverpool and ask how they might mine their approach in order to mimic their success. Liverpool stand now as a paradigm for how data might be incorporated into the way a team is run and the way the game is played. In analytics, Ignacio Palacios-Huerta, a former director at the Spanish team Athletic Bilbao and a professor at the London School of Economics, told the *Financial Times*, 'There is clear leadership by one club: Liverpool. They have a group of four or five PhDs in maths and physics, and they know football.' It is regarded as, arguably, the most efficient elite club on the planet, a beacon of modernity, the gold standard.

And yet the scale and the significance of Liverpool's success runs deeper even than that. In the autumn of 2021, Edwards announced that he would leave the club in the summer of 2022; he had decided, he said, that the time was right for a new challenge. The imminent departure of the 'laptop guru' who had cost Brendan Rodgers his job and championed the 'Moneyball' approach was not greeted as a blessed relief for Liverpool. It was not even dismissed as an irrelevance.

It was, instead, treated by fans as a terrible blow, and framed by the media as a looming crisis. There was frenzied speculation that Edwards might be about to join Real Madrid, or Paris Saint-Germain, or Arsenal, or even Newcastle United, recently added to the portfolio of the Public Investment Fund, the sovereign wealth fund of the state of Saudi Arabia. It was quite a turnaround, to put it mildly, and it mirrored the seismic shift the game had experienced as a direct result of Liverpool's success.

All of those trophies might have been testament to Klopp's talent, but they also served to vindicate all of the work Edwards, Graham and their team had done over the previous decade. There is a reason, as Edwards put it when announcing his resignation, that he named his dog Bobby, after Firmino. That vindication did not go unnoticed. Liverpool's success gave English football a begrudging epiphany. It fundamentally altered the way the game regarded data and analytics. No longer was it an unwelcome import, a non-native species, an alien idea pitched by snake-oil salesmen and charlatans and, worst of all, Americans. Instead, because they could see that it worked, it became yet another sphere in which clubs sought to compete with each other, to outdo each other, to find an edge. The clubs that spend time and money on their data resources are no longer regarded as outliers, accused of grasping at smoke; instead, it is the teams who do not invest who are considered outdated, old-fashioned, faintly neolithic. Liverpool gave football the proof it needed – the only proof it really values, the kind that can be weighed in silver and gold – that the beautiful game could be quantified, and that in doing so it lost none of its soul.

THE RISE OF THE OUTSIDERS

The first time Ashwin Raman read the message, he assumed it was a joke. It had to be. There were several reasons why he could not genuinely have been offered a job – an actual, paying job – working as an analyst for one of Scotland's bigger clubs. He had no qualifications, for a start. Or any experience, for that matter. Neither of those were desperately surprising, of course, because he was still only 16. He had not even finished school, let alone started at university. He was still living at home, with his parents and younger sister. And that home was in the Indian city of Bangalore, some 6,000 miles away from his prospective new employer in Dundee. That also seemed like a problem.

But the offer, it turned out, was real. A few years earlier, when he was in his early teens, Raman had started a blog. He had been a football fan since the 2014 World Cup, but the nascent analytics scene had captured his imagination. He did not consider himself a maths enthusiast, but a relative had loaned him a copy of *Soccernomics* and he had devoured it in an evening. Numbers seemed much more appealing in the context of football. *The Numbers Game* and *Soccermatics* followed. He started following the work of StatsBomb and Analytics FC and, after a while, thought he might as well join in.

He did not know whether many people were reading his work, not really, and he did not particularly mind. He was writing for himself, and for the small circle of acquaintances – drawn from Britain and Europe and the United States – who followed him on Twitter. He was not doing it as an advertising pitch. 'Of course, I'd always wanted to work at a club at some point, but I'd considered it completely out of the realm of possibility,' he said. Particularly, he knew, because he was only 16, and he lived at home, with his parents, in Bangalore.

Among his followers, though, was a progressive Scottish coach and analyst who was, at the time, working as the technical director for an Indian team. Stevie Grieve made a point of keeping up-to-date with the work of the analytics hobbyists – heirs to the community that had gathered a decade or so before around Chris Anderson, Sarah Rudd and others – most of whom congregated on Twitter to promote and critique each other's work. Much of it, he found, was vaguely impenetrable, suffused with a jargon borrowed from the influential but highly technical German website Spielverlagerung. Several of that site's alumni had gone on to work for clubs, most notably René Marić, plucked by the Red Bull network and on his way to becoming assistant manager at Borussia Dortmund. Those who hoped to follow in his path had adopted the same house style as a marker of sophistication.

Raman's writing, on the other hand, was clear, concise and authentic. 'Ashwin wrote what he saw,' Grieve said. 'He gave examples, he explained why Player X had done one thing when he might have done something else. His graphics were consistent and clear. He had some tactical understanding of the game, and some of the coding skills, and the rest he could learn.' He knew he was young – 'youngish, anyway, maybe 19 or 20' – but he was sufficiently impressed to get in touch.

Raman was a little star-struck by the blossoming friendship: Grieve had, a few years previously, hosted *The Mind Game*, a tactics and analysis show on Indian television. He was encouraged, perhaps even a little flattered, by Grieve's approval. He did not expect, though, to wake up one morning to receive a message from him, offering him a job. In 2019, Grieve had returned to his native Scotland, taking up a post as head of analysis at Dundee United. He wanted to make the club smarter, more sophisticated, more advanced, but he had precious little money to play with; recruiting full-time analysts would be close to impossible. Instead, he came up with a scheme. He would tap into the public analytics community, offering those writers who had most impressed him the chance to put their theories to the test on a part-time basis, and he would pay for it out of his own pocket. Raman was one of the first he contacted.

Initially, Grieve tasked him with conducting the club's regular performance reviews – gauging how they were doing against a set of pre-determined metrics – and creating easily digestible visualisations that could be passed on to the manager or the club's board of directors. Though he was only working a few hours every week – with breaks for exams – Raman's role soon expanded into recruitment, the area he found most interesting: working with data from Wyscout's video analysis platform, Grieve asked him to build a system that allowed the club to scout more effectively in different countries and different positions. 'I also often ended up over-enthusiastically looking for players, with no real direction,' Raman said. 'I'd mention who stood out in the data and the video. It was so much fun to do the stuff I'd been doing with the blog, but with some tangible effect and, well, pay.' Often, his suggestions were a little too expensive for a club of Dundee United's size – 'there were a few where it just would not have been possible for us to sign them,' Grieve said – but he appreciated the enthusiasm, and the effort.

The arrangement lasted for a couple of years, before Grieve moved on, for nearby St Johnstone, and Raman decided that he was in need of a break. 'I wanted to focus on college,' he said. 'I really enjoyed the work, but I felt a little burned out. I reached a point where most of the football I was watching was for work.' The break did him good: by the spring of 2022, he was watching games in great volumes again, writing about them for fun, his interest and his passion revived.

Whether that will translate into a career he isn't quite sure, not yet. Grieve, for one, would work with him again in a heartbeat: 'The football industry is about trust, and I trust him,' he said. 'So if I have a job when he's finished his studies, I'd find a place for him.' Raman himself, though, is not entirely sure. Quite how 'exploitative' the football industry can be for analysts and scouts, with low wages and unsociable hours even for relatively senior positions, puts him off. He is intending to study history or sociology. He might choose to see where that takes him, instead. 'I'm going to make sure I have a foot in both doors,' he said.

The fact working in football is even an option for him, though, lays bare the profound shift the game has undergone in the last decade or so. Data, as Billy Beane said, has the power to 'democratise' a sport. It opens doors that have previously been closed to anyone who has not enjoyed an illustrious career as a player to anyone talented enough to get through them. The part of his, and the A's', legacy that brings him most pride is the sense that baseball is now among 'the smartest industries' on the planet, recruiting from the same pool as Wall Street and Silicon Valley, drafting some of the brightest minds in the world on a fraction of the salaries they might earn in Palo Alto or Manhattan simply because of a love of the game.

Football is, of course, not quite so far down that road, but the direction of travel is clear. It is not just Liverpool who have recruited astrophysicists and theoretical mathematicians. Laurie Shaw, the lead artificial intelligence scientist at Manchester City, counts Britain's Treasury among his former employers; he studied astrophysics at both Harvard and Yale. Dominic Jordan, the Director of Data Science at Manchester United, is an expert in geospatial analytics. In one of his previous roles, he helped design public transport systems by examining the movement of people.

They are just the high-level appointments. Beneath them, out of the limelight, are scores more people like Raman – scientists and physicists and statisticians and hobbyists, the young and the gifted – who had effectively been locked out of football for more than a century. They want to work in football because they love the game; the game wants to hire them because they might, just might, be able to further our understanding of how it could, and how it should, be played. So slowly as to be almost imperceptible, their arrival makes the game a little smarter, a little more inclusive, a little more global. For a couple of years, Dundee United employed as an analyst a teenager working out of his bedroom at his parents' house in Bangalore. For a long time, that would not have been possible. Now, thanks to the rise of data, it is.

At all times, Monchi holds his phone close, nestling it in the palm of his hand, as though it might go off at any moment, bringing him some information so crucial, so urgent that he cannot afford to waste a millisecond retrieving it from his pocket. When he does work up the courage to put it down, he places it carefully, as one would a precious vase, on the table in front of him. He does his best to ignore it, but the temptation is too great. His eyes drift to its screen, dark and quiet, every few seconds. He watches it warily, anxiously, obsessively.

Monchi's phone is the secret to his, and his club's, success. Over the last 20 years, Sevilla's sporting director has forged a reputation as the man who has tamed football's chimerical transfer market. When he started, in 2003, Sevilla was an ailing backwater, far adrift not just of Spain's twin titans, Real Madrid and Barcelona, but excluded even from the rank of ambitious clubs – Atlético Madrid, Valencia, Real Betis – beneath them. Two decades on, Sevilla has become a regular presence in the Champions League. The club has lifted the Europa League no fewer than six times, and the Copa del Rey four times. That transformation is down, in no small part, to Monchi, and his eye for talent and his nose for a deal.

The list of players that Monchi can claim as triumphs is extraordinary. He was the man who brought Daniel Alves to Europe. He was the man who signed Ivan Rakitic for just £2 million. He was the man who spotted Julio Baptista and Luis Fabiano and Jules Koundé. He brought them all to Seville, their gifts lifting the club's horizons, and then sold most of them on, for multiples of their original costs, allowing the club to spend just a little more on their replacements, allowing the team to become a little stronger every time it seemed to have to start again. There are plenty of sporting directors or chief scouts or managers, even, who have pulled that trick once, or even twice. Most estimates have it that at least 50 per cent of transfers are doomed to failure. Monchi has been defying that consistently for two decades. The methods he has devised have been shaped by experience and necessity. He knows the value, for a club like Sevilla, of striking early, so he tends to focus his energies, and those of his staff, on markets that he knows well: the French second division, for example, where many teams might be reluctant to tread; Brazil, rather than Argentina, where the clubs are more transactional, and deals simpler. In those areas, he maintains a broad network of agents and scouts and contacts; the transfer market, after all, is built largely on relationships. He learned early on that the market can change in a flash, when he lost Sergio Ramos to Real Madrid on the final day of the transfer window in 2005 and had to shop around, at the last minute, to find a replacement central defender; now, his scouts have to submit a full team of potential signings from their territories every month, just so Sevilla are never caught quite so short again.

He takes great care, too, to make sure he is recruiting the right sort of person, not just the right sort of player. Emilío De Díos, his scouting manager, spends much of his time performing due diligence on what a player is like away from the pitch, speaking to their families and friends and colleagues and coaches. Monchi has long been conscious that a player can only thrive if they are comfortable in their environment. Seville is not London or Paris or Milan; Sevilla are not Real Madrid or Barcelona or Manchester United. Different types of players succeed in different types of environment; it is a source of great pride to him that so many of his alumni continue to retain affection for their former club. He knows that he is signing players who will one day move on, if all goes well; that is the model, after all. But he wants to be sure that, while they are at Sevilla, they feel at home.

He is, in other words, the archetype of football's traditional way of doing things: the sporting director who knows everyone and everything, who instinctively understands the forces that drive the market, who keeps the phone close because an opportunity can arise at any given moment, and then there really is not a millisecond to waste.

And yet, for all that, Monchi has, in recent years, given himself over to analytics. It is not just that all of his staff's reports are now filed onto a bespoke server, where performance data can be contrasted according to their age or their position or their value. It is not just that he has seen the ranks of the scouting department swelled not by former players but by mathematicians and engineers. It is that Sevilla, the club that mastered the old transfer market, has invested heavily in artificial intelligence and data pipelines and proprietary algorithms. Its database now includes details of 18,000 players, all of them prospective targets, all of them easily assessed and compared. 'Big Data is the future of football,' Monchi said. 'With the financial landscape we have, it can keep us in the elite in Spain, in Europe, and around the world.'

No less striking than the fact that even Monchi, the Platonic ideal of the transfer market guru, is using data is that he has incorporated it so naturally. To him, it is not an alien incursion, a way of automating what has always been a very human process. It is simply another way of doing what he has always done. All of that research, all of those man-hours, are designed to make sure Sevilla spend their money as wisely as possible. Data is just another check. 'You are not going to sign a player based on data, but it reduces the risk, and helps us make decisions,' he said.

The vast majority of clubs have, in recent years, come to precisely the same realisation. While it may only be a handful who place data front and centre in their work, there are very few clubs who do not incorporate it in some way in their recruitment strategies. Most, even away from the moneyed elite, have the full suite of subscriptions: Wyscout and Scout7 and InStat and STATS Perform and all the rest. Many use the video footage or the raw data available on those platforms to whittle down the number of players they might be interested in watching in the flesh, and then dispatch their scouts to see a refined list of targets. Others might use the data as a form of due diligence, checking that there is not a cheaper, more suitable alternative to the player they have previously identified. Almost everyone uses it as a way to compare and contrast potential targets with players they have in their squads already. Not everyone, of course, quite knows what they are looking for; often, the qualitative difference now is not so much that some clubs are using data and some clubs are not, but in some clubs using it well and some clubs using it poorly. Manchester United, famously, claimed to have examined the credentials of 804 right-backs before signing Aaron Wan-Bissaka. It is not hard to see why they might, belatedly, have chosen to appoint a Director of Data Science.

Data has started to prove more popular on the other side of transfers, too. In 2020, when the young German forward Kai Havertz was considering leaving Bayer Leverkusen, his agents commissioned a study to assess which of his suitors would provide the best fit for his style of play. Barcelona had expressed an interest; they were ruled out on the grounds that Havertz tended to produce his best work in areas of the field occupied by a diminutive Argentinean playmaker. In the end, he signed for Chelsea, not simply because of the economic package the club put together but because Petr Cech, the club's technical director, had the clearest idea of how he might grow in the team.

Havertz is not alone. 21st Group has provided similar assessments to the likes of Patrick Bamford, Nathan Redmond, Dominic Solanke and Marcus Rashford, as their representatives try to establish which clubs would suit them and which would not. Raheem Sterling used data to state his case in his ultimately futile contract negotiation with Liverpool in 2015. Knowledge is power, on both sides of a deal.

That is not to say, of course, that the old virtues in the transfer market are not still important. Scouts need to watch players, live. Clubs need to research the characters, the flaws, the foibles of stars they might spend tens of millions of pounds on hiring. Monchi still needs to keep his phone close to him, at all times, because transfers are still about relationships and reputations.

If anything, it has to be closer still, because the prevalence of data, the availability of information, has eroded so many of the edges he spent years carefully cultivating. He was able to sign Dani Alves, for example, because he was the only representative of a European club at a South American youth tournament. Now, of course, not only are dozens of European teams dispatching emissaries to any youth tournament they can think of, but every team in Europe with a Wyscout package is already fully aware of any and every player who might be taking part in it. Data has made the world smaller, and the advantages more slender. It has changed the way teams sign players, and which players they sign. But that is just the start. It has also changed the way those players play.

One of the first counter-intuitive insights contained in *The Numbers Game* regarded the essential futility of the corner kick. Corners, traditionally, had always been regarded as a good thing. They were, particularly in northern European countries, seen not just as relatively reliable sources of both chances and goals, but they had come to be used as a sort of proxy measure for supremacy, similar to the idea of 'territory' in rugby. The team that had won the most corners, as a rule, had probably spent more time near the opposition penalty area.

Chris Anderson and David Sally sought to overturn that. Corners, they suggested, were not nearly as exciting as we had assumed them to be. Using data from StatDNA, the firm that would later come under the auspices of Arsenal, they studied almost 1,500 corners from a Premier League season, and realised that the vast majority of them, some 80 per cent, did not even lead to a shot on goal. The chances of anyone actually scoring, directly or indirectly, from a corner, were vanishingly small. The numbers suggested that most teams only scored from a corner once every ten games or so. As far as Anderson and Sally were concerned, corners were 'next to worthless'.

It is curious, then, that at least three of the teams at the heart of data's rise in football – Liverpool, Brentford and Midtjylland – have come to precisely the opposite conclusion. Rasmus Ankersen takes great pride in Midtjylland's status as the best side in Europe at set-pieces. Brentford have employed specialist coaches. Liverpool scored more goals from set-pieces than any other team from Europe's big five leagues on their way to winning the Champions League in 2019. Ajax, another team that has invested heavily in data, won a reputation that year for playing an ornate, intricate style in keeping with the club's traditions. They also scored more goals from set-pieces than anyone else in the tournament. They came within a few seconds of reaching the final.

All of those teams would recognise the inherent truth of what Anderson and Sally proclaimed: corners are, without question, deeply inefficient. A team has something like a 1.8 per cent chance of scoring from any given set-piece, according to a paper submitted to the Sloan conference in 2018 by the statistician Paul Power. But instead of seeing a limitation, as Anderson and Sally's initial reading might have suggested, those teams saw an opportunity. The very inefficiency of set-pieces made them the game's juiciest low-hanging fruit. Even making small gains in how effective they could be, shaving the finest of margins, would bestow a considerable and immediate competitive advantage. The data did not render corners obsolete. If anything, it afforded them a renewed focus. That is the thing with numbers: they do not always mean what they seem to mean.

It is striking, though, that it is not possible to dismiss any of the standard-bearers for the use of data within modern football as mere long-ball teams, consumed by production over process. That has not always been the case. Twenty years earlier, one of the earliest teams to embrace data, Sam Allardyce's Bolton, placed enormous value on set-pieces, too. Corners and free-kicks were, after all, almost the Platonic ideal of the Positions of Maximum Opportunity advocated by Charles Hughes. Those managers that followed his school of thought – including Allardyce – saw set-pieces as a short cut, a source of cheap goals, a far easier way to level the playing field than training underpowered squads to pick their way through opposing defences: the logic being that if you can't go through them, you may as well go over them.

And yet their modern successors – particularly Liverpool and Brighton – have little else in common with Allardyce's teams. None of them could accurately be dismissed as 'long-ball' sides. None of them have sacrificed aesthetics for effectiveness quite as willingly, quite as comprehensively, as the apostles of what might be termed early data: Allardyce, Tony Pulis, John Beck. They all stand as powerful retorts to the longstanding idea that data would lead to a simplistic, utilitarian approach to football.

Data did not land in football in a vacuum. The game is not static. It is continually evolving and refining and distilling itself, buffeted by a whole host of forces, only one of which is what is going on behind the scenes. Styles rise and fall. Best practice spreads. Ideas are shared, developed, and then undermined and discredited. Fashions come and go and then, often, come again, subject to the same kind of thinly disguised rebrand as Alan Partridge's rebadged Mini Metro.

That makes it difficult to say, with absolute certainty, which elements of elite football in its current form – the style of play that is *à la mode* among the game's aristocrats – can be traced back entirely to data. There is, put simply, too broad a suite of influences. There has, for example, been a notable demise in the popularity of the long-range shot. In the 2003/04 season, the Premier League's players took more than 5,000 shots from outside the penalty area. By 2020/21, that had collapsed to 3,333. That is a substantive change in the nature of the spectacle of a football match: two decades ago, fans in any given Premier League stadium would have been treated to roughly 13 long-range efforts every game; almost half the shots taken in any fixture came from outside the box. Now, it is only a little more than a third: just eight or so speculative efforts every game.

It seems likely that is testament to the increased awareness among teams – even those who are not quite so devoted to data as Brighton and Brentford and Liverpool – of metrics like Expected Goals; it is reasonable to assume that, five years or so since it first appeared on *Match of the Day*, most coaches have worked out that taking a shot from long distance is often less valuable than retaining possession and waiting for a better opportunity to present itself. But it is also possible that it has been driven by a desire to ape the style popularised by the dominant club teams of the era: Pep Guardiola's masterpieces at Barcelona, Bayern Munich and Manchester City. Their predilection to keep the ball circulating until the perfect chance arose was not – or at least not solely – because of an innate understanding of probability, but because of a deliberate philosophical choice made by their manager.

Crossing, like long-range shooting, has fallen from fashion, too. Twenty years ago, there were nearly 16,000 crosses from open play in the Premier League; in 2021, that had dropped below 10,000. At the same time, the number of passes in any given game has increased by a third: up from 545 in the early 2000s to almost 800 at the start of this decade. Both of those might be consequences of a more data-led approach that encourages teams to retain the ball and discourages the reckless gamble of the hopeful cross. Or it could be the influence, again, of Guardiola, whose teams standardised the idea of playing wingers on their 'unnatural' sides – a right-footed forward on the left, and vice versa – and made keeping hold of the ball at all costs a central part of their identity.

The likelihood is, of course, that the football we see played out in the rarefied airs of the Premier League and the Champions League is the creation of both Guardiola – and, through him, the legacy of coaches like Arrigo Sacchi and Johan Cruyff – and his fellow super-coaches and the sport's embrace of data. It is both philosophical and pragmatic.

Most elite teams, now, believe ardently in the idea of 'counter-pressing'. The concept first gained traction, in its current form, in Germany, where it was proselytised by the likes of Ralf Rangnick, Jürgen Klopp and Thomas Tuchel. Its popularity and its pre-eminence can be attributed, largely, to the fact that it works: it was the approach that allowed Rangnick to build the Red Bull empire from scratch, Klopp to lead Borussia Dortmund to consecutive titles and Bayern Munich to be crowned champions of Europe in both 2013 and 2020.

But at its heart is a single data-driven insight. At RB Leipzig, Rangnick installed a custom-made clock at the training ground. During small-sided training games, it would be started, ticking loud enough for the players to hear. It gave them eight seconds to win the ball off their opponents, and ten seconds after that to have a shot on goal. If they failed, they had to give the ball back. The principle, for Rangnick, was simple. The greatest moment of danger for any team is in the moment when they switch from a defensive mode to an offensive one. His team, therefore, had the best chance of creating a goal-scoring opportunity if they won the ball back quickly after losing possession, and then wasted no time in moving it as close to goal as possible. He did not just believe that. He knew it, because that is what the data told him.

That idea has since spread around Europe, disseminated not only by the diaspora of German and German-influenced coaches but by the natural competitive mechanism by which football absorbs new ideas. It has been absorbed into what is regarded as the game's best practice; the high press is now a cornerstone of the dogma espoused by most progressive, ambitious coaches. It has been normalised, internalised, standardised as a central tenet of elite, modern football, but it has its roots in data. The same is true for much of the football we see now on the fields of the Premier League and the Champions League. The form elite football now takes is a direct product of the game's digital age.

Daryl Morey stands alongside Billy Beane as one of the pioneers of data analysis in American sports: his work for the Houston Rockets and then the Philadelphia 76ers is credited in no small way with doing for basketball what the Oakland A's did for baseball. He has also, over the years, become something of a football devotee, exposed to the growing science of football analytics in his role as the founder of MIT Sloan Sports Analytics Conference.

As recently as 2019, though, his verdict on the sport's attempts to incorporate data was damning. The revolution the sport had anticipated for more than a decade at that point, as far as he could tell, was dead in the water. Speaking at one of Sloan's football-themed presentations that year, he was credited with saying that the game's 'data sucks, no-one cares, and no-one should'.

Strangely, many of those who have spent a considerable part of their working lives furthering the cause of data within football would have some sympathy with that blunt, bleak assessment. The sporting director at one data-infused Premier League team believes that there are no more than a handful of teams in English football doing anything even vaguely useful with analytics. Another longstanding executive, who has worked with several elite teams across Europe for a number of years, does not see any reason to describe any team – even those who are considered standard-bearers for the discipline – as truly 'data first'. Even the most positive analysts feel all football has done, so far, is clear the lowest bar possible. 'It is better to have the data than to not have the data,' as Morey put it on stage in Boston.

That such a view should be so pervasive, even with the impact of data clearly visible in the way clubs are structured, the way clubs play, the way they are covered and even the way we speak about the game, is not easily explained. To some extent, of course, it can be attributed to the veil of secrecy under which all clubs operate. Until recently, only Midtjylland – thanks to Rasmus Ankersen's evangelist streak – were willing to discuss their work in analytics in public. Liverpool and Brentford have subsequently become a little more forthcoming, but even they remain light on detail. Brighton still keep their cards close to their chests.

That tendency applies within the game itself. There exists an esprit de corps among analysts, but the nature of the work that teams are doing is guarded as if it was a state secret. Clubs know how quickly knowledge spreads; if they believe they have identified an edge, there is no competitive benefit to giving it away. Even those immersed in the world do not know, not with any certainty, exactly what their rivals are doing. Often – for reasons of personal pride and professional justification – the impression they give is that they, and only they, are the true carriers of the flame; other teams, and particularly any outside influences, are dismissed as charlatans and posers, little more than salesmen hoping to palm their snake-oil off on executives who do not understand the product. Even those teams who are accepted by consensus as being at the cutting edge – Arsenal, Liverpool, a handful of others – remain something of a mystery. They know they are doing something, and something that works, but they do not know quite what it is.

There are other factors at play, too. Many of those who have spent years trying to promote analytics within a sport that was inattentive and inhospitable have felt that struggle on an intensely personal level. For a long time, they felt if not entirely alone, then certainly part of a small, vaguely heretical community, one that found it hard to be heard, to be understood, even to be accepted. Everyone working in the sphere has a story to tell about a manager who ignored them or a coaching staff who dismissed them or a club that pledged fealty to the idea of data but was, in reality, simply ticking a box. More than one person compared football's attitude to analytics to its approach to community work: the desire to be seen to be doing something is much stronger than the desire to actually do it. They carry those scars with them. It does not look much like a revolution when you are locked in a continual battle for recognition and for existence. It does not feel like change when the ground gained can be measured in inches.

Perhaps most of all, though, the analytics community inside football finds it hard to see how far it has come when it is so keenly aware of how far it has to go. Whatever progress has been made is, in all likelihood, barely a fraction of the progress that might be to come. Ten years after the publication of *The Numbers Game,* and more than twenty since the advent of Opta and ProZone, football has still only scratched the surface of what analytics might yet do.

There is still, after all, not just more data to collect, but better data, too. In 2018, Ted Knutson, the founder of StatsBomb, decided to expand from the analysis his firm had been doing for years and into the far more expensive, far more time-consuming business of data collection: the equivalent, perhaps, of a chef choosing to move into farming. He had felt, like Morey, that not enough of the data available to football clubs was of a high enough standard: it was not clean enough, not comprehensive enough and often not meaningful enough. The traditional providers did not seem, to his eye, to be interested in changing that. He believed that StatsBomb, which had been working with clubs and agencies to tell them what the data meant, could. The result, StatsBomb Data, runs a data collection centre in Egypt, where employees spend up to 16 hours coding a game. They record, on average, more than 3,000 events for each fixture in 84 different competitions around the world. Knutson is confident that what they produce is not only more detailed, but more useful to clients than what their competitors might be able to provide, taking into account not just things like where a shot was taken, but digging deeper still, and measuring how much pressure the player with the ball was under. The appetite among clubs, Knutson said, proved to be ferocious. 'It's like being a vacuum salesman,' he said. 'People want what you have, so they come to you.' Lyon were the company's first paying client; a few months later, Paris Saint-Germain joined up, too. StatsBomb started with six customers; by the summer of 2021, Knutson could count on 125. 'When you think of something like Wikipedia or Google Maps, the world would never go backward,' said Knutson. 'It feels like data is the same. There will come a point where operating without it would make you feel like you have lost a sense.'

Event data, though, is just the start. The Golden Fleece for data providers is what is referred to as 'broadcast tracking', a system that would allow either the companies themselves or clubs to use the footage of games shot for television networks as a source for data not just on what is happening on the ball, but off it, too: a large-scale, widespread version of the system Ian Graham introduced at Liverpool. No longer would teams need an elaborate network of cameras, the kind first used by ProZone, in order to work out exactly what was happening, and where, at any given moment in a game; in turn, that would allow more teams to be able to determine which players were contributing most to their teams' attacking performances. Most in the field believe that easily accessible tracking data drawn from broadcast feeds is the next great leap forward.

At that point, the question will no longer be which teams are working with high-quality data, but which is working with it best.

That is why Manchester City and Manchester United and Barcelona are appointing mathematicians and physicists and engineers as keenly – although not, admittedly, at quite such great expense – as they are signing new midfielders: it is to make sure they are as well positioned as possible in what they perceive to be football's looming space race. Success, in the future, will to some extent be determined by which teams have the best players, the finest coaches and – of course – the most money. But it will also be dependent on who has the best models, who has the most sophisticated algorithms, who can find the signals in the noise. The clubs that parse the data best will, if the early years of the digital era have illustrated anything, make more good decisions or, at the very least, fewer bad ones. That will, in the future, be the difference between success and failure. 'It is moving so fast that, in five or ten years, the gap could be very large indeed,' Javier Fernandez, Barcelona's former head of data analysis, told *El País*.

That there is still much to do, that their field remains relatively young, though, should not obscure the scale of the change that football has undergone since the dawn of its data age. There is a difference between most clubs not using data and most clubs not using data well, and it is one that should not be overlooked.

It would be an exaggeration to suggest that, inside teams, all resistance to analytics has melted away; that is demonstrably not true. Many analysts are still fighting the same battles they have always fought. But, for the first time, they can be sure the conceptual battle has long since been won. Football, once a sideshow at Sloan, the most influential conference in all of sport, is now an established part of it; no longer do the emissaries of Premier League teams have to skulk in corners, desperately trying to identify familiar faces. Each year, the conference runs a competition to determine the best sports-themed research paper from submissions from hundreds of academics and practitioners. Football's presence among their number is growing exponentially. In 2021, both first and second place were taken by football-themed papers. In 2022, football had two of the seven finalists. The OptaPro forum, too, has grown exponentially, from the meeting of a few dozen enthusiasts in the bowels of a university building in London at its inception in 2014, to a slick, professional affair attended by dozens of clubs and almost a thousand guests less than a decade later. The game as a whole has accepted, on some level, the utility of data; it no longer has to operate in the shadows. Analytics is now an established part of recruitment. It is has started to affect, in some small way, the way teams play. Expected Goals flashes up on our television screens during every broadcast and has started to influence our discourse. That is football's data revolution. That we do not yet know where it will end does not mean it has not started.

Chris Anderson never quite shook the feeling that he had experienced on those day trips out to Sheffield and to Birmingham and to all of the other places he and David Sally had visited on their research trips up and down England. He loved being close to football – the grandeur of it, the romance of it, the sweep of the stands and the lushness of the grass – but for a long time he felt like a tourist to it. Even when he was in it, he never really felt of it.

He had expected that. He and Sally had written in *The Numbers Game* that football was dominated by a central, native core that monopolised power through the perpetuation of some 'secret knowledge'. If you had not played the game, they believed, you could not understand the game; if you could not understand the game, then you were not welcome in it. Football, he could see from afar, did not welcome outsiders.

The rise of data, the story of this book, has been the unravelling of that resistance. Football is now awash with those it might once have considered outsiders. The most famous cases, perhaps, are in the ranks of analysts and data scientists that are attached to the vast majority of elite teams: the physicists and the mathematicians and the experts in the migratory patterns of bison whose appointments still tend to inspire a sort of wide-eyed, vaguely comical wonder.

But they are not just there. They are in scouting departments and executive suites and directors' boxes. Rasmus Ankersen and Michael Edwards and Bastian Quentmeier and almost every single one of the characters in this book are outsiders. Indeed, increasingly, being a transplant to football is seen as a source of strength, rather than weakness; a number of teams in Italy, France and Germany, in particular, have appointed sporting directors – or equivalent – with little or no background in the sport. That way, ownership groups think, they are less likely to be beholden to certain agents or managers or old friends. That should not be a surprise, really, given that more and more of the most powerful people in the game, the owners, are frequently not lifelong fans. Football's ownership ranks have been swelled by groups coming to the sport with fresh eyes, fresh ideas, too, often from the United States and, as the sale of Chelsea in the light of the Russian invasion of Ukraine in the spring of 2022 proved, ordinarily backed by private equity. Football is a game, now, for the outsiders.

That includes Anderson. When he left Coventry, he could at least reflect that his unanticipated mid-life career change had not done anyone any harm, in the end. His family had settled in London. Kathleen had been appointed to a prestigious teaching post at the London Business School. The boys, Nick and Eli, had gone through school, and were getting ready to apply to university; they both intended to continue their studies back in the United States. He had been able, as it turned out, to resume his career as an academic, as though the strange, five-year interlude in which he tried to buy a football team never happened. He took up a professorship, first at Warwick, then the London School of Economics; in 2022, he was appointed as the inaugural Ralf Dahrendorf Professor of European Politics and Society. He had his status, and with it at least part of his old identity back.

But the thing with football is that once you are in, it is very difficult to get out. Nobody truly leaves football, not really; at best, you might be allowed a brief period of leave. David Sally had made a clean break, writing a book on the art of negotiation, returning to his roots in business school, but Anderson, as the man on the ground, had established a network; he had become something of a node himself. American investors would get in touch, seeking a connection or an introduction; others would tap him up for advice, for a little project work here or there. Enough to keep his hand in. Enough for him not to have to let go, not entirely.

And so, when David Blitzer suggested that he might like to do a little work for the group he had helped put together, Anderson could not resist. Blitzer had evidently fallen for the game; the idea that this investment might be more fun than most had clearly proven to be true. As well as Crystal Palace, he was interested in taking stakes in a handful of other teams: not quite so high profile, of course, but the sorts of places that might prove fruitful in identifying and developing talented players. Together with a handful of partners, he was looking at a club in Belgium, and one in Portugal, and one in Spain. They would add to it later, taking a stake in the Bundesliga team Augsburg and, in 2022, completing a takeover of the Major League Soccer team Real Salt Lake. He liked him, he trusted him and he wanted him on board. He wanted to give him a chance to do what he had set out to do. Blitzer invited Anderson to act as an advisor for the network.

It was the sort of opportunity that, a decade earlier, Anderson assumed to be impossible. Even when he had taken all sorts of risks, and asked his family to make all sorts of sacrifices to pursue it, it still seemed far-fetched. And yet here he was, here he is, part of the game once again. That is a measure of how hard he worked, of course, and it is testament to the strength of his ideas, but it is also a gauge of how far football has come. It has done more than embrace the concept that data might have some use. It has realised that a range of perspectives and thoughts and expertise can add value, that the alloy is always stronger than the base metal. For the first time, it is a place where outsiders can feel at home.

THANKS

The story of football's data revolution is, obviously, a story about ideas and numbers and equations and algorithms and things that I cannot even pretend to understand. But like all stories, it is mainly about people; it was the willingness of those people who have done so much to change the game to share their stories that made this book possible.

Those names, if you have made it this far, will be familiar: Ram Mylvaganam, Sarah Rudd, Ravi Ramineni, Henry Stott, Duncan Alexander, Simon Wilson, Sam Green, Omar Chaudhuri, Simon Gleave, Miles Jacobson, Ted Knutson, Hendrik Almstadt, Rasmus Ankersen, Danny Finkelstein, Billy Beane, Damien Comolli, Luke Bornn, Bill Gerrard, Mike Forde, Chris Brady, Jonas Boldt, Bastian Quentmeier, Keith Harris, Ralf Rangnick, Stevie Grieve, Ashwin Raman, Jamie Carragher, Richard Hughes, Steve Houghton, Micah Richards and Monchi. Particular thanks go to Lukas Keppler and Leo Lachmuth at Impect, in Germany and the Philippines, both of whom answered a frankly troubling volume of emails, and kindly introduced me to Ashley Flores. I should point out that the version of the game's recent history told in this book is not a comprehensive one; there have, certainly, countless contributors to the rise of data who have not been given the prominence they deserve in this telling. To them, I apologise.

And then there is the whole other cast of characters, the ones whose work behind the scenes made telling those stories possible, the central nodes of the story. Their help was enormously appreciated, too: Phil Hay, Adam Crafton, Steve Horowitz, Rob Tilliss, Dominic Fifield, Garth Brameld, Jonathan Wilson, Jack Pitt-Brooke, Miguel Delaney, Jonathan Liew, Jackie Cruz, Rosie Bass, Neil Atkinson, Tony Barrett and Matt McCann. All of the books and outlets used as source material are acknowledged, but Christoph Biermann's *Football Hackers*, Simon Kuper and Stefan Szymanski's *Soccernomics*, *Inverting the Pyramid* by the omnipresent Jonathan Wilson and, obviously, *The Numbers Game* were invaluable.

The support and understanding of my colleagues at the *New York Times* – particularly Tariq Panja and Andy Das – has been invaluable; it was the willingness of first Jason Stallman and then Randy Archibold to allow me to wander into whatever areas of football peaked my interest that allowed me to discover many of the stories that would, in time, become this book in the first place. Jack Fogg, at HarperCollins, believed that book might be worth reading; Adam Humphrey guided me through the process.

Everyone always thanks their agents, normally as some sort of afterthought, but this book genuinely would not have happened without David Luxton. It was David who encouraged me when I had doubts and mollified me when I was overcome with angst, because that's what good agents do, and he's a good agent. (He also had to do quite a lot of negotiating and reassuring because, as it turns out, writing a book when you have a newborn baby is a dreadful idea.) But it was also David who first introduced me to Chris Anderson and David Sally, and in that sense David is really the origin story of this book.

The first time I met Chris and Dave was a couple of hours before the opening ceremony of London 2012, over a video call (this was before Zoom was even a thing; they truly were ahead of their time). They had written a book, and kindly asked me to imbue with it a little more expertise in football, the game. There is a reasonably good chance you have read it. If not, you should. *The Numbers Game* was the starting point for my interest in the growing role of data in football, and my ongoing fascination in their adventures in the game. Chris, in particular, was kind enough to share (some of) his story with me in real time in those years that he spent traipsing the streets of Mayfair, hoping to find one paved with gold, offering me a rare insight into the peculiar mechanics of football, the industry, in the process. I can't thank him enough for trusting me, a decade on, to put that story down in ink and/or pixels. It was a privilege and a responsibility, and I hope I have done it justice.

The biggest thanks of all, though, go to my family – to Mum, Dad, Rachel and Boony – for understanding that sometimes it can take several weeks to reply to a WhatsApp, to Ann and Ken for stepping in and doing quite a lot of the parenting that I should have been doing, and to my wife, Kate, who for some reason affords me an apparently limitless supply of support and patience. Ed and Aurelie were absolutely no help at all, but I'll discuss that with both of them when they're older.

Lastly, I want to thank my brother, Robert. Rob isn't here anymore, but every time I felt even vaguely tempted to step away from the yawning chasm of emptiness that was meant to be a manuscript, I thought of him. He would have read this book without telling me and he would never have given me any feedback, but more than anything else I wanted to dedicate something to him. I love you, mate, and I miss you every day.